The Soup
Cookbook

The Soup
Cookbook

Consultant editor:
Anne Sheasby

LORENZ BOOKS

This edition is published by Lorenz Books

Lorenz Books is an imprint of Anness Publishing Ltd
Hermes House, 88–89 Blackfriars Road, London SE1 8HA
tel. 020 7401 2077; fax 020 7633 9499
www.lorenzbooks.com; info@anness.com

© Anness Publishing Ltd 2004

UK agent: The Manning Partnership Ltd, 6 The Old Dairy, Melcombe Road,
Bath BA2 3LR; tel. 01225 478444; fax 01225 478440; sales@manning-partnership.co.uk

UK distributor: Grantham Book Services Ltd, Isaac Newton Way,
Alma Park Industrial Estate, Grantham, Lincs NG31 9SD; tel. 01476 541080;
fax 01476 541061; orders@gbs.tbs-ltd.co.uk

North American agent/distributor: National Book Network, 4501 Forbes Boulevard,
Suite 200, Lanham, MD 20706; tel. 301 459 3366; fax 301 429 5746; www.nbnbooks.com

Australian agent/distributor: Pan Macmillan Australia, Level 18, St Martins Tower,
31 Market St, Sydney, NSW 2000; tel. 1300 135 113; fax 1300 135 103;
customer.service@macmillan.com.au

New Zealand agent/distributor: David Bateman Ltd, 30 Tarndale Grove,
Off Bush Road, Albany, Auckland; tel. (09) 415 7664; fax (09) 415 8892

A CIP catalogue record for this book is available from the British Library.

Editorial Director: Judith Simons
Project Editor: Felicity Forster
Jacket and Text Design: Chloë Steers
Typesetting: Jonathan Harley and Diane Pullen
Illustrations: Angela Wood

Recipes: Matthew Drennan, Brian Glover,
Becky Johnson, Debra Mayhew,
Ysanne Spevack and Marlena Spieler
Editorial Reader: Lindsay Zamponi
Production Controller: Darren Price

1 3 5 7 9 10 8 6 4 2

NOTES
Bracketed terms are intended for American readers.
For all recipes, quantities are given in both metric and imperial measures and,
where appropriate, measures are also given in standard cups and spoons.
Follow one set, but not a mixture, because they are not interchangeable.
Standard spoon and cup measures are level.
1 tsp = 5ml, 1 tbsp = 15ml, 1 cup = 250ml/8fl oz
Australian standard tablespoons are 20ml. Australian readers should use 3 tsp
in place of 1 tbsp for measuring small quantities of gelatine, flour, salt, etc.
Medium (US large) eggs are used unless otherwise stated.

CONTENTS

INTRODUCTION

Soups are very versatile and can be made using many different ingredients. One of the great things about soup is that you can put a selection of fresh, raw and sometimes cooked ingredients into a pan with some well-flavoured stock, let the mixture bubble away for a short while, and within no time at all you have created a delicious, flavourful, home-made soup with very little effort.

Many soups are quick and easy to make and simply combine a few key ingredients with added flavourings, such as herbs or spices, whereas other soups – perhaps those ideal for a special occasion or a more substantial meal – may require a little more preparation. Whichever kind you choose, it is well worth the effort to create fresh and flavourful soups in your own kitchen.

Many soups make ideal starters to a meal, and they are always a popular choice, while other soups are substantial enough to be meals in themselves, served with plenty of fresh crusty bread as an accompaniment.

There are light and refreshing soups that are chilled, ideal for summer dining *al fresco*; rich and creamy soups, perfect for meals shared with family and friends; warming soups for winter suppers; hearty soups that are ideal for a substantial wholesome lunch or supper; or special occasion soups for smart dinner parties or entertaining friends.

An essential ingredient in most soups is a good well-flavoured stock, and one that is preferably home-made. Stock (bouillon) cubes and stock powder save time, but it is hard to beat the flavour and quality of home-made stocks, and they are relatively easy and inexpensive to make. Once you have a good

basic stock, whether it is vegetable, fish, meat or chicken stock, there is a huge range of soups that you can create in your kitchen. However, remember that your stock will only be as good as the quality of ingredients used to make it – you can't produce a good, tasty stock from old, limp, past-their-best vegetables! However, if you are really short of time, choose one of the chilled fresh stock products available from some supermarkets and delicatessens.

Very little specialist equipment is needed to make soups, although you will find that a food processor or blender is invaluable and will save time and effort when you want to purée soup mixtures before serving, although pressing the soup through a sieve (strainer) or using a hand-held blender are perfectly good alternatives.

The addition of an attractive garnish, perhaps a sprinkling of chopped fresh herbs or a swirl of cream added at the last minute, will enhance even the simplest of soups. Soups may be served on their own or topped with a few crunchy croûtons. Slices or chunks of fresh crusty bread or bread rolls, served warm or cold, make an ideal accompaniment to many soups.

This book presents an eclectic, appetizing selection of soups from all over the world to suit all occasions. Choose from light and refreshing dishes such as Chilled Asparagus Soup or Summer Tomato Soup, or tempting recipes for rich Broccoli & Stilton Soup, Cream of Spinach Soup or Shrimp & Corn Bisque, or select warming winter favourites such as Nettle Soup, Sweet Potato & Parsnip Soup or Spicy Carrot Soup with Garlic Croûtons.

Alternatively, try flavourful combinations such as Italian Rocket & Potato Soup, Chunky Bean & Vegetable Soup or Pear & Watercress Soup, or travel further afield for more exotic choices such as Coconut & Seafood Soup, Moroccan Vegetable Soup, Thai Chicken Soup or Wonton Soup.

ANNE SHEASBY

VEGETABLES

Using vegetables offers the cook an infinite number of culinary possibilities, including creating a wide range of delicious and flavourful soups. The choice of vegetables is immense, and the growing demand for organic produce has led to pesticide-free vegetables becoming widely available. Vegetables are an essential component of a healthy diet and have countless nutritional benefits. They are at their most nutritious when freshly picked.

CARROTS

The best carrots are not restricted to the cold winter months. Summer welcomes the slender, sweet new crop, often sold with their green, feathery tops.

Look for firm, smooth carrots – the smaller they are, the sweeter they are. Carrots should be prepared just before use to preserve their valuable nutrients. They are delicious in classic soups such as Carrot & Coriander Soup or Carrot Soup with Ginger, as well as being an important ingredient in many other soups. Raw carrots, cut into thin julienne strips, also create an unusual and attractive garnish for soup.

BEETROOT

Deep ruby-red in colour, beetroot (beet) adds a vibrant hue and flavour to all sorts of dishes including delicious soups. Beetroot and orange is a classic combination for a soup, as in Beetroot Soup with Ravioli, or

why not try an unusual but delicious combination of flavours with Beetroot & Apricot Swirl soup, which is a light and refreshing choice. If cooking beetroot whole, wash carefully, in order not to damage the skin, or the nutrients and colour will leach out. Trim the stalks to about 2.5cm/1in above the root. Small beetroots are sweeter and more tender than larger ones.

CELERIAC

Strictly speaking, celeriac is a root vegetable, since it is the root of certain kinds of celery. It is bumpy with a patchy brown/white skin and has a similar but less pronounced flavour than celery. When cooked it is more akin to potatoes. It is used in soups and broths such as Cream of Celeriac & Spinach Soup.

SWEDE

The globe-shaped swede (rutabaga) has pale orange-coloured flesh with a delicate sweet flavour. Trim off the thick peel, then treat in the same way as other root vegetables. For soups, swede is usually peeled and diced, then cooked with other vegetables and stock until tender. It may be finely chopped and used in chunky vegetable soups, or chopped, cooked with stock and other ingredients, then puréed to create a smooth soup, before serving.

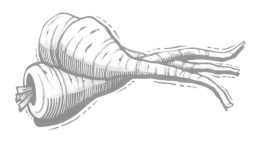

PARSNIPS
These winter root vegetables have a sweet, creamy flavour and are a delicious element in many soups. Parsnips are best purchased after the first frost of the year, as the cold converts their starches into sugar, enhancing their sweetness. Scrub well before use and peel only if the skin is tough. Avoid large roots, which can be woody.

TURNIPS
Turnips have many health-giving qualities, and small turnips with their green tops intact are especially nutritious. Their crisp, ivory flesh, which is enclosed in white, green and pink-tinged skin, has a pleasant, slightly peppery flavour, the intensity of which depends on their size and the time of harvesting. Turnips add a lovely flavour and substance to vegetable-based soups.

POTATOES
There are thousands of potato varieties, and many lend themselves to particular cooking methods. Main crop potatoes, such as Estima and Maris Piper, and sweet potatoes (preferably the orange-fleshed variety which have a better flavour than the cream-fleshed type), are ideal for using in soups. New potatoes or salad potatoes can also be used for some soup recipes. Potatoes are also good (especially when mashed or puréed) as a thickener for some soups. Discard any potatoes with green patches. Vitamins and minerals are stored in, or just beneath the skin, so it is best to use potatoes unpeeled.

BROCCOLI
This nutritious vegetable should be a regular part of everyone's diet. Two types are commonly available: purple-sprouting, which has fine, leafy stems and a delicate head, and calabrese, the more substantial green variety with a tightly budded top and thick stalk. Choose broccoli that has bright, compact florets. Yellowing florets, a limp woody stalk and a pungent smell are an indication of overmaturity. Trim stalks before cooking, although young stems can be eaten, too. Broccoli adds flavour and texture as well as a lovely colour to soups. Once cooked, it is often puréed to create an attractive green-coloured soup. It is a versatile vegetable and combines well in soups with other ingredients such as Stilton (blue) cheese and almonds, or in more unusual combinations, such as Broccoli, Anchovy & Pasta Soup.

CAULIFLOWER
The cream-coloured compact florets, or curds, should be encased in large, bright green leaves. There are also varieties with purple or green florets. Raw or cooked cauliflower has a mild flavour and is delicious when combined with other ingredients to make tasty soups such as Cauliflower & Walnut Cream or Cauliflower, Flageolet & Fennel Seed Soup.

SPINACH

This dark green leaf is a superb source of cancer-fighting antioxidants. It contains about four times more beta carotene than broccoli. It is also rich in fibre, which can help to lower harmful levels of LDL cholesterol in the body, reducing the risk of heart disease and stroke. Spinach does contain iron but not in such a rich supply as was once thought. It also contains oxalic acid, which inhibits the absorption of iron and calcium in the body. However, eating spinach with a vitamin C-rich food will increase absorption. Spinach also contains vitamins C and B6, calcium, potassium, folate, thiamine and zinc. Spinach and other leafy green vegetables are ideal shredded and added to soups or cooked in them and then puréed to create flavourful, nutritious dishes with a lovely deep green colour, ideal for swirling cream into to garnish just before serving.

PUMPKINS

These are native to America, where they are traditionally enjoyed at Thanksgiving. Small pumpkins have sweeter, less fibrous flesh than the larger ones. Deep orange in colour, pumpkin can be used in soups. Squash, such as the butternut variety, makes a tasty alternative to pumpkin, if pumpkin is not available.

COURGETTES

The most widely available summer squash, courgettes (zucchini) have most flavour when they are small and young. Young courgettes have glossy, bright green or yellow skin and cream-coloured flesh. Standard courgettes, as well as baby courgettes, may be used on their own or with other flavourings and ingredients, such as mint, yogurt or even Dolcelatte cheese, to create delicious soups.

CUCUMBER

The Chinese say food should be enjoyed for its texture as well as flavour; cucumbers have a unique texture and refreshing, cool taste. Varieties include English cucumbers, ridged cucumbers, gherkins and kirbys. Cucumbers are ideal for chilled soups such as Cucumber & Yogurt Soup with Walnuts.

CORN

There are five main varieties of corn – popcorn, sweetcorn, dent corn, flint corn and flour corn. Dent corn is the most commonly grown worldwide, for animal feeds and oil, and the corn we eat on the cobs is sweetcorn (corn). Baby corn cobs are picked when immature and are cooked and eaten whole. Corn and baby corn, as well as canned or frozen sweetcorn kernels are all used in creative soup recipes such as Sweetcorn & Scallop Chowder or Clam & Corn Chowder.

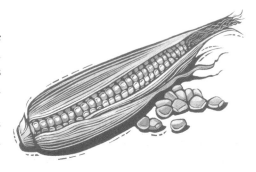

TOMATOES

There are dozens of varieties to choose from, which vary in colour, shape and size. The egg-shaped plum tomato is perfect for many types of cooking, including soups, as it has a rich flavour and a high proportion of flesh to seeds – but it must be used when fully ripe. Too often, store-bought tomatoes are bland and tasteless because they have been picked too young. Vine-ripened and cherry tomatoes together with large beefsteak tomatoes have good flavour and are also good for soups. Sun-dried tomatoes add a rich intensity to soups as well as sauces and stews. Genetically engineered tomatoes are now sold in some countries; check the label. If tomatoes are cooked with their skins on, you will find that many tomato-based soups may need puréeing and sieving (straining) to remove skins and seeds before reheating and serving.

Buying and Storing Tomatoes

Look for deep-red fruit with a firm, yielding flesh. Tomatoes that are grown and sold locally will have the best flavour. To improve the flavour of a slightly hard tomato, leave it to ripen fully at room temperature. It is best to avoid refrigeration because this stops the ripening process and adversely affects the taste and texture of the tomato.

PEPPERS

In spite of their name, (bell) peppers have nothing to do with the spice pepper used as a seasoning. They are actually members of the capsicum family and are called sweet peppers, bell peppers and even bull-nose peppers and come in a variety of colours – red, green, yellow, white, orange and dark purple-black. The colour of the pepper tells you something about its flavour. Green peppers are the least mature and

PEELING AND SEEDING TOMATOES

Tomato seeds can give soups a bitter flavour. Removing them and the tomato skins will also give a smoother result which is preferable for many soups.

1 *Immerse the tomatoes in boiling water and leave for about 30 seconds – the base of each tomato can be slashed to make peeling easier.*
2 *Lift out the tomatoes with a slotted spoon, rinse in cold water to cool slightly, and peel off the skin.*
3 *Cut the tomatoes in half, then scoop out the seeds with a teaspoon and remove the hard core. Dice or coarsely chop the flesh according to the recipe.*

have a fresh "raw" flavour. Red peppers are ripened green peppers and are distinctly sweeter. Yellow/orange peppers taste more or less like red peppers, although perhaps slightly less sweet. Black peppers have a similar flavour to green peppers but when cooked are a bit disappointing, as they turn green. Peppers add a lovely flavour and colour to soups, such as Roasted Pepper Soup or Red Pepper Soup with Lime.

AVOCADO

Strictly a fruit rather than a vegetable, the avocado has been known by many names – butter pear and alligator pear to name but two. There are four varieties: Hass, the purple-black small bumpy avocado, the Ettinger and Fuerte, which are pear-shaped and have smooth green skin, and the Nabal, which is rounder in shape. The black-coloured Hass has golden-yellow flesh, while green avocados have pale green to yellow flesh. Avocados can be used successfully to make tempting soups such as Miami Chilled Avocado Soup and Cream of Avocado Soup.

ASPARAGUS

There are two main types: white asparagus is picked just before it sprouts above the surface of the soil; while green-tipped asparagus is cut above the ground and develops its colour when it comes into contact with sunlight. Before use, scrape the lower half of the stalk with a vegetable peeler, then trim off the woody end. Briefly poach whole spears in a frying pan containing a little boiling salted water, or tie the spears in a bundle and boil upright in an asparagus boiler or tall pan, if the recipe calls for cooked asparagus. Otherwise, chop the prepared raw asparagus and use as directed in the recipe. Chilled Asparagus Soup is delicious, light and refreshing, ideal for summer eating.

CELERY

Celery has a distinct and individual flavour – it is sharp and savoury, which makes it an excellent flavouring for soups. The tangy, astringent flavour and crunchy texture of celery contrasts well with the other ingredients. Most supermarkets sell both green and white celery (when celery grows naturally the stalks are green; banking up earth against the shoots makes it pale and white). Look for celery with fresh-looking leaves, and avoid any with outer stalks missing. Try delicious recipes such as Mushroom, Celery & Garlic Soup, Winter Vegetable Soup or Curried Celery Soup.

ONIONS

Every cuisine in the world includes onions in one form or another. They are an essential flavouring, offering a range of taste sensations, from the sweet and juicy red onion and powerfully pungent white onion to the light and fresh spring onion (scallion). Pearl onions and shallots are the babies of the family. Onions are an essential ingredient in many soups, as they add extra flavour, and will liven up the flavour of many. Shallots and leeks can be used in place of onions in many recipes, and they also add delicious flavour. Additionally, spring onions may be used as a flavouring or garnish for some soups.

Buying and Storing Onions

When buying, choose onions that have dry, papery skins and are heavy for their size. They will keep for 1–2 months in a cool, dark place.

GARLIC

An ingredient that almost everyone who does any cooking at all will need, garlic is a bulb that is available in many varieties. Their papery skins can be white, pink or purple. Colour makes no difference to taste, but the attraction of the large purple bulbs is that they make a beautiful display in the kitchen. As a general rule, the smaller the garlic bulb, the stronger it is likely to be.

LEEKS

Like onions and garlic, leeks have a long history and are very versatile, having their own distinct, subtle flavour. They are less pungent than onions, but are still therapeutically beneficial. Excellent in soups, leeks add delicious flavour and texture to many recipes. A classic combination of leeks and potatoes produces the popular soup Vichyssoise, which can be served hot or cold, as a light and refreshing starter. Commercially grown leeks are usually about 25cm/10in long, but you may occasionally see baby leeks, which are very mild and tender and can also be used in soups. Try some excellent winter soups such as Leek & Thyme Soup, Leek, Parsnip & Ginger Soup and Chicken & Leek Soup with Prunes & Barley.

MUSHROOMS

The most common cultivated variety of mushroom is actually one type in various stages of maturity. The button (white) mushroom is the youngest and has, as its name suggests, a tight, white, button-like cap. It has a mild flavour. Cap mushrooms are slightly more mature and larger in size, while the flat field (portabello) mushroom is the largest and has dark, open gills. Flat mushrooms have the most prominent flavour. Mushrooms are a useful ingredient in many soups, and add flavour and texture, as well as colour (especially the brown cap/chestnut [cremini] or field mushrooms). Fresh and dried wild mushrooms also add delicious taste to some soup recipes, such as Wild Mushroom Soup.

Several varieties of wild mushroom are now available in supermarkets, for example oyster mushrooms and shiitake mushrooms.

Oyster mushrooms are ear-shaped fungi that grow on rotting wood. Cap, gills and stem are all the same colour, which can be

greyish brown, pink or yellow. They are now widely cultivated, although they are generally thought of as wild mushrooms. Delicious in both flavour and texture, they are softer than button (white) mushrooms when cooked but seem more substantial, having more "bite" to them.

Shiitake mushrooms are Japanese fungi from the variety of tree mushrooms (called *take* in Japan, the *shii* being the hardwood tree from which they are harvested). They have a meaty, slightly acid flavour and a distinct slippery texture, and they need to be cooked through (takes 3–5 minutes) before eating.

Buying and Storing Mushrooms

Buy mushrooms that smell and look fresh. Avoid ones with damp, slimy patches and any that are discoloured. Store in a paper bag in the refrigerator for up to 4 days. Wipe mushrooms with damp kitchen paper before use but never wash or soak them.

WATERCRESS

As its name suggests, watercress is grown in water. It is perhaps the most robustly flavoured of all the salad ingredients, with its distinctive "raw" flavour, both peppery and slightly pungent. As well as salads, watercress makes a great addition to recipes such as Watercress & Orange Soup or Watercress Soup.

LEGUMES

Pulses, lentils and peas provide the cook with a diverse range of flavours and textures, and they are a great addition to soups. They have long been a staple food in the Middle East, South America, India and the Mediterranean. Low in fat and high in complex carbohydrates, vitamins and minerals, legumes are also an important source of protein for vegetarians, matching animal-based sources when eaten with cereals.

PULSES

The edible seeds from plants belonging to the legume family, pulses are packed with protein, vitamins, minerals and fibre, and are low in fat. For the cook, their ability to absorb the flavours of other foods means that pulses can be used as the base for an infinite number of dishes, and many are ideal for use in soups.

RED KIDNEY BEANS

These are dark red-brown kidney-shaped beans that keep their shape and colour when cooked. They are excellent in soups as well as many other dishes. Raw kidney beans contain a substance that cannot be digested and which may cause food poisoning if the toxins are not extracted. It is therefore essential that you fast-boil red kidney beans for 15 minutes before use, then change the water, bring to the boil and simmer for at least 30 minutes until they are cooked and tender enough to eat.

BROAD BEANS

Usually eaten in their fresh form, broad (fava) beans change in colour from green to brown when dried, making them difficult to recognize. The outer skin can be very tough and chewy, and some people prefer to remove it after cooking. Broad beans add delicious flavour to soups – try Fresh Broad Bean & Arborio Rice Soup.

HARICOT BEANS

Most commonly used for canned baked beans, these versatile, ivory-coloured beans are small and oval in shape. Called navy or Boston beans in the USA, they make delicious soups, such as minestrone and Provençal Vegetable Soup.

CANNELLINI BEANS

These small, white, kidney-shaped beans – sometimes called white kidney beans – have a soft, creamy texture when cooked and are popular in Italian cooking. They can be used in place of haricot (navy) beans and make a tasty addition to soups such as Fresh Tomato & Bean Soup.

CHICKPEAS

Also known as garbanzo beans, robust and hearty chickpeas have a delicious nutty flavour and creamy texture. They need lengthy cooking and are much used in Mediterranean and Middle Eastern cooking, including soups such as Chickpea & Spinach Soup with Garlic.

SOYA BEANS

These small, oval beans vary in colour from creamy-yellow through brown to black. Soya beans contain all the nutritional properties of animal products but without the disadvantages. They are extremely dense and need to be soaked for up to 12 hours before cooking. They combine well with robust ingredients such as garlic, herbs and spices, and they make a healthy addition to soups. Soya beans are also used to make tofu, tempeh, textured vegetable protein (TVP), flour and the different versions of soy sauce. Try an unusual soup – Japanese Crushed Tofu Soup, which uses tofu as an ingredient.

Buying and Storing Beans

Look for plump, shiny beans with unbroken skins. Beans toughen with age so, although they will keep for up to a year in a cool, dry place, it is best to buy them in small quantities from stores with a regular turnover of stock. Avoid any beans that look dusty or dirty or smell musty, and store them in an airtight container in a cool, dark and dry place.

LENTILS AND PEAS

These are among our oldest foods. Lentils are hard even when fresh, so they are always sold dried. Unlike other pulses, they do not need soaking before cooking.

RED LENTILS

Bright orange-coloured red split lentils, sometimes known as Egyptian lentils, are the most familiar variety. They cook in just 20 minutes, eventually disintegrating into a thick purée. They are ideal for thickening soups. Try creative recipes such as Spiced Lentil Soup, Green Lentil Soup or Lentil & Pasta Soup.

SOAKING BEANS

Most pulses require soaking in cold water for several hours or even overnight before use, so it is wise to plan ahead. If you are short of time, the long soaking process can be speeded up: first, cook the beans in boiling water for 2 minutes, then remove the pan from the heat. Cover and leave for 2 hours. Drain, rinse and cover with fresh cold water before cooking.

1–2 hours
Split peas, whole peas

3–4 hours
Aduki, black, borlotti, broad, butter, cannellini, flageolet, haricot, kidney, lima, mung, navy, pinto

5–8 hours
Chickpeas, ful medames, soya beans

PEAS

Dried peas come from the field pea not the garden pea, which is eaten fresh. Unlike lentils, peas are soft when young and require drying. They are available whole or split; the latter have a sweeter flavour and cook more quickly. Like split lentils, split peas do not hold their shape when cooked, making them perfect for soups. They take about 45 minutes to cook. Dried peas require soaking overnight before use. Split Pea & Ham Soup makes a great hearty lunch or supper dish.

Buying and Storing Lentils and Peas

Although lentils and peas can be kept for up to a year, they toughen with time. Buy from stores with a fast turnover of stock and store in airtight containers in a cool, dark place. Look for bright, unwrinkled pulses.

MEAT

Packed with high-quality protein, meat is an excellent food and is used in a variety of soup recipes. Careful rearing means leaner animals and hence healthier cuts of meat, making it perfectly possible to follow current dietary advice while still enjoying meat and poultry. Nowadays we are spoilt for choice with all the types and cuts of meat available. Most butchers and many supermarkets with fresh meat counters are only too happy to advise you on the best cuts of meat to use for all your recipes, including soups.

CHICKEN
The stock from cooking chicken makes an ideal basis for many delicious soups. Choose corn-fed or free-range birds for the best flavour. Cuts used in soups include breasts, legs and thighs. Boneless thighs or breasts are a good buy.

DUCK
There isn't much meat on a duck, so buy big rather than small birds or choose duck breasts. Although leaner than it used to be, duck is still a fatty meat, so remove as much of the fat as possible before cooking. Duck Consommé is a classic recipe, and lean duck can be used instead of chicken in some soups.

TURKEY
A turkey isn't just for Christmas – today's smaller birds are perfect for soups. Try recipes such as Chinese Chicken & Asparagus Soup, Chicken & Almond Soup, or Chicken, Leek & Celery Soup, using turkey in place of chicken.

BACON
Used in soups to add flavour, bacon can be bought sliced, in lardons (thin strips or dice), or in a piece. Available smoked or unsmoked (green). Bacon is an ingredient in Lentil Soup with Rosemary.

BEEF, LAMB AND PORK
Some soup recipes call for the addition of beef, lamb or pork. These not only bring flavour to a dish, but also make a valuable contribution in terms of nutrition, since they are a source of high-quality protein. When making soup, the best cuts of beef, lamb and pork are steak, chops or fillet, although other cuts such as pork belly, neck of lamb and minced beef, lamb or pork are also used, so be guided by the recipe or ask your butcher for advice. Meat bones are also used for making stocks.

PANCETTA
Pancetta is belly of pork that is cured with salt and spices, and it is eaten either raw in very thin slices, or cut more thickly and used in cooking. It is used widely in Italian cooking, such as in the Umbrian Onion & Pancetta Soup, and is available in many regional variations. Pancetta is sold in supermarkets and butchers, but smoked streaky (fatty) or back (lean) bacon is a good substitute if pancetta is not available.

FISH

Fish is one of the quickest and easiest foods to cook, and as well as being delicious to eat, it is also very nutritious and a great source of easily digestible protein as well as other important nutrients such as B vitamins. White fish such as skinless cod, haddock and monkfish are naturally low in fat. Oily fish such as salmon, trout and mackerel are rich in omega-3 fats, which are beneficial to health, and we are actively encouraged to eat oily fish at least once a week in our diets. Oily fish are also a good source of B vitamins as well as vitamins A and D.

TYPES OF FISH

We have access to a wide range of fresh sea fish, as well as river and lake fish, some caught from our local shores and others imported from further afield. Although some fish is seasonal, many varieties are available all year round at good fishmongers (fish dealers), supermarkets and town markets. Many different types of fish are used as an ingredient in soups, and it is always best to buy firm, fresh fish.

ROUND SEA FISH

This is a large group of fish that includes cod, haddock, whiting and mackerel, as well as more exotic varieties such as John Dory (or porgy), red mullet and parrot fish. Round sea fish have a rounded body shape with eyes at each side of the head, and they swim with the dorsal fin uppermost. These fish are normally sold whole, in fillets or in cutlets or steaks.

FLAT SEA FISH

Plaice, dabs, turbot, sole and skate are common examples of flat sea fish. Flat fish swim on their sides and have both eyes on top of their head. They usually have a white (blind) side and a darker upper surface, which is coloured to camouflage them within their local habitat. Flat fish are usually sold whole or filleted.

FRESHWATER FISH

Freshwater fish may live in freshwater rivers or lakes and include varieties such as salmon, trout and pike. They are usually sold whole, in fillets or in steaks or cutlets.

SMOKED FISH

Fish is usually smoked by one of two main methods – hot smoke or cold smoke. Typical examples of smoked fish include haddock, cod, salmon, mackerel, trout and kippers. Smoked fish are sold in various forms including whole, as fillets or in thin slices.

Both white fish such as cod, haddock, monkfish and mullet and oily fish such as mackerel and salmon are used as an ingredient in creative soup recipes. Smoked fish such as smoked haddock or smoked cod are also used to create flavourful soups. We include a range of delicious fish-based soups such as Creamy Cod Chowder and Salmon Chowder. Or choose from tempting combinations such as Smoked Mackerel & Tomato Soup or Provençale Fish Soup with Pasta.

SHELLFISH

We are fortunate to have a good selection of fresh and frozen shellfish available all year round, either shellfish caught off our local shores, or varieties caught further afield and imported. Shellfish are at their best when eaten fresh and in season. Frozen shellfish are also available and are a good substitute if fresh is not available.

Once purchased, keep fresh shellfish chilled, and store in a refrigerator until it is ready to use. As a general rule, fresh shellfish, as well as frozen (defrosted) shellfish, is best eaten on the day you purchase it or used within 24 hours – your fishmonger (fish dealer) will be able to advise you more on the length of time recommended for this.

Many shellfish and crustaceans have wonderfully exotic names and almost all shellfish is considered edible, from clams to razor-shells, sea snails and small scallops. Shrimps and prawns come in all sizes and colours, from vibrant red to pale grey, while crustaceans range from blue-black lobsters to bright orange crawfish.

CHOOSING SHELLFISH
When buying fresh shellfish such as scallops, mussels, clams and oysters, look for those with tightly closed shells. They are still alive when sold fresh, and any sign of

an open shell may indicate that they are far from fresh. A sharp tap on the shell may persuade the shellfish to close up, but otherwise, avoid it. When buying cooked shellfish such as crab, lobster and prawns (shrimp), make sure the shells are intact. They should feel quite heavy and have a fresh, agreeable smell.

SHRIMPS AND PRAWNS
There are many varieties of shrimps and prawns, which are known collectively as shrimp in the United States. The smallest are small pink or brown shrimp. Next in size come the pink prawns with a delicate flavour. Then there are the larger variety of prawn, which turn bright red when they are cooked. They are highly prized for their fine, strong flavour. Best, and most expensive of all, are large succulent king prawns (jumbo shrimp) which have a superb flavour and texture. Similar to these is the cicala, which resembles a small, flat lobster.

Shrimp and prawns can be used in a large number of recipes, including a variety of different tasty soups such as Prawn Bisque, Pork & Noodle Broth with Prawns, Prawn Creole or Prawn & Egg-knot Soup.

Buying Shrimps and Prawns
Shrimps and prawns should have bright shells that feel firm; if they look limp or smell of ammonia, do not buy them.

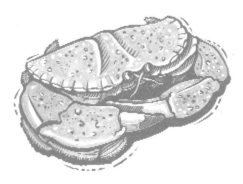

CRAB

Crabmeat, both fresh and drained, can be used in creative soup recipes. Try recipes such as Corn & Crab Bisque or Creamed Corn & Crab Meat Soup.

SCALLOPS

Scallops are a useful ingredient in some soups, such as Corn & Scallop Chowder, Seafood Wonton Soup and Thai Fish Soup.

LOBSTERS AND OYSTERS

Lobsters and oysters are used as ingredients in delicious soups such as Lobster Bisque and Oyster Soup.

SQUID AND CUTTLEFISH

Despite their appearance, squid and cuttlefish are actually molluscs, whose shell is located inside the body. They are indistinguishable in taste, but cuttlefish have a larger head and a wider body with stubbier tentacles. Once the bone has been removed, cuttlefish are very tender. The shell of a squid is nothing more than a long, thin, transparent quill. Both squid and cuttlefish have ten tentacles. Squid is more commonly used in soup recipes.

Small squid and cuttlefish should be cooked briefly, just until they turn opaque, or they will become rubbery and tough. Larger specimens need long, slow cooking to make them tender, making them ideal for use in some soups. Try recipes such as Coconut & Seafood Soup or Seafood Laksa.

MUSSELS

These shellfish have a smooth texture and sweet flavour. Both whole and shelled mussels may be used in soups, and they also make an attractive garnish, cooked and served in their open shells. Try flavourful soups such as Spiced Mussel Soup or Saffron Mussel Soup.

CLAMS

There are many different types of clam, ranging from tiny smooth-shelled clams to long, thin razor shells and the large Venus clams with beautiful ridged shells. All have a sweet flavour and a slightly chewy texture. Because they vary so much in size, it is best to ask the fishmonger how many clams you will need for a particular soup or be guided by the recipe. Try tempting recipes such as Clam Chowder or Clam & Pasta Soup.

PREPARING SQUID

To clean squid, hold the body in one hand and the head in the other, and pull away the head gently but firmly. The entrails will come away. Cut off the tentacles and remove the dark ink sac from the head. Pull out the transparent quill and rinse the body. Peel off the purplish membrane. Unless the squid are tiny enough to serve whole, cut the body into 5mm/¼in rings and the tentacles into manageable pieces.

Pasta & Noodles

The wide range of fresh and dried pasta available to us today is impressive, and the shapes and types of pasta readily available ensure that you have plenty of choice when it comes to selecting which pasta to cook. Pasta is also a nutritious food and it plays an important part in a healthy, well-balanced diet. Pasta is low in fat and provides a good source of carbohydrate, hence it is a good source of energy, as well as being a useful source of protein and some vitamins and minerals. Pasta, especially small pasta such as stellette or pastina is ideal for use in soups and is an important ingredient in recipes such as minestrone.

Soup Pasta

These tiny shapes, of which there are many different ones, are mostly made from plain durum wheat pasta, although you may find them made with egg and even flavoured with carrot or spinach.

Types of Soup Pasta

Teeny-weeny pasta shapes are called pastina in Italian, and there are literally hundreds of different ones to choose from. In Italy they are always served in broths and clear soups, and are regarded almost as nursery food because they are so often served for children's meals.

Shapes of pastina vary enormously, and seem to get more and more fanciful as the market demands. The smallest and most plain *pasta per minestre* (pasta for soups) are like tiny grains. Some look like rice and are in fact called risi or risoni, while others are more like barley and are called orzi. Fregola, from Sardinia, look like couscous, and have a similar nutty texture and flavour. Semi di melone are like melon seeds, as their name suggests, while acini de pepe or peperini are named after peppercorns, which they resemble in shape and size if not in colour. Coralline, grattini and occhi are three more very popular tiny shapes.

The next size up are the ones that are most popular with children. These include alfabeti and alfabetini (alphabet shapes), stelline and stellette (stars), rotellini (tiny wagon wheels) and anellini, which can be tiny rings, sometimes with ridges that make them look very pretty, or larger hoops. Ditali are similar to anellini but slightly thicker, while tubettini are thicker still.

Another category of *pasta per minestre* consists of slightly larger shapes, more like miniature versions of familiar types of short pasta. Their names end in "ine", "ette" or "etti", denoting that they are the diminutive forms. These include conchigliette (little shells), farfalline and farfallette (little bows), funghetti (little mushrooms), lumachine (little snails), quadretti and quadrettini (little squares), orecchiettini (little ears), renette (like baby penne) and tubetti (little tubes). The size of these varies: the smaller ones are for use in clear broths, while the larger ones are more often used in thicker soups.

Buying and Storing Soup Pasta

The quality of pasta varies tremendously – choose good-quality Italian brands made from 100 per cent durum wheat, and buy fresh pasta from an Italian delicatessen rather than pre-packed pasta from the supermarket.

Dried pasta will keep almost indefinitely, but if you keep it in a storage jar, it is a good idea to use it all up before adding any from a new packet.

Fresh pasta is usually sold loose and is best cooked the same day, but can be kept in the refrigerator for a day or two. Fresh pasta from a supermarket is likely to be packed in plastic packs and bags and will keep for 3–4 days in the refrigerator. Fresh pasta freezes well and should be cooked from frozen. Convenient packs of supermarket pasta have the advantage of being easy to store in the freezer.

We include several flavourful pasta soups such as Roasted Tomato & Pasta Soup, Tiny Pasta in Broth, Chicken Minestrone and Meatball & Pasta Soup.

NOODLES

The fast food of the East, noodles can be made from wheat flour, rice, mung bean flour or buckwheat flour.

Wheat noodles are available in two types: plain and egg. Plain noodles are made from strong flour and water, they can be flat or round and come in various thicknesses. Egg noodles are more common than the wheat variety, and are sold both fresh and dried. The Chinese types are available in various

thicknesses. Very fine egg noodles, which resemble vermicelli, are usually sold in individual coils. More substantial wholewheat egg noodles are widely available from larger supermarkets.

Rice noodles are very fine and delicate, and are opaque-white in colour. They come in various widths, from the very thin strands known as rice vermicelli to the thicker rice sticks.

Made from mung bean starch, cellophane noodles are translucent and do not need to be boiled; they are simply soaked in boiling water for 10–15 minutes. They have a fantastic texture which they retain when cooked, never becoming soggy.

Soba are the best-known type of buckwheat noodles. They are a much darker colour than wheat noodles. In Japan they are traditionally used in soups.

Both fresh and dried noodles are readily available in health food stores and Asian stores as well as most supermarkets. Noodles can be used in a variety of flavourful soup recipes. Try some tasty soups such as Chiang Mai Noodle Soup, Beef Noodle Soup or Thai Chicken Soup.

Buying and Storing Noodles

Packets of fresh noodles are found in the chiller cabinets of Asian stores and some supermarkets. They must be stored in the refrigerator or freezer. Dried noodles will keep for many months in an airtight container in a cool, dry place.

HERBS & SPICES

Herbs, the aromatic and fragrant plants that we use to add flavour and colour to our dishes, have been cultivated all over the world for centuries. The majority of herbs are familiar as culinary herbs, but many are also good for medicinal and cosmetic purposes. In cookery, herbs are chosen mainly for their flavouring and seasoning properties as well as adding colour and texture to dishes. Herbs, both fresh and dried, add delicious flavour and aroma to a whole variety of dishes, including many hot and chilled soups.

HERBS
Herbs can make a significant difference to the flavour and aroma of a soup, and they can enliven the simplest of dishes.

BASIL
This delicate aromatic herb is widely used in Italian and Thai cooking. The leaves bruise easily, so they are best used whole or torn, rather than cut with a knife.

CORIANDER
Warm and spicy, coriander (cilantro) looks similar to flat leaf parsley, but its taste is completely different.

MINT
Mint, a popular herb, has deep green leaves with an unmistakable strong and tangy scent and flavour. It is used in many dishes, including some soup recipes such as Green Pea & Mint Soup.

OREGANO
This is a wild variety of marjoram, but it has a more robust flavour that goes well with tomato-based soups.

PARSLEY
There are two types of parsley: flat leaf and curly. Both taste relatively similar, but the flat leaf variety is preferable in cooked dishes. Parsley is an excellent source of vitamin C, iron and calcium.

TARRAGON
This small, perennial plant bears slim green leaves, and its distinctive taste is said to be a cross between aniseed and mint. It marries well with chicken and shellfish in soups and other dishes.

THYME
This robustly flavoured aromatic herb is good in tomato-based soups, and with soups containing lentils and beans. It is also an essential ingredient in a classic bouquet garni, used for flavouring many soups.

Buying and Storing Herbs
Fresh herbs are widely available, sold loose, in packets or growing in pots. Place stems in a jar half-filled with water and cover with a plastic bag. Sealed with an elastic band, the herbs should keep for about a week.

SPICES

Highly revered for thousands of years, spices – the seeds, fruit, pods, bark and buds of plants – add flavour, colour and interest to the most unassuming of ingredients, while the evocative aroma of spices stimulates the appetite. Spices add delicious flavour to many soup recipes.

CHILLIES

Chillies are available fresh as well as in dried, powdered and flaked form. Dried chillies tend to be hotter than fresh, and this is certainly true of chilli flakes, which contain both the seeds and the flesh. The best pure chilli powders do not contain added ingredients, such as onion and garlic. All types of chilli may be used in a variety of soup recipes.

CORIANDER

Alongside cumin, ground coriander is a key ingredient in Indian curry powders and garam masala, and in northern Europe the ivory-coloured seeds are used as a pickling spice. Coriander seeds have a sweet, earthy, burnt-orange flavour that is more pronounced than the fresh leaves. The ready-ground powder rapidly loses its flavour and aroma, so it is best to buy whole seeds, which are easily ground in a mortar using a pestle, or in a coffee grinder. Before grinding, lightly dry-roast the seeds in a frying pan to enhance their flavour. Coriander adds delicious flavour and warmth to soups.

CUMIN

Cumin is a familiar component of Indian, Mexican, North African and Middle Eastern cooking and is added to soups to give a delicious flavour and aroma. The seeds have a robust aroma and slightly bitter taste, which is tempered by dry-roasting. Black cumin seeds are milder and sweeter. Ground cumin can be harsh, so it is best to buy the whole seeds and grind them just before use to be sure of a fresh flavour.

LEMON GRASS

This long fibrous stalk has a fragrant citrus aroma and flavour when cut. It is a familiar part of South-east Asian cooking and may be used as an ingredient in soups from this region. To use, remove the tough, woody outer layers, trim the root, then cut off the lower 5cm/2in and slice or pound in a mortar using a pestle. Bottled chopped lemon grass and lemon grass purée are also available.

PEPPER

Undoubtedly the oldest, most widely used spice in the world, pepper is a very versatile seasoning and is invaluable for soups, because it not only adds flavour of its own to a dish, but also brings out the flavour of the other ingredients.

SALT

Salt is also an important flavouring in soups. However, it is usually best to leave the seasoning of stocks and soups until the last minute, just before serving. Add salt a little bit at a time, until you have the seasoned flavour you require.

Buying and Storing Spices

Always buy spices in small quantities from a store with a regular turnover of stock. Store in airtight jars in a cool place.

OTHER FLAVOURINGS

There are many other flavourings that are used to add depth to many dishes, including soups – for example, olive oil, flavoured oils and vinegars, alcohol, chilli sauce, pesto and soy sauce, as well as more exotic flavourings such as dashi or fish sauce. Many add that important final touch or richness to a soup, contributing an important element to the overall character of the soup. We detail just a few of these flavourings below, out of a wide range that are used in the recipes in this book.

OILS AND VINEGARS

Flavoured oils and vinegars are brilliant for splashing into finished soups to pack an extra punch. Consider chilli oil for a super-fiery flavour in a spicy soup, or basil or rocket oil to enliven a fish or Mediterranean-style soup. Infuse virgin olive oil with chillies, roasted whole garlic cloves, whole spices, woody herbs or citrus peel instead of buying flavoured oil. Flavour and colour oil with soft aromatic herbs such as basil. Vinegar adds bite to some soups, so look out for the many types available, including wine vinegars, balsamic vinegar, sherry vinegar and fruit-flavoured vinegars, such as raspberry.

ALCOHOL

Add to soups in moderation. The golden rule is to simmer the soup for a few minutes to cook off the strong alcohol, leaving the flavour. White wine, Pernod and vermouth work very well with creamy fish soups.

FLAVOURED CREAMS

These provide a wonderful way of introducing contrasting flavour to a finished soup. Crème fraîche or whipped double (heavy) cream can be transformed by adding a purée of fresh herbs, grilled (bell) peppers or sun-dried tomatoes. Infused saffron and pesto can also be added.

CHILLI SAUCE

For those who like very hot food, chilli sauce can be offered at the table, or a dash can be added to flavour soups during cooking or to individual servings of soup.

PESTO AND PISTOU

Pesto and pistou are closely related, the latter hailing from southern France, where it is stirred into a rich vegetable soup. Both are made by mixing crushed garlic, basil and olive oil, and pesto also contains pine nuts and Parmesan cheese. Stir into soup to add flavour and colour.

FLAVOURED BUTTERS

Flavoured butters can be spread on warm bread to accompany a soup, or added to each bowl just before serving. Flavourings range from herbs and spices to shellfish.

SOY SAUCE

Made from fermented soya beans, soy sauce is one of Asia's most important contributions to the global pantry. There are three types of Chinese soy sauce on the market: light, dark and regular. As a rule, light soy sauce is used for soups. Light soy sauce is the initial extraction, like the first pressing of virgin olive oil. It has the most delicate flavour and is light brown in colour with a lovely "beany" fragrance.

There are several different types of Japanese soy sauce, too. Usukuchi soy sauce is light in colour and tastes less salty than the Chinese light soy. Tamari is dark and thick with a strong flavour, and is even less salty than the light type. Shoyu is a full-flavoured sauce that is aged for up to two years. In between, there is the very popular Kikkoman, which is a brand name for the equivalent of the Chinese regular soy sauce – neither too weak, nor too strong.

The Indonesian kecap manis is thick and black, with a powerful aroma, but a surprisingly sweet taste.

Soy sauce is used as a flavouring in some Chinese, Thai and Japanese soups such as Wonton Soup, Clear Soup with Meatballs, Japanese Crushed Tofu Soup and Prawn & Egg-knot Soup.

FISH SAUCE

Fish sauce is an essential seasoning for Thai and Vietnamese cooking, in much the same way that soy sauce is important to the

DASHI

This stock, based on kombu (a type of seaweed) and dried bonito flakes (from a small tuna), is the basis of most Japanese soups; it can also be used instead of water in any dish that requires a delicately flavoured stock.

Makes 800ml/27fl oz/3½ cups
10cm/4in square of kombu
900ml/1½ pints/3¾ cups water
40g/1½oz katsuobushi (dried bonito flakes)

1 Wipe the kombu with a damp cloth. Cut it into 3–4 strips and put in a pan. Pour over the water, making sure that the seaweed is submerged, and soak for an hour.

2 Place the pan over a medium heat. Just before the water boils, lift out the seaweed (shred and use for soup).

3 Stir in the katsuobushi, bring to the boil, remove from the heat and leave to stand until the flakes have sunk to the bottom of the pan. Strain through a muslin-lined sieve (cheesecloth-lined strainer). Use as required.

Chinese and the Japanese. In Vietnam it is often made using shrimp, but in Thailand, the sauce is more often made using salted, fermented fish.

All types of fish sauce have a pungent flavour and aroma and are very salty. Thai nam pla has a slightly stronger flavour and aroma than the Vietnamese or Chinese versions. The colour of fish sauce can vary considerably; lighter-coloured sauces are considered to be better than darker versions. Fish sauce is used as a seasoning in some soup recipes such as Smoked Mackerel & Tomato Soup, Pork & Noodle Broth with Prawns, and Ginger, Chicken & Coconut Soup.

TECHNIQUES & EQUIPMENT

One advantage of making your own soups is that you won't need any specialist equipment to try a wide range of tasty recipes. You will need basic equipment such as good knives and a chopping board or two, as well as a good-quality heavy-based pan and utensils such as wooden spoons, etc. One additional piece of equipment that is very useful in soup-making is a food processor or blender, to enable you to purée cooked soups, if desired. However, if you don't have one of these, many of the soups that require puréeing can simply be hand-pressed to make them smooth.

CHOOSING A PAN
For making soups you should choose a good-quality heavy-based pan. For the health-conscious, choose a good-quality non-stick pan, and you may be able to slightly reduce the amount of butter or oil used to sauté the vegetables.

CHOPPING AN ONION
Use a small knife to trim the root end of the onion and remove the skin with the tough layer underneath. Cut the onion in half. Place the cut side down on a chopping board and use a large sharp knife to slice down through the onion without cutting through the root. Slice horizontally through the onion. Finally, cut down across the original cuts and the onion will fall apart into fine dice.

PEELING VEGETABLES
The quickest way to peel vegetables is to use a swivel peeler. For example, trim off the top and end of a carrot, then hold the carrot in one hand and run the peeler away from you down its length, turning the carrot as you work. Use a julienne peeler or cutter to cut vegetables such as carrots and courgettes into thin julienne strips. Use julienne strips of vegetables in recipes or as an attractive garnish for chilled or cooked hot soups.

CHOPPING FRESH HERBS
Rinse and thoroughly dry the herbs and remove the leaves from the stalks, if necessary (this is necessary when chopping herbs such as rosemary, where the tender leaves should be removed from the tough stalks before chopping).

Place the herbs on a chopping board and, using a sharp knife, cut the herbs into small pieces (as finely or as coarsely as you wish), holding the tip of the blade against the board and rocking the blade back and forth.

CHOPPING FRESH HERBS WITH A MEZZALUNA
Alternatively, use a mezzaluna (which means 'half-moon' in Italian) – a curved crescent-shaped blade attached to two handles, which rocks back and forth over the herbs to chop them effectively. It is good for chopping a lot of herbs at the same time.

COOKING SOUPS

Use a wooden spoon to stir soups at all stages of cooking. This will not damage the base of the pan (important if the pan is non-stick). However, wood absorbs flavours, so wash and dry the spoon well after use. And don't leave the spoon in the soup while it is cooking.

COOKING VEGETABLES

Use a heavy-based pan to cook or sweat chopped vegetables for soups. A good pan that conducts and holds heat well allows the vegetables to cook for longer before browning, so that they can be softened without changing colour.

WHISKING

A balloon whisk is useful when making some soups, for quickly incorporating ingredients such as eggs and cream, which could curdle, or flour mixtures that can form lumps.

SIEVING SOUPS

A wooden mushroom (or champignon, which looks like a large, flat toadstool) is useful for pressing ingredients efficiently through a fine sieve (strainer) to give a smooth purée. The back of a large spoon or ladle also works, but it is a little slower.

PURÉEING SOUPS

A hand-held blender is brilliant, as it allows you to blend the soup directly in the pan. Controlling the speed is easy, to give the required consistency. Be careful when using a hand-held blender in a non-stick pan, and be sure not to let the blender touch the base or sides of the pan because it will cause damage to the surface.

A more traditional method is to use a mouli-legume, a cooking instrument from France that is a cross between a sieve (strainer) and a food mill. It sits over a bowl and has a blade to press the food through two fine sieves. The blade is turned by hand to push the soup through the sieves, leaving all the fibres and solids behind. It can grind food quickly into a coarse or fine texture.

The most common items of equipment for puréeing soups are food processors and free-standing blenders. Both types of machine are quick and efficient, but the food processor does not produce as smooth a result as a conventional blender, and for some recipes the soup will need to be sieved (strained) afterwards. Food processors can also be used for finely chopping and slicing vegetables for salsas and garnishes, as well as for the soup itself.

COOK'S TIPS

• *Before puréeing vegetable soups, reserve a ladleful or two of the cooked, finely chopped vegetables, then add them to the puréed soup to add texture and appeal to the finished soup.*
• *Remember to avoid overfilling a food processor or blender, as liquid can seep out from around the blade or through the lid. Most soups will have to be processed in two or three batches.*

MAKING STOCKS

Fresh stocks are indispensable for creating good home-made soups. They add a depth of flavour that plain water just cannot achieve. Although many supermarkets now sell tubs of fresh stock, these may be expensive, especially if you need large quantities for your cooking. Making your own is surprisingly easy and much more economical, particularly if you can use leftovers.

Home-made stocks aren't just cheaper, they're also a lot tastier, and they're much more nutritious too, precisely because they're made with fresh, natural ingredients. You can, of course, use stock cubes, granules or bouillon powder, but be sure to check the seasoning as these tend to be particularly high in salt. One good idea for keen and regular soup makers is to freeze portions of concentrated home-made stock in plastic freezer bags, or ice-cube trays, so you always have a supply at your disposal whenever you need some. Frozen stock can be stored in the freezer for up to three months (fish stock for up to 2 months). Ensure that you label each stock carefully for easy identification.

Use the appropriate stock for the soup you are making. Onion soup, for example, is improved with a good beef stock. Be particularly careful to use a vegetable stock if you are catering for vegetarians.

Recipes are given on the following pages for vegetable stock, fish stock, chicken stock, meat stock and basic stocks for Chinese and Japanese cooking.

VEGETABLE STOCK

Use this versatile stock as the basis for all vegetarian soups. Vegetable stock may also be used for meat, poultry or fish-based soups. Use your own selection of fresh, flavourful vegetables for this stock, to vary the flavour a little.

Ingredients
Makes 2.5 litres/4½ pints/10 cups
2 leeks, roughly chopped
3 celery sticks, roughly chopped
1 large onion, unpeeled, roughly chopped
2 pieces fresh root ginger, chopped
1 yellow (bell) pepper, seeded and chopped
1 parsnip, chopped
mushroom stalks
tomato peelings
45ml/3 tbsp light soy sauce
3 bay leaves
a bunch of parsley stalks
3 sprigs of fresh thyme
1 sprig of fresh rosemary
10ml/2 tsp salt
freshly ground black pepper
3.5 litres/6 pints/15 cups cold water

1 Put all the ingredients into a stockpot or large pan. Bring slowly to the boil, then lower the heat and simmer for 30 minutes, stirring from time to time.
2 Allow to cool. Strain, then discard the vegetables. The stock is ready to use or can be frozen for future use.

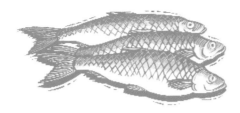

FISH STOCK

Fish stock is much quicker to make than poultry or meat stock. Ask your fishmonger for heads, bones and trimmings from white fish. Lobster or crab shell pieces (taken after boiling lobster or crab and scooping out the meat) can also be used in place of fish trimmings to make a tasty fish stock, together with the other flavourings listed.

Ingredients

Makes about 1 litre/1¾ pints/4 cups
675g/1½lb heads, bones and trimmings
   from white fish
1 onion, sliced
2 celery sticks with leaves, chopped
1 carrot, sliced
½ lemon, sliced (optional)
1 bay leaf
a few sprigs of fresh parsley
6 black peppercorns
1.35 litres/2¼ pints/6 cups cold water
150ml/¼ pint/⅔ cup dry white wine

1 Rinse the fish heads, bones and trimmings well under cold running water. Put in a stockpot or large pan with the vegetables and lemon, if using, the herbs, peppercorns, water and wine.
2 Bring to the boil, skimming the surface frequently, then reduce the heat and simmer for 25 minutes.
3 Strain the stock without pressing down on the ingredients in the sieve (strainer).
4 If not using immediately, leave to cool and then refrigerate. Fish stock should be used within 2 days, or it can be frozen for up to 2 months.

CHICKEN STOCK

A good home-made poultry stock is invaluable in the kitchen. If poultry giblets are available, add them (except the livers) with the wings. Once made, chicken stock can be kept in an airtight container in the refrigerator for 3–4 days, or frozen for longer storage (up to 3 months).

Ingredients

Makes about 2.5 litres/4½ pints/10 cups
1.2–1.3kg/2½–3lb chicken or turkey
   (wings, backs and necks)
2 onions, unpeeled, quartered
1 tbsp olive oil
4 litres/7 pints/16 cups cold water
2 carrots, roughly chopped
2 celery sticks, with leaves if possible,
   roughly chopped
a small handful of parsley stalks
a few sprigs of fresh thyme or
   5ml/1 tsp dried thyme
1 or 2 bay leaves
10 black peppercorns, lightly crushed

1 Combine the poultry wings, backs and necks in a stockpot or large pan with the onion quarters and the oil. Cook over a moderate heat, stirring occasionally, until the poultry and onions are lightly and evenly browned.
2 Add the water and stir well to mix in the sediment on the bottom of the pan. Bring to the boil and skim off the impurities as they rise to the surface of the stock.
3 Add the chopped carrots and celery, fresh parsley, thyme, bay leaf and black peppercorns. Partly cover the stockpot and gently simmer the stock for about 3 hours.
4 Strain the stock through a sieve (strainer) into a bowl and leave to cool, then chill in the refrigerator for an hour.
5 When cold, carefully remove the layer of fat that will have set on the surface.

MEAT STOCK

The most delicious meat soups rely on a good home-made stock for success. A stock cube will do if you do not have time to make your own, but fresh home-made stock will give a much better flavour and basis for soups, so it's well worth spending a little time making your own stock. Once it is made, meat stock can be kept in the refrigerator for up to 4 days, or frozen for up to 3 months.

Ingredients

Makes about 2 litres/3½ pints/8 cups
1.8kg/4lb beef bones, such as shin, leg, neck and shank, or veal or lamb bones, cut into 6cm/2½in pieces
2 onions, unpeeled, quartered
2 carrots, roughly chopped
2 celery sticks, with leaves if possible, roughly chopped
2 tomatoes, coarsely chopped
4.5 litres/7½ pints/18¾ cups cold water
a handful of parsley stalks
few sprigs of fresh thyme or 5ml/1 tsp dried thyme
2 bay leaves
10 black peppercorns, lightly crushed

1 Preheat the oven to 230°C/450°F/Gas 8. Put the bones in a roasting pan or casserole dish and roast, turning occasionally, for 30 minutes until they start to brown.
2 Add the onions, carrots, celery and tomatoes and baste with the fat in the pan.

Roast for a further 20–30 minutes until the bones are well browned. Stir and baste occasionally.
3 Transfer the bones and roasted vegetables to a stockpot or large pan. Spoon off the fat from the roasting pan. Add a little of the water to the roasting pan or casserole and bring to the boil on top of the stove, stirring well to scrape up any browned bits. Pour this liquid into the stockpot.
4 Add the remaining water to the pot. Bring just to the boil, skimming frequently to remove all the foam from the surface. Add the parsley, thyme, bay leaves and peppercorns.
5 Partly cover the stockpot and simmer the stock for 4–6 hours. The bones and vegetables should always be covered with liquid, so top up with a little boiling water from time to time if necessary.
6 Strain the stock through a colander, then skim as much fat as possible from the surface. If possible, cool the stock and then refrigerate it; the fat will rise to the top and set in a layer that can be removed easily.

COOK'S TIPS

• *Meat stock needs long, slow cooking in order to extract as much flavour as possible from the bones.*
• *To remove fat from the surface of stock effectively, add a few ice cubes. When the fat has set around the ice, lift it off.*
• *When making stock, add fresh (not limp or old) leftover vegetables, trimmings or peelings to add extra flavour to the stock. Do not use potatoes or potato trimmings, as these tend to make the stock cloudy.*

STOCK FOR CHINESE COOKING

This stock is an excellent basis for soup-making, and is ideal for tasty Chinese soups such as Wonton Soup.

Ingredients

Makes 2.5 litres/4½ pints/11 cups
675g/1½lb chicken portions
675g/1½lb pork spareribs
3.75 litres/6½ pints/15 cups cold water
3–4 pieces fresh root ginger, unpeeled, crushed
3–4 spring onions (scallions), each tied into a knot
45–60ml/3–4 tbsp Chinese rice wine or dry sherry

1 Trim off any excess fat from the chicken and spareribs and chop them into pieces.
2 Place the chicken and sparerib pieces into a stockpot or large pan with the water. Add the ginger and spring onion knots.
3 Bring to the boil and, using a sieve (strainer), skim off the froth. Reduce the heat and simmer, uncovered, for 2–3 hours.
4 Strain the stock, discarding the chicken, pork, ginger and spring onions. Add the wine or sherry and return to the boil. Simmer for 2–3 minutes.
5 Refrigerate the stock when cool. It will keep for up to 4 days. Alternatively, it can be frozen in small containers for up to 3 months and defrosted when required.

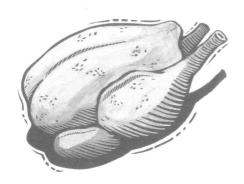

STOCK FOR JAPANESE COOKING

Dashi is the stock that gives the characteristically Japanese flavour to many dishes. Known as Ichiban-dashi, it is used for delicately flavoured dishes, including soups. Of course instant stock is available in all Japanese supermarkets, either in granule form, in concentrate or even in a tea-bag style. Follow the instructions on the packet.

Ingredients

Makes about 800ml/1⅓ pints/3½ cups
10g/¼oz dried kombu seaweed
10–15g/¼–½oz dried bonito flakes

1 Wipe the kombu seaweed with a damp cloth and cut two slits in it with scissors, so that it flavours the stock effectively.
2 Soak the kombu in 900ml/1½ pints/3¾ cups cold water for 30–60 minutes.
3 Heat the kombu in its soaking water in a pan over a moderate heat. Just before the water boils, remove the seaweed. Add the bonito flakes and bring to the boil over a high heat, then remove the pan from the heat.
4 Leave the stock until all the bonito flakes have sunk to the bottom of the pan. Line a sieve (strainer) with kitchen paper or muslin and place it over a large mixing bowl, then gently strain the stock. Use as required or cool and refrigerate for up to 2 days.

THICKENING SOUPS

Soups can be thickened in a variety of ways, using ingredients such as a butter and flour paste, cream, cornflour (cornstarch) or arrowroot, breadcrumbs, beaten eggs or ground almonds. However, many soups, once cooked and puréed will not need any thickening ingredients added, as the puréed soup is thick enough. Vegetables such as potatoes, onions and carrots, once cooked and puréed in a soup, will often help to thicken the soup sufficiently. If your soup does need thickening, try one of the methods below.

BEURRE MANIÉ

This smooth flour and butter paste is used to thicken soups at the end of the cooking time. Equal quantities of plain flour and butter are kneaded together, then a small knob of the paste is added to the soup and whisked until it is fully incorporated before adding the next. The soup is brought to the boil and simmered for about 1 minute, until thickened and to avoid a raw flour flavour. A similarly useful paste can be made using flour and cream.

CREAM

Double (heavy) cream can be used to thicken a fine soup. It is added towards the end of cooking, then the soup is brought to the boil and simmered gently for a few minutes until the soup is slightly reduced and thickened.

GROUND ALMONDS

Ground almonds can be used as a thickener in soups, and they add extra flavour as well as texture to the soup. The delicate flavour of almonds blends particularly well with fish- and chicken-based soups. However, ground almonds do not thicken soup in the same way that ingredients such as flour and cornflour (cornstarch) do, to make a thick, smooth soup. Instead they add body, texture, flavour and richness to the soup.

CORNFLOUR OR ARROWROOT

These fine flours are mixed with a little cold water (about double the volume of the dry ingredient) to make a smooth, thick, but runny, paste. (This is known as slaking.) The paste is stirred into the hot soup and simmered, stirring, until thickened. Cornflour (cornstarch) takes about 3 minutes to thicken completely and lose its raw flavour. Arrowroot achieves maximum thickness on boiling and tends to become slightly thinner if it is allowed to simmer for any length of time, so this is usually avoided. Cornflour gives an opaque result, but arrowroot becomes clear when it boils, so it is useful for thickening clear liquids and soups.

BREADCRUMBS

The more rustic approach is to use fresh white breadcrumbs to thicken soup. They can be toasted in oil before being stirred into a simmering soup, or added directly to a finished dish.

EGGS

Beaten eggs, egg yolks, or a mixture of eggs and a little cream can be used to enrich and slightly thicken a smooth soup. Whisk the eggs or egg and cream into the hot soup, but do not allow it to boil once they are added or it will curdle.

GARNISHES

Garnishes should look attractive, be edible, complement the flavour of the soup and add that final finishing touch to it. Some typical garnishes include sprinkling the soup with chopped herbs or stirring them into it just before serving, or topping thick, rich soups with a fresh herb sprig or two for an attractive garnish. Croûtons, made from either plain or flavoured bread, add appeal and crunch to many soups. Below are some typical garnishes, as well as a few tips for some more unusual ones.

HERBS

Adding a handful of chopped fresh herbs to a bowl of soup just before serving can make a good soup look great. A bundle of chives makes a dainty garnish. Cut 5–6 chives to about 6cm/2½in long and tie them in a bundle using another length of chive.

FRIED CROÛTONS

This classic garnish adds texture as well as flavour to soups. To make croûtons, cut bread into small cubes and fry the cubes in a little oil. Toss the bread continuously so that the cubes are golden all over, then drain on kitchen paper.

GRILLED CROÛTES

Topped with grilled cheese, croûtes not only look good, but taste great in all sorts of soups. To make them, toast small slices of baguette on both sides. If you like, you can rub the toast with a cut clove of garlic, then top with grated Cheddar or Parmesan, a crumbled blue cheese, such as Stilton, or a slice of goat's (chèvre) cheese. Then grill briefly until the cheese is beginning to melt.

CRISP-FRIED SHALLOTS

Finely sliced shallots make a quick garnish for smooth lentil and vegetable soups. Cut them crossways into rings, then shallow fry in hot oil until crisp and golden.

CRISPS

Use these to add a crunchy dimension to smooth and rustic soups. Try shop-bought thick-cut crisps (US potato chips) or tortilla chips; alternatively, make your own vegetable crisps (chips). Wafer-thin slices of fresh raw beetroot (beet), pumpkin or parsnips can all be deep-fried in hot oil for a few moments to produce delicious crisps.

VEGETABLE JULIENNE

An effective way of preparing ingredients for adding a splash of colour to soup is to cut them into julienne strips. Shreds of spring onions (scallions) or red and green chillies make great garnishes. Alternatively, finely dice peeled and seeded tomatoes.

CREAM AND YOGURT

A swirl of cream is the simplest soup garnish and is good for smooth soups. If the soup is very thin, then whip the cream lightly so that it floats. Crème fraîche and natural (plain) yogurt can also be used.

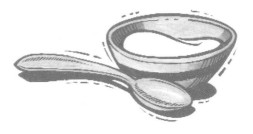

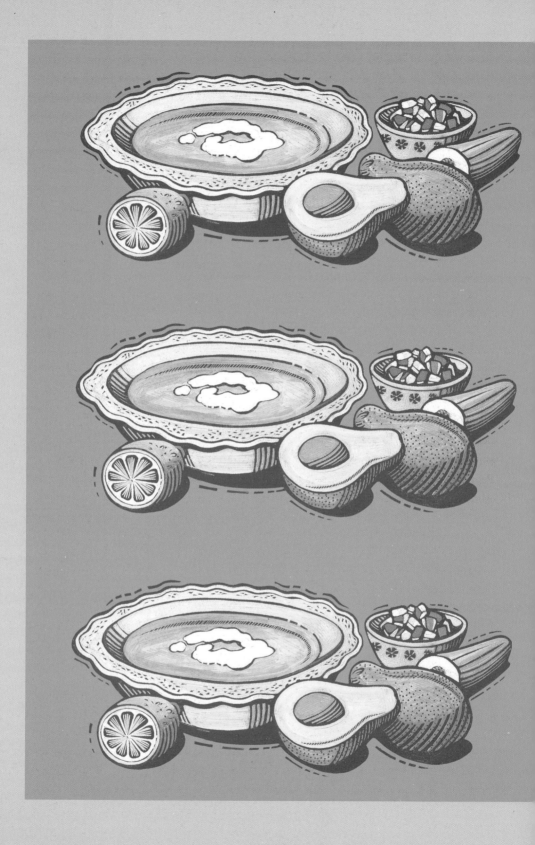

LIGHT &
REFRESHING SOUPS

You may not immediately associate the summer months as a time of year when you might be serving soup for lunch or supper. Many of the recipes in this chapter are for chilled soups, and these, as well as hot soups, create a delicious, light and refreshing dish ideal for an appetizer, light lunch or quick supper. Select from tempting soups such as Summer Tomato Soup, Roasted Pepper Soup or classic Vichyssoise, or try something a bit different such as Chilled Almond Soup, Chicken Stellette Soup or Duck Consommé.

CHILLED ASPARAGUS SOUP

This delicate, pale green soup, garnished with a swirl of cream or yogurt, is as pretty as it is delicious. The rich flavour of asparagus makes it a luxury soup.

SERVES 6

INGREDIENTS
900g/2lb fresh asparagus
60ml/4 tbsp butter or olive oil
175g/6oz/1½ cups sliced leeks or spring onions (scallions)
45ml/3 tbsp flour
1.5 litres/2½ pints/6¼ cups chicken stock or water
120ml/4fl oz/½ cup single (light) cream or natural (plain) yogurt
15ml/1 tbsp chopped fresh tarragon or chervil
salt and freshly ground black pepper

COOK'S TIP
Top each garnish of cream or yogurt with a fresh herb sprig or a sprinkling of chopped herbs.

1 Cut the top 6cm/2½in off the asparagus spears and blanch in boiling water for 5–6 minutes until just tender. Drain thoroughly. Cut each tip into two or three pieces and set aside.

2 Trim the ends of the stalks, removing any brown or woody parts. Chop the stalks into 1cm/½in pieces.

3 Heat the butter or oil in a heavy-based pan. Add the sliced leeks or spring onions and cook over a low heat for 5–8 minutes until softened but not browned. Stir in the chopped asparagus stalks, cover and cook for another 6–8 minutes until the stalks are tender.

4 Add the flour and stir well to blend. Cook for 3–4 minutes, uncovered, stirring occasionally.

5 Add the stock or water. Bring to the boil, stirring frequently, then reduce the heat and simmer for 30 minutes. Season with salt and pepper.

6 Purée the soup in a food processor or food mill. If necessary, strain it to remove any coarse fibres. Stir in the asparagus tips, most of the cream or yogurt, and the herbs. Chill well. Stir before serving and check the seasoning. Garnish each bowl with a swirl of cream or yogurt.

VARIATIONS
Use onions or shallots in place of leeks or spring onions (scallions). Use well-flavoured vegetable stock in place of chicken stock. Use milk in place of cream or yogurt.

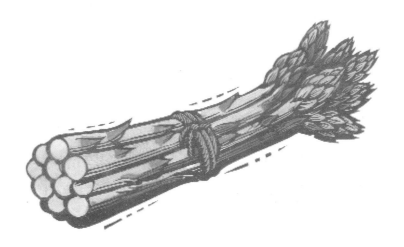

MIAMI CHILLED AVOCADO SOUP

Avocados are combined with lemon juice, dry sherry and an optional dash of hot pepper sauce to make this subtle chilled soup. The texture of avocados makes them easy to blend, so they are ideal as soup ingredients.

SERVES 4

INGREDIENTS
2 large or 3 medium ripe avocados
15ml/1 tbsp fresh lemon juice
75g/3oz/³⁄₄ cup coarsely chopped peeled cucumber
30ml/2 tbsp dry sherry
25g/1oz/¹⁄₄ cup coarsely chopped spring onions (scallions), with some of
    the green stems
475ml/16fl oz/2 cups mild-flavoured chicken stock
5ml/1 tsp salt
hot pepper sauce (optional)
natural (plain) yogurt or cream, to garnish

1 Cut the avocados in half, remove the stones and peel. Roughly chop the flesh and place in a food processor or blender. Add the lemon juice and process until very smooth.

2 Add the cucumber, sherry and most of the spring onions, reserving a few for the garnish. Process again until smooth.

3 In a large bowl, combine the avocado mixture with the chicken stock. Whisk until well blended. Season with the salt and a few drops of hot pepper sauce, if liked. Cover the bowl and place in the refrigerator to chill thoroughly.

4 To serve, fill individual bowls with the soup. Place a spoonful of yogurt or cream in the centre of each bowl and swirl with a spoon. Sprinkle with the reserved chopped spring onions.

BEETROOT & APRICOT SWIRL

This soup is most attractive if you swirl together the two differently coloured mixtures, but if you prefer they can be mixed together to save on both time during the preparation and in the washing-up afterwards.

SERVES 4

INGREDIENTS
4 large cooked beetroots (beets), roughly chopped
1 small onion, roughly chopped
600ml/1 pint/2½ cups chicken stock
200g/7oz/1 cup ready-to-eat dried apricots
250ml/8fl oz/1 cup orange juice
salt and freshly ground black pepper

1 Place the roughly chopped beetroot and half the onion in a pan with the stock. Bring to the boil, then reduce the heat, cover and simmer for about 10 minutes. Place the mixture in a food processor or blender and purée until completely smooth.

2 Place the rest of the onion in a pan with the apricots and orange juice, cover and simmer gently for about 15 minutes, until tender. Purée in a food processor or blender.

3 Return the two mixtures to the pans and reheat. Season to taste with salt and pepper, then gently swirl them together in individual soup bowls for a decorative marbled effect.

COOK'S TIP
The apricot mixture should be the same consistency as the beetroot (beet) mixture – if it is too thick, add a little more orange juice.

GAZPACHO

This is a traditional chilled Spanish soup, perfect for a summer lunch. Make sure that all the ingredients are in peak condition for the best flavour.

SERVES 6

INGREDIENTS
1 green (bell) pepper, seeded and roughly chopped
1 red (bell) pepper, seeded and roughly chopped
½ cucumber, roughly chopped
1 onion, roughly chopped
1 fresh red chilli, seeded and roughly chopped
450g/1lb ripe plum tomatoes, roughly chopped
900ml/1½ pints/3¾ cups passata (bottled strained tomatoes) or tomato juice
30ml/2 tbsp red wine vinegar
30ml/2 tbsp olive oil
15ml/1 tbsp caster (superfine) sugar
salt and freshly ground black pepper
crushed ice, to garnish (optional)

1 Reserve a small piece of green and red pepper, cucumber and onion. Finely chop these and set aside as a garnish.

2 Process all the remaining ingredients (except the ice) in a food processor or blender until smooth. You may need to do this in batches.

3 Pass the soup through a sieve (strainer) into a clean glass bowl, pushing it through with a spoon to extract the maximum amount of flavour.

4 Adjust the seasoning and chill. Serve sprinkled with the reserved chopped green and red pepper, cucumber and onion. For an extra special touch, add a little crushed ice to the garnish.

SUMMER TOMATO SOUP

The success of this soup depends on having ripe, full-flavoured tomatoes, such as the oval plum variety, so make it when the tomato season is at its peak.

SERVES 4

INGREDIENTS
15ml/1 tbsp olive oil
1 large onion, chopped
1 carrot, chopped
1 kg/2¼lb ripe tomatoes, quartered
2 garlic cloves, chopped
5 sprigs of fresh thyme, or 1.5ml/¼ tsp dried thyme
4 or 5 sprigs of fresh marjoram, or 1.5ml/¼ tsp dried marjoram
1 bay leaf
45ml/3 tbsp crème fraîche, sour cream or natural (plain) yogurt, plus a little extra
   to garnish
salt and freshly ground black pepper

1 Heat the olive oil in a large, preferably stainless-steel pan or flameproof casserole.

2 Add the onion and carrot and cook over a medium heat for 3–4 minutes until just softened, stirring occasionally.

3 Add the quartered tomatoes, chopped garlic and herbs. Reduce the heat and simmer, covered, for 30 minutes.

4 Discard the bay leaf and pass the soup through a food mill or press through a sieve (strainer). Leave to cool, then chill in the refrigerator.

VARIATION
If you prefer, you can use oregano instead of marjoram, and parsley instead of thyme.

WATERCRESS & ORANGE SOUP

This is a healthy and refreshing soup, which is delicious served either hot or chilled. The oranges add a zingy bite to the vegetable flavour.

SERVES 4

INGREDIENTS
1 large onion, chopped
15ml/1 tbsp olive oil
2 bunches or bags of watercress
grated rind and juice of 1 large orange
600ml/1 pint/2½ cups vegetable stock
150ml/¼ pint/⅔ cup single (light) cream
10ml/2 tsp cornflour (cornstarch)
salt and freshly ground black pepper
a little thick cream or natural (plain) yogurt, to garnish
4 orange wedges, to serve

COOK'S TIPS
Always remember to cool the soup slightly before blending. It is often easier to blend the soup in batches rather than trying to blend it all at once. This will also ensure an even consistency throughout.

1 Soften the onion in the oil in a large pan. Add the watercress, unchopped, to the onion. Cover and cook for about 5 minutes until the watercress is softened.

2 Add the orange rind and juice and the stock to the watercress mixture. Bring to the boil, cover and simmer for 10–15 minutes.

3 Blend or liquidize the soup thoroughly, and sieve (strain) if you want to increase the smoothness of the finished soup. Blend the cream with the cornflour until no lumps remain, then add to the soup. Season to taste.

4 Bring the soup gently back to the boil, stirring until just slightly thickened. Check the seasoning.

5 Serve the soup with a swirl of cream or yogurt, and a wedge of orange to squeeze in at the last moment.

6 If serving the soup chilled, thicken as above and leave to cool, before chilling in the refrigerator. Garnish with cream or yogurt and orange, as above.

VARIATIONS
Use 2 leeks or 6 shallots in place of the onion. Use crème fraiche or milk in place of cream.

Cucumber & Yogurt Soup with Walnuts

This is a particularly refreshing cold soup, using a classic combination of cucumber and yogurt. The chopped walnuts add a tasty, nutty flavour.

SERVES 5–6

INGREDIENTS
1 cucumber
4 garlic cloves
2.5ml/½ tsp salt
75g/3oz/¾ cup walnut pieces
40g/1½oz day-old bread, torn into pieces
30ml/2 tbsp walnut or sunflower oil
400ml/14fl oz/1⅔ cups natural (plain) yogurt
120ml/4fl oz/½ cup cold water or chilled still mineral water
5–10ml/1–2 tsp lemon juice

FOR THE GARNISH
40g/1½oz/scant ½ cup walnuts, coarsely chopped
25ml/1½ tbsp olive oil
sprigs of fresh dill

COOK'S TIP
If you prefer your soup smooth, purée it in a food processor or blender before serving.

1 Cut the cucumber in half and peel one half of it. Dice the cucumber flesh and set aside.

2 Using a large mortar and pestle, crush together the garlic and salt well, then add the walnuts and bread.

3 When the mixture is smooth, slowly add the walnut or sunflower oil and combine well.

4 Transfer the mixture into a large bowl and beat in the yogurt and diced cucumber. Add the cold water or mineral water and lemon juice to taste.

5 Pour the soup into chilled soup bowls to serve. Garnish with the chopped walnuts and drizzle with the olive oil. Finally, arrange the sprigs of dill on top and serve immediately.

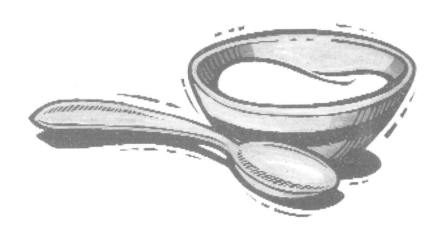

ROASTED PEPPER SOUP

Grilling intensifies the flavour of sweet red and yellow (bell) peppers and helps this delicious soup to keep its stunning colour.

SERVES 4

INGREDIENTS
3 red (bell) peppers
1 yellow (bell) pepper
1 medium onion, chopped
1 garlic clove, crushed
750ml/1¼ pints/3 cups vegetable stock
15ml/1 tbsp plain (all-purpose) flour
salt and freshly ground black pepper
diced red and yellow (bell) pepper, to garnish

> VARIATION
> *If preferred, garnish the soup with a swirl of natural (plain) yogurt instead of the diced (bell) peppers.*

1 Preheat the grill (broiling) pan. Cut the peppers in half, remove their stalks, cores and white pith, and scrape out the seeds.

2 Line a grill pan with foil and arrange the halved peppers, skin-side up, in a single layer on the foil. Grill (broil) until the skins have blackened and blistered.

3 Transfer the peppers to a plastic bag and leave until cool, then peel away their skins and discard. Roughly chop the pepper flesh.

4 Put the onion, garlic clove and 150ml/¼ pint/⅔ cup of the stock in a large pan. Boil for about 5 minutes until the stock has reduced in volume. Reduce the heat and stir until softened and just beginning to colour.

5 Sprinkle the flour over the onion, then gradually stir in the remaining stock and stir.

6 Add the chopped, roasted peppers and bring to the boil. Cover and simmer for a further 5 minutes.

7 Leave to cool slightly, then purée in a food processor or blender until smooth. Season to taste with salt and freshly ground black pepper. Return to the pan and reheat until piping hot.

8 Ladle into four soup bowls and garnish each with a sprinkling of differently coloured diced peppers.

Red Pepper Soup with Lime

The beautiful, rich red colour of this soup makes it an attractive appetizer or light lunch. For a special dinner, toast some tiny croûtons and sprinkle them into the soup.

SERVES 4–6

INGREDIENTS
1 large onion, chopped
4 red (bell) peppers, seeded and chopped
5ml/1 tsp olive oil
1 garlic clove, crushed
1 small fresh red chilli, sliced
45ml/3 tbsp tomato purée (paste)
900ml/1½ pints/3¾ cups chicken stock
finely grated rind and juice of 1 lime
salt and freshly ground black pepper
shreds of lime rind, to garnish

1 Cook the onion and peppers gently in the oil in a covered pan for about 5 minutes, shaking the pan occasionally, until just softened.

2 Stir in the garlic, chilli and tomato purée. Add half the stock, then bring to the boil. Cover and simmer for 10 minutes.

3 Cool slightly, then purée in a food processor or blender. Return to the pan and add the remaining stock, the lime rind and juice and salt and pepper.

4 Bring the soup back to the boil, then serve at once, with a few strips of lime rind scattered into each bowl.

VARIATIONS
Use 2 leeks or 6 shallots in place of the onion. Use 1 small fresh green chilli if red chillies are not available. Use the finely grated rind and juice of 1 small lemon in place of the lime.

SPINACH & RICE SOUP

Use very fresh young spinach leaves and risotto rice to prepare this surprisingly light, refreshing soup. The grated Pecorino cheese makes a delicious Italian garnish.

SERVES 4

INGREDIENTS
675g/1½lb fresh spinach, washed
45ml/3 tbsp extra-virgin olive oil
1 small onion, finely chopped
2 garlic cloves, finely chopped
1 small fresh red chilli, seeded and finely chopped
115g/4oz/generous ½ cup risotto rice
1.2 litres/2 pints/5 cups vegetable stock
salt and freshly ground black pepper
60ml/4 tbsp grated Pecorino cheese, to serve

1 Place the spinach in a large pan with just the water that clings to its leaves after washing. Add a large pinch of salt. Heat gently until the spinach has wilted, then remove from the heat and drain, reserving any liquid. Use a knife to chop finely.

2 Heat the oil in a large pan and cook the onion, garlic and chilli for 4–5 minutes until softened. Stir in the rice until well coated, then pour in the stock and reserved spinach liquid.

3 Bring to the boil, lower the heat and simmer for 10 minutes. Add the spinach and cook for 5–7 minutes more, until the rice is tender. Season with salt and freshly ground black pepper and serve with the Pecorino cheese.

Courgette Soup with Pasta

This is a pretty, fresh-tasting soup, which is always a welcome dish in hot weather. Courgettes (zucchini) are quick to cook and, unlike other squashes, they are available all year round. The taste best when eaten immediately after they have been picked.

SERVES 4–6

INGREDIENTS
60ml/4 tbsp olive or sunflower oil
2 onions, finely chopped
1.5 litres/2½ pints/6¼ cups chicken stock
900g/2lb courgettes (zucchini)
115g/4oz small soup pasta (stellette)
a little lemon juice
30ml/2 tbsp chopped fresh chervil
salt and freshly ground black pepper
sour cream, to serve

1 Heat the oil in a large pan and add the onions. Cover and cook gently for about 20 minutes, stirring occasionally, until soft but not coloured.

2 Pour the chicken stock into the pan and gradually bring the mixture to the boil.

3 Meanwhile, grate the courgettes and stir into the boiling stock with the pasta. Reduce the heat, cover the pan and simmer for 15 minutes until the pasta is tender.

4 Season to taste with lemon juice, salt and pepper. Stir in the chopped fresh chervil. Pour into bowls and add a swirl of sour cream before serving.

VARIATIONS
You can use cucumber instead of courgettes (zucchini), if you prefer, and other soup pasta such as tiny shells.

VICHYSSOISE

Serve this flavourful soup with a dollop of crème fraîche or sour cream and sprinkle with a few snipped fresh chives – or, for special occasions, you could garnish the dish with a small spoonful of caviar.

SERVES 6–8

INGREDIENTS
450g/1lb/about 3 large potatoes, peeled and cubed
1.5 litres/2½ pints/6¼ cups chicken stock
350g/12oz leeks, trimmed
150ml/¼ pint/⅔ cup crème fraîche or sour cream
salt and freshly ground black pepper
45ml/3 tbsp snipped fresh chives, to garnish

1 Put the cubed potatoes and chicken stock in a pan or flameproof casserole and bring to the boil. Reduce the heat and simmer for 15–20 minutes.

2 Make a slit along the length of each leek and rinse well under cold running water to wash away any soil. Slice thinly.

3 When the potatoes are barely tender, stir in the leeks. Taste then season with salt and freshly ground black pepper and simmer for 10–15 minutes until both the vegetables are soft, stirring from time to time. If the soup is too thick, thin it down with a little more stock or water.

4 Purée the soup in a food processor or blender. If you prefer a very smooth soup, pass it through a food mill or press through a coarse sieve (strainer). Stir in most of the cream, cool and then chill. To serve, ladle into chilled bowls and garnish with a swirl of cream and the snipped chives.

> VARIATION
> *To make a low-fat soup, use low-fat fromage frais instead of crème fraîche or sour cream.*

Green Pea & Mint Soup

Green peas and mint are perfect partners and really capture the flavours of summer. Using frozen peas eliminates the labour involved in shelling fresh peas, but without compromising the flavour.

SERVES 4

INGREDIENTS
50g/2oz/4 tbsp butter
4 spring onions (scallions), chopped
450g/1lb fresh or frozen peas
600ml/1 pint/2½ cups vegetable stock
2 large sprigs of fresh mint
600ml/1 pint/2½ cups milk
a pinch of sugar (optional)
salt and freshly ground black pepper
small sprigs of fresh mint, to garnish
single (light) cream, to serve

1 Heat the butter in a large pan, add the chopped spring onions and cook gently on a low heat until they are softened but not browned.

2 Stir the peas into the pan, add the stock and mint, and bring to the boil. Cover and simmer gently for about 30 minutes if you are using fresh peas (15 minutes if you are using frozen peas), until they are tender. Remove about 45ml/3 tbsp of the peas, and reserve to use for a garnish.

3 Pour the soup into a food processor or blender, add the milk and purée until smooth. Season to taste, adding a pinch of sugar, if liked. Leave to cool, then chill lightly in the refrigerator.

4 Pour the soup into bowls. Swirl a little cream into each, then garnish with the mint and the reserved peas.

CHILLED ALMOND SOUP

Unless you are prepared to spend time pounding all the ingredients for this soup by hand, a food processor or blender is essential. Then you will find that this Spanish soup is simple to make and refreshing to eat on a hot day.

SERVES 6

INGREDIENTS
115g/4oz fresh white bread
750ml/1¼ pints/3 cups cold water
115g/4oz/1 cup blanched almonds
2 garlic cloves, sliced
75ml/5 tbsp olive oil
25ml/1½ tbsp sherry vinegar
salt and freshly ground black pepper

FOR THE GARNISH
toasted flaked almonds
seedless green and black grapes, halved and skinned

1 Break the bread into a bowl and pour 150 ml/¼ pint/⅔ cup of the water on top. Leave for 5 minutes.

2 Put the almonds and garlic in a food processor or blender and process until finely ground. Blend in the soaked bread.

3 Gradually add the oil until the mixture forms a smooth paste. Add the sherry vinegar, then the remaining cold water, and process until smooth.

4 Transfer to a bowl and season with salt and pepper, adding a little more water if the soup is too thick. Chill for at least 2–3 hours. Serve scattered with the toasted almonds and grapes.

CHILLED GARLIC & ALMOND SOUP WITH GRAPES

This creamy chilled summer soup is based on an ancient Moorish recipe from Andalucia in southern Spain. Almonds and pine nuts are typical ingredients of this sun-drenched region.

SERVES 6

INGREDIENTS
75g/3oz/¾ cup blanched almonds
50g/2oz/½ cup pine nuts
6 large garlic cloves, peeled
200g/7oz good-quality day-old bread, crusts removed
900ml–1 litre/1½–1¾ pints/3¾–4 cups still mineral water, chilled
120ml/4fl oz/½ cup extra virgin olive oil, plus extra to serve
15ml/1 tbsp sherry vinegar
30–45ml/2–3 tbsp dry sherry
250g/9oz grapes, peeled, halved and seeded
salt and freshly ground white pepper
ice cubes and snipped fresh chives, to garnish

COOK'S TIPS
• Toasting the nuts slightly accentuates their flavour, but you can omit this step if you prefer a paler soup.
• Blanching the garlic softens its flavour.

1 Roast the almonds and pine nuts together in a dry pan over a moderate heat until they are very lightly browned. Cool, then grind to a powder.

2 Blanch the garlic in boiling water for 3 minutes. Drain off the water and rinse the cooked cloves.

3 Soak the bread in 300ml/½ pint/1¼ cups of the water for 10 minutes, then squeeze dry. Process the garlic, bread, nuts and 5ml/1 tsp salt in a food processor or blender until they form a paste.

4 Gradually blend in the olive oil and sherry vinegar, followed by sufficient water to make a smooth soup with a creamy consistency.

5 Stir in 30ml/2 tbsp of the sherry. Adjust the seasoning and add more dry sherry to taste. Chill for at least 3 hours, then adjust the seasoning again and stir in a little more chilled water if the soup has thickened. Reserve a few of the grapes for the garnish and stir the remainder into the soup.

6 Ladle the soup into bowls – glass bowls look particularly good – and garnish with ice cubes, the reserved grapes and snipped fresh chives. Serve with additional extra virgin olive oil to drizzle over the soup to taste just before it is eaten.

TAMARIND SOUP WITH PEANUTS & VEGETABLES

Known in Indonesia as Sayur Asam, *this is a colourful and refreshing soup from Jakarta with more than a hint of sharpness.*

SERVES 4 AS A STARTER OR 8 AS PART OF A BUFFET

INGREDIENTS
5 shallots or 1 medium red onion, sliced
3 garlic cloves, crushed
2.5cm/1in galangal, peeled and sliced
1–2 fresh red chillies, seeded and sliced
25g/1oz/¼ cup raw peanuts
1cm/½ in cube shrimp paste, prepared
1.2 litres/2 pints/5 cups well-flavoured stock
50–75g/2–3oz/½–¾ cup salted peanuts, lightly crushed
15–30ml/1–2 tbsp soft dark brown sugar
5ml/1 tsp tamarind pulp, soaked in 75ml/5 tbsp warm water for 15 minutes
salt

FOR THE VEGETABLES
1 chayote, thinly peeled, seeds removed, flesh finely sliced
115g/4oz French (green) beans, trimmed and finely sliced
50g/2oz corn kernels (optional)
*a handful of green leaves, such as watercress, rocket (arugula) or Chinese leaves,
    finely shredded*
1 fresh green chilli, sliced, to garnish

COOK'S TIP
Ingredients such as shrimp paste, galangal and tamarind pulp may be available in some larger supermarkets, otherwise specialist grocers or Chinese supermarkets are likely to stock them.

1 Grind the shallots or onion, garlic, galangal, chillies, raw peanuts and shrimp paste in a food processor, or using a pestle and mortar.

2 Pour in some of the stock to moisten and then pour this mixture into a pan or wok, adding the rest of the stock. Cook for 15 minutes with the crushed salted peanuts and sugar.

3 Strain the pre-soaked tamarind pulp, discarding any seeds that remain. Reserve the juice.

4 About 5 minutes before serving, add the chayote slices, beans and corn, if using, to the soup and cook fairly rapidly. At the last minute, add the green leaves and salt to taste.

5 Add the tamarind juice and adjust the seasoning. Serve at once, garnished with slices of green chilli.

VARIATIONS

Use 1 standard onion or 2 small leeks in place of shallots or red onion. Use small broccoli florets or fresh (shelled) peas in place of French (green) beans.

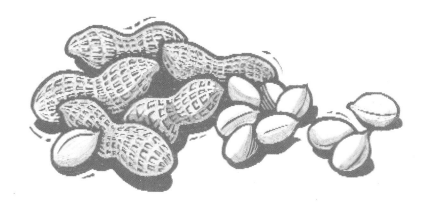

SPINACH & TOFU SOUP

This is an extremely delicate and mild-flavoured soup, which can be used to counterbalance the heat from a hot Thai curry.

SERVES 4–6

INGREDIENTS
30ml/2 tbsp dried shrimp
1 litre/1¾ pints/4 cups chicken stock
225g/8oz fresh tofu, drained and cut into 2cm/¾ in cubes
30ml/2 tbsp fish sauce
350g/12oz fresh spinach
freshly ground black pepper
2 spring onions (scallions), finely sliced, to garnish

1 Rinse and drain the dried shrimp. Combine the shrimp with the chicken stock in a large pan and bring to the boil. Add the tofu and simmer for about 5 minutes. Season with fish sauce and black pepper to taste.

2 Wash the spinach leaves thoroughly and tear into bite-size pieces. Add to the soup. Cook for another 1–2 minutes.

3 Pour the soup into warmed bowls, sprinkle the chopped spring onions on top to garnish, and serve.

COOK'S TIPS
Dried shrimp and fish sauce are available in Chinese grocers or supermarkets. Thinly pared strips of lemon or lime rind will also make an attractive garnish for this soup.

VARIATIONS
Use vegetable or fish stock in place of chicken stock. Use shredded dark green cabbage leaves, watercress or rocket (arugula) in place of spinach.

HOT & SOUR PRAWN SOUP

This classic seafood soup, known as Tom Yam Goong, is probably the most popular and best-known soup from Thailand.

SERVES 4–6

INGREDIENTS
450g/1lb king prawns (shrimp)
1 litre/1¾ pints/4 cups chicken stock or water
3 lemon grass stalks
10 kaffir lime leaves, torn in half
225g/8oz can straw mushrooms, drained
45ml/3 tbsp fish sauce
50ml/2fl oz/¼ cup lime juice
30ml/2 tbsp chopped spring onion (scallion)
15ml/1 tbsp fresh coriander (cilantro) leaves
4 fresh red chillies, seeded and chopped
2 spring onions (scallions), finely chopped, to garnish

1 Shell and devein the prawns and set aside. Rinse the prawn shells and place in a large pan with the stock or water and bring to the boil.

2 Bruise the lemon grass stalks with the blunt edge of a chopping knife and add them to the stock, together with half the lime leaves. Simmer gently for 5–6 minutes until the stalks change colour and the stock is fragrant.

3 Strain the stock, return to the pan and reheat. Add the mushrooms and prawns, then cook until the prawns turn pink.

4 Stir in the fish sauce, lime juice, spring onion, coriander, red chillies and the rest of the lime leaves. Taste and adjust the seasoning. The soup should be sour, salty, spicy and hot. Garnish with finely chopped spring onions before serving.

CHICKEN STELLETTE SOUP

Provided you have some good chicken stock to hand, this light, clear soup is very simple and quick to prepare. It is as easy on the palate as it is on the eye.

SERVES 4–6

INGREDIENTS
900ml/1½ pints/3¾ cups chicken stock
1 bay leaf
4 spring onions (scallions), sliced
225g/8oz button (white) mushrooms, sliced
115g/4oz cooked chicken breast
50g/2oz small soup pasta (stellette)
150ml/¼ pint/⅔ cup dry white wine
15ml/1 tbsp chopped parsley
salt and freshly ground black pepper

1 Put the stock and bay leaf into a large pan and bring to the boil. Add the sliced spring onions and mushrooms.

2 Remove the skin from the chicken and discard. Slice the chicken thinly, add to the soup and season to taste with salt and pepper. Heat through for 2–3 minutes.

3 Add the pasta to the soup, cover and simmer for 7–8 minutes until the pasta is *al dente*.

4 Just before serving, add the wine and chopped parsley and heat through for 2–3 minutes. Pour into individual soup bowls.

VARIATIONS
Use 2 shallots in place of the spring onions (scallions). Use cooked turkey or duck breast in place of chicken. Use chopped fresh chives, oregano or marjoram in place of parsley.

Jalapeño-style Soup

Chicken, chilli and avocado combine to make this simple but unusual soup. Use chilli discreetly, however – you can't take the heat away if you make a mistake.

SERVES 6

INGREDIENTS
1.5 litres/2½ pints/6¼ cups chicken stock
2 cooked chicken breast fillets, skinned and cut into large strips
1 drained canned chipotle or jalapeño chilli, rinsed
1 avocado

1 Heat the stock in a large pan and add the chicken and chilli. Simmer over a very gentle heat for 5 minutes to heat the chicken through and release the flavour from the chilli.

2 Cut the avocado in half, remove the stone and peel off the skin. Slice the avocado flesh neatly lengthways.

3 Using a slotted spoon, remove the chilli from the stock and discard it. Pour the soup into heated serving bowls, distributing the chicken evenly among them.

4 Carefully add a few decorative avocado slices to each bowl and serve the soup immediately.

COOK'S TIP
When using canned chillies, it is important to rinse them thoroughly before adding them to a dish so as to remove the flavour of any pickling liquid.

CHINESE CHICKEN & ASPARAGUS SOUP

This is a very delicate and delicious soup. When fresh asparagus is not in season, tinned white asparagus is an acceptable substitute.

SERVES 4

INGREDIENTS
140g/5oz chicken breast fillet
pinch of salt
1 tsp egg white
1 tsp cornflour (cornstarch) paste
115g/4oz asparagus
700ml/1¼ pints/3 cups chicken stock
salt and freshly ground black pepper
fresh coriander (cilantro) leaves, to garnish

1 Cut the chicken meat into thin slices, each about the size of a postage stamp. Mix with a pinch of salt, then add the egg white, and finally the cornflour paste.

2 Cut off and discard the tough stems of the asparagus, and diagonally cut the tender spears into short, even lengths.

3 In a wok or pan, bring the stock to a rolling boil, add the asparagus and bring back to the boil, cooking for 2 minutes. (You do not need to do this if you are using tinned asparagus.)

4 Add the chicken, stir to separate and bring back to the boil once more. Adjust the seasonings. Serve hot, garnished with fresh coriander leaves.

PORK & PICKLED MUSTARD GREENS SOUP

This highly flavoured soup makes an interesting start to a meal. Pickled mustard leaves are members of the cabbage family, and are used in traditional Asian cooking.

SERVES 4–6

INGREDIENTS
225g/8oz pickled mustard leaves, soaked
50g/2oz cellophane noodles, soaked
15ml/1 tbsp vegetable oil
4 garlic cloves, finely sliced
1 litre/1¾ pints/4 cups chicken stock
450g/1lb pork ribs, cut into large chunks
30ml/2 tbsp fish sauce
a pinch of sugar
freshly ground black pepper
2 fresh red chillies, seeded and finely sliced, to garnish

1 Cut the pickled mustard leaves into bite-size pieces. Taste to check the seasoning. If they are too salty, soak them for a little longer.

2 Drain the cellophane noodles, discarding the soaking water, and cut them into pieces about 5cm/2in long.

3 Heat the oil in a small frying pan, add the garlic and stir-fry until golden. Transfer to a bowl and set aside.

4 Put the stock in a pan, bring to the boil, then add the pork ribs and simmer gently for 10–15 minutes.

5 Add the pickled mustard leaves and cellophane noodles. Bring back to the boil. Season to taste with fish sauce, sugar and freshly ground black pepper.

6 Pour the soup into individual serving bowls. Garnish with the fried garlic and the red chillies and serve hot.

DUCK CONSOMMÉ

The Vietnamese community in France has had a profound influence on French cooking, as this soup demonstrates – it is light and rich at the same time, with intriguing flavours of South-east Asia.

SERVES 4

INGREDIENTS

*1 duck carcass (raw or cooked), plus 2 legs or any giblets, trimmed of
    as much fat as possible
1 large onion, unpeeled, with root end trimmed
2 carrots, cut into 5cm/2in pieces
1 parsnip, cut into 5cm/2in pieces
1 leek, cut into 5cm/2in pieces
2–4 garlic cloves, crushed
2.5cm/1in piece fresh root ginger, peeled and sliced
15ml/1 tbsp black peppercorns
4–6 sprigs of fresh thyme or 5ml/1 tsp dried thyme
1 small bunch of coriander (cilantro) (6–8 sprigs), leaves and stems separated*

FOR THE GARNISH
*1 small carrot
1 small leek, halved lengthways
4–6 shiitake mushrooms, thinly sliced
soy sauce
2 spring onions (scallions), thinly sliced
watercress or finely shredded Chinese leaves
freshly ground black pepper*

> COOK'S TIP
> *Use a julienne cutter or peeler to prepare the carrot and leek for the garnish.*

1 Put the duck carcass and legs or giblets, onion, carrots, parsnip, leek and garlic in a large, heavy pan or flameproof casserole. Add the ginger, peppercorns, thyme and coriander stems, cover with cold water and bring to the boil over a medium-high heat, skimming off any foam that rises to the surface.

2 Reduce the heat and simmer gently for 1½–2 hours, then strain through a muslin-lined sieve (cheesecloth-lined strainer) into a bowl, discarding the bones and vegetables. Cool the stock and chill for several hours or overnight. Skim off any congealed fat and blot the surface with kitchen paper to remove any traces of fat.

3 To make the garnish, cut the carrot and leek into 5cm/2in pieces. Cut each piece lengthways in thin slices, then stack and slice into thin julienne strips. Place in a large pan with the sliced mushrooms.

4 Pour over the stock and add a few dashes of soy sauce and some pepper. Bring to the boil over a medium-high heat, skimming any foam that rises to the surface. Adjust the seasoning. Stir in the spring onions and watercress or Chinese leaves. Ladle the consommé into warmed bowls and sprinkle with the coriander leaves before serving.

VARIATIONS
Use a chicken carcass and chicken legs or a small turkey carcass and turkey legs in place of duck and duck legs. Use 2 small turnips in place of carrots. Use fresh flat leaf parsley in place of coriander (cilantro).

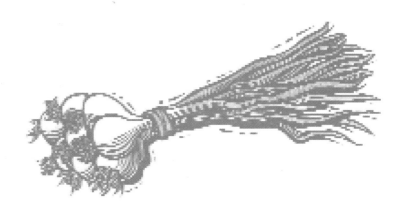

RICH & CREAMY SOUPS

This tempting selection of rich and creamy soups brings together a variety of tastes and flavours from all over the world. They are ideal served for a special occasion or dinner party or as a tasty snack or appetizer for all the family to enjoy. Choose from flavourful soups such as Broccoli & Stilton Soup, Cream of Avocado Soup or Creamy Corn Soup. Or tempt your tastebuds with delights including Carrot Soup with Ginger, Fresh Pea Soup St Germain, Spiced Parsnip Soup or Coconut & Seafood Soup.

BROCCOLI & ALMOND SOUP

The creaminess of the toasted almonds in this soup combines perfectly with the slightly bitter taste of the broccoli.

SERVES 4–6

INGREDIENTS
50g/2oz/½ cup ground almonds
675g/1½lb broccoli
900ml/1½ pints/3¾ cups vegetable stock or water
300ml/½ pint/1¼ cups skimmed milk
salt and freshly ground black pepper

1 Preheat the oven to 180°C/350°F/Gas 4. Spread the ground almonds evenly on a baking sheet and toast in the oven for about 10 minutes until golden. Reserve one quarter of the almonds and set aside to garnish the finished dish.

2 Cut the broccoli into small florets and steam for about 6–7 minutes until they are tender.

3 Place the remaining toasted almonds, broccoli, stock or water and milk in a food processor or blender and process until smooth. Season with salt and pepper to taste.

4 Reheat the soup over a medium heat and serve, sprinkled with the reserved toasted almonds.

BROCCOLI & STILTON SOUP

This is a very easy but rich soup – choose something simple to follow, such as plainly roasted or grilled (broiled) meat, poultry or fish.

SERVES 4

INGREDIENTS
350g/12oz broccoli
25g/1oz/2 tbsp butter
1 onion, chopped
1 leek, white part only, chopped
1 small potato, cut into chunks
600ml/1 pint/2½ cups hot chicken stock
300ml/½ pint/1¼ cups milk
45ml/3 tbsp double (heavy) cream
115g/4oz Stilton cheese, rind removed, crumbled
salt and freshly ground black pepper

1 Break the broccoli into florets, discarding any tough stems. Set aside two small florets to garnish the finished dish.

2 Melt the butter in a large pan and cook the onion and leek until soft but not coloured. Add the broccoli and potato, then pour in the stock. Cover and simmer for 15–20 minutes, until the vegetables are tender.

3 Cool slightly, then pour into a food processor or blender and purée until smooth. Strain the mixture through a sieve (strainer) back into the rinsed pan.

4 Add the milk and double cream to the pan. Season to taste with salt and freshly ground black pepper. Reheat gently. Add the cheese at the last minute, stirring until it just melts. Do not boil.

5 Meanwhile, blanch the reserved broccoli florets and cut them vertically into thin slices. Ladle the soup into warmed bowls and garnish with the sliced broccoli and a generous grinding of black pepper.

CREAMY TOMATO SOUP

Tomato soup is an old favourite. This version is made special by the addition of fresh herbs and whipping cream.

SERVES 4

INGREDIENTS
25 g/1 oz/2 tbsp butter or margarine
1 onion, chopped
900 g/2 lb tomatoes, peeled and quartered
2 carrots, chopped
450 ml/³/4 pint/scant 2 cups chicken stock
30 ml/2 tbsp chopped fresh parsley
2.5 ml/¹/2 tsp fresh thyme leaves, plus extra to garnish
75 ml/5 tbsp whipping cream (optional)
salt and freshly ground black pepper

1 Melt the butter or margarine in a large pan. Add the onion and cook for 5 minutes until softened.

2 Stir in the tomatoes, carrots, chicken stock, parsley and thyme. Bring to the boil. Reduce the heat to low, cover the pan, and simmer for 15–20 minutes until the vegetables are tender.

3 Purée the soup in a vegetable mill until it is smooth. Return the puréed soup to the pan.

4 Stir in the cream, if using, and reheat gently. Season the soup to taste with salt and freshly ground black pepper. Ladle into warmed soup bowls and serve piping hot, garnished with fresh thyme leaves.

COOK'S TIP
Meaty and flavourful, Italian plum tomatoes are the best choice for this soup..

Egg & Cheese Soup

In this classic Roman soup, eggs and cheese are beaten into hot broth, producing a slightly "curdled" texture, which is a characteristic of the dish.

SERVES 6

INGREDIENTS
3 eggs
45 ml/3 tbsp fine semolina
90 ml/6 tbsp grated Parmesan cheese
a pinch of freshly grated nutmeg
1.5 litres/2½ pints/6¼ cups meat or chicken stock
salt and freshly ground black pepper
12 slices French bread, to serve

1 Beat the eggs in a bowl with the semolina and cheese. Add the nutmeg. Beat in 250 ml/8 fl oz/1 cup of the cool stock.

2 Meanwhile, gently heat the leftover stock to simmering point in a large pan over a medium heat.

3 When the stock is hot, whisk the egg mixture into the stock. Raise the heat slightly and bring it barely to the boil. Season with salt and pepper. Cook for 3–4 minutes. As the egg cooks, the soup will lose its smooth consistency.

4 To serve, toast the slices of French bread and place 2 of them in the bottom of each soup plate. Ladle the hot soup on top of the bread and serve immediately.

TOMATO & BLUE CHEESE SOUP

The concentrated flavour of roasted tomatoes strikes a great balance with strong blue cheese. Some blue cheeses you could try include Roquefort, Stilton or Gorgonzola.

SERVES 4

INGREDIENTS
1.5 kg/3lb ripe tomatoes, peeled, quartered and seeded
2 garlic cloves, minced
30ml/2 tbsp vegetable oil or butter
1 leek, chopped
1 carrot, chopped
1.2 litres/2 pints/5 cups chicken stock
115g/4oz blue cheese, crumbled
45ml/3 tbsp whipping cream
several large fresh basil leaves, or 1–2 fresh parsley sprigs, plus extra to garnish
175g/6oz bacon, cooked and crumbled, to garnish
salt and freshly ground black pepper

1 Preheat the oven to 200°C/400°F/Gas 6. Spread the tomatoes in a shallow ovenproof dish. Sprinkle with the garlic and some salt and pepper. Place in the oven and bake for 35 minutes.

2 Heat the oil or butter in a large pan. Add the leek and carrot and season lightly with salt and pepper. Cook over low heat, stirring often, for about 10 minutes until softened.

3 Stir in the stock and baked tomatoes. Bring to the boil, then lower the heat, cover and simmer for about 20 minutes.

4 Add the blue cheese, cream and basil or parsley. Transfer to a food processor or blender and process until smooth (work in batches if necessary). Taste and adjust the seasoning.

5 Reheat the soup, but do not boil. Serve garnished with bacon and a sprig of fresh herbs.

CAULIFLOWER & WALNUT CREAM

Even though there's no cream added to this soup, the puréed cauliflower gives it a delicious, rich, creamy white texture.

SERVES 4

INGREDIENTS
1 medium cauliflower
1 medium onion, roughly chopped
450ml/³⁄4 pint/scant 2 cups chicken or vegetable stock
450ml/³⁄4 pint/scant 2 cups skimmed milk
45ml/3 tbsp walnut pieces
salt and freshly ground black pepper
paprika and chopped walnuts, to garnish

1 Trim the cauliflower of outer leaves and break into small florets. Place the cauliflower, onion and stock in a large pan.

2 Bring to the boil, cover and simmer for about 15 minutes until soft. Add the milk and walnut pieces, then purée in a food processor or blender until smooth.

3 Season the soup to taste with salt and pepper, then reheat and bring to the boil. Serve sprinkled with a dusting of paprika and chopped walnuts.

VARIATION
If you prefer, you can make this soup using broccoli instead of cauliflower.

JERUSALEM ARTICHOKE SOUP

The Jerusalem artichoke is a white-fleshed root related to the sunflower. Topped with saffron cream, this soup is wonderful on a chilly day.

SERVES 4

INGREDIENTS
50g/2oz/4 tbsp butter
1 onion, chopped
450g/1lb Jerusalem artichokes, peeled and cut into chunks
900ml/1½ pints/3¾ cups chicken stock
150ml/¼ pint/⅔ cup milk
150ml/¼ pint/⅔ cup double (heavy) cream
a good pinch of saffron powder
salt and freshly ground black pepper
snipped fresh chives, to garnish

1 Melt the butter in a large, heavy-based pan and cook the onion for 5–8 minutes until soft but not browned, stirring from time to time.

2 Add the Jeruslaem artichokes to the pan and stir until coated in the butter. Cover and cook gently for 10–15 minutes, being careful not to allow the artichokes to brown. Pour in the chicken stock and milk, then cover and simmer for 15 minutes. Cool slightly, then process in a food processor or blender until smooth.

3 Strain the soup back into the pan. Add half the cream, season to taste and reheat gently. Lightly whip the remaining cream and the saffron powder. Ladle the soup into warmed soup bowls and put a spoonful of saffron cream in the centre of each. Scatter the snipped chives over the top and serve immediately.

CREAM OF AVOCADO SOUP

Avocados make wonderful soup – pretty, delicious and refreshing. When combined with cream, their texture is wonderfully soft and smooth.

SERVES 4

INGREDIENTS
2 large ripe avocados
1 litre/1¾ pints/4 cups chicken stock
250ml/8fl oz/1 cup single (light) cream
salt and freshly ground white pepper
15ml/1 tbsp finely chopped fresh coriander (cilantro), to garnish (optional)

1 Cut the avocados in half, remove the stones and mash the flesh. Put the flesh into a sieve (strainer) and press it through the sieve with a wooden spoon into a warm soup bowl.

2 Heat the chicken stock with the cream in a pan. When the mixture is hot, but not boiling, whisk it into the puréed avocado in the bowl.

3 Season to taste with salt and white pepper. Serve immediately, sprinkled with the coriander, if using. The soup may be served chilled, if preferred.

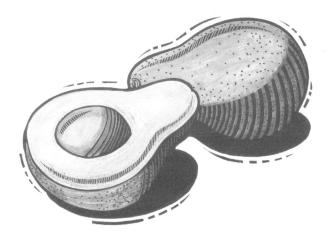

Watercress Soup

Watercress stalks add a distinctive peppery, pungent flavour to soups, and the leaves make an attractive garnish as well. This is a delicious and nutritious soup that should be served with fresh crusty bread.

Serves 4

Ingredients
15ml/1 tbsp sunflower oil
15g/½oz/1 tbsp butter
1 medium onion, finely chopped
1 medium potato, diced
about 175g/6oz watercress
400ml/14fl oz/1⅔ cups vegetable stock
400ml/14fl oz/1⅔ cups milk
lemon juice, to taste
salt and freshly ground black pepper
sour cream, to serve

Cook's Tip
If you don't have a food processor or blender, purée the cooked soup by tipping it into a large sieve (strainer) over a bowl (do this in several batches, if necessary), and squash them through the sieve using the back of a ladle. Return the crushed vegetables to the stock or soup and reheat before serving.

1 Heat the oil and butter in a large pan and fry the onion over a gentle heat until soft but not browned. Add the potato, fry gently for 2–3 minutes and then cover and sweat for 5 minutes over a gentle heat, stirring from time to time.

2 Strip the watercress leaves from the stalks and set aside. Roughly chop the watercress stalks.

3 Add the stock and milk to the pan, stir in the chopped stalks and season. Bring to the boil and simmer gently, partially covered, for 10–12 minutes until the potatoes are tender. Add all but a few of the watercress leaves and simmer for 2 minutes more.

4 Process the soup in a food processor or blender, then pour into a clean pan and heat gently with the reserved watercress leaves.

5 Taste the soup when hot, add a few drops of lemon juice and adjust the seasoning to taste.

6 Pour the soup into warmed soup bowls and garnish with a little sour cream in the centre just before serving.

VARIATION
For a low-calorie alternative, omit the sour cream when serving this healthy soup.

CREAM OF CELERIAC & SPINACH SOUP

Celeriac has a wonderful flavour that is reminiscent of celery, but also adds a slightly nutty taste. Here it is combined with spinach to make a delicious soup.

SERVES 6

INGREDIENTS
1 litre/1¾ pints/4 cups water
250ml/8fl oz/1 cup dry white wine
1 leek, thickly sliced
500g/1¼lb celeriac, diced
200g/7oz fresh spinach leaves
freshly grated nutmeg
salt and freshly ground black pepper
25g/1oz/¼ cup pine nuts, to garnish

1 Mix the water and wine in a jug. Place the leek, celeriac and spinach in a deep pan and pour the liquid over the top. Bring to the boil, lower the heat and simmer for 10–15 minutes until the vegetables are soft.

2 Pour the celeriac mixture into a food processor or blender and purée until smooth, in batches if necessary. Return to the clean pan and season to taste with salt, freshly ground black pepper and nutmeg. Reheat gently.

3 Heat a non-stick frying pan (do not add any oil) and add the pine nuts. Roast until golden brown, stirring occasionally so that they do not stick. Sprinkle them over the soup and serve.

COOK'S TIP
If the soup is too thick, thin it with a little water or semi-skimmed (low-fat) milk when puréeing.

CREAM OF SPINACH SOUP

This is a deliciously creamy soup, and if you love spinach and coconut, you'll find yourself making this dish over and over again.

SERVES 4

INGREDIENTS
25g/1oz/2 tbsp butter
1 small onion, chopped
675g/1½lb fresh spinach, chopped
1 litre/1¾ pints/4 cups vegetable stock
100ml/6½ tbsp coconut milk
freshly grated nutmeg
300ml/½ pint/1¼ cups single (light) cream
salt and freshly ground black pepper
fresh snipped chives, to garnish

1 Melt the butter in a pan over a moderate heat and sauté the onion for a few minutes until soft. Add the spinach, cover the pan and cook gently for 10 minutes, until the spinach has wilted and reduced.

2 Pour the spinach mixture into a food processor or blender and add a little of the stock. Blend until smooth.

3 Return the mixture to the pan and add the remaining stock and the coconut milk, with salt, pepper and nutmeg to taste. Simmer gently for 15 minutes to thicken.

4 Add the cream to the pan, stir well and heat through, but do not boil. Serve hot, garnished with long strips of chives.

CREAM OF RED PEPPER SOUP

Grilling (bell) peppers gives them a sweet, smoky flavour, which is delicious in salads or, as here, in a velvety soup with a secret flavouring of rosemary to add aromatic depth. This soup is equally good served hot or chilled, as you prefer.

SERVES 4

INGREDIENTS
4 red (bell) peppers
25g/1oz/2 tbsp butter
1 onion, finely chopped
1 sprig of fresh rosemary
1.2 litres/2 pints/5 cups chicken or light vegetable stock
45ml/3 tbsp tomato purée (paste)
120ml/4fl oz/½ cup double (heavy) cream
paprika
salt and freshly ground black pepper

COOK'S TIP
For extra heat and flavour, finely chop and seed a small fresh red chilli and sauté with the onion and rosemary.

1 Preheat the grill (broiling) pan. Put the peppers under the grill and turn them regularly until the skins have blackened all around. Put them into polythene bags, sealing them closed. Leave them for 20 minutes.

2 Peel the blackened skin off the peppers. If possible avoid rinsing them under the tap because this removes some of the natural oil and hence the flavour.

3 Halve the peppers, removing the seeds, stalks and pith as you go, then roughly chop the flesh.

4 Melt the butter in a deep pan. Add the onion and rosemary, and cook gently over a low heat for about 5 minutes. Remove the rosemary and discard.

5 Add the peppers and stock to the onion, bring to the boil and simmer for 15 minutes. Stir in the tomato, then process or sieve (strain) the soup to make a smooth purée.

6 Stir in half the cream and season with paprika. Add a little salt, if necessary, and some pepper.

7 Serve the soup hot or chilled, with the remaining cream swirled delicately on top. Speckle the cream very lightly with a pinch of paprika.

VARIATIONS
Use 30ml/2 tbsp olive oil in place of butter. Use 4 shallots in place of the onion. Use crème fraiche in place of double (heavy) cream.

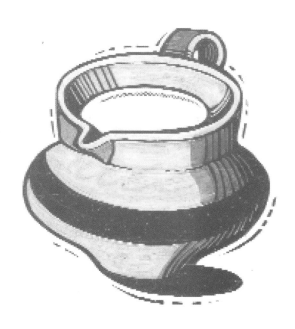

Simple Cream & Onion Soup

This wonderfully soothing soup has a deep, buttery flavour that is complemented by crisp croûtons or snipped chives, sprinkled over just before serving.

Serves 4

Ingredients
115g/4oz/½ cup unsalted butter
1kg/2¼lb yellow onions, sliced
1 fresh bay leaf
105ml/7 tbsp dry white vermouth
1 litre/1¾ pints/4 cups good chicken or vegetable stock
150ml/¼ pint/⅔ cup double (heavy) cream
a little lemon juice (optional)
salt and freshly ground black pepper
croûtons or snipped fresh chives, to garnish

> ### Cook's Tip
> *Adding the second batch of onions gives texture and a lovely buttery flavour to this soup. Make sure that the onions do not brown.*

1 Melt 75g/3oz/6 tbsp of the butter in a large heavy-based pan. Set about 200g/7oz of the onions aside and add the rest to the pan with the bay leaf. Stir to coat in the butter, then cover and cook very gently for about 30 minutes. The onions should be very soft and tender, but not browned.

2 Add the vermouth, increase the heat and boil rapidly until the liquid has evaporated. Add the stock, 5ml/1 tsp salt and pepper to taste. Bring to the boil, lower the heat and simmer for 5 minutes, then remove from the heat.

3 Leave the soup to cool, then discard the bay leaf and process it in a food processor or blender. Return the soup to the rinsed pan.

4 Meanwhile, melt the remaining butter in another pan and cook the remaining onions slowly, covered, until soft but not browned. Uncover and continue to cook gently until golden yellow.

5 Pour the cream into the soup and reheat it gently until hot, but do not allow it to boil. Taste and adjust the seasoning, adding a little lemon juice if liked.

6 Add the buttery onions and stir for 1–2 minutes, then ladle the soup into bowls. Sprinkle with croûtons or snipped chives and serve.

VARIATIONS

Use shallots in place of yellow onions. Use dry white wine in place of vermouth. Use crème fraiche in place of cream. Use a fresh or dried bouquet garni in place of the bay leaf.

CREAM OF SPRING ONION SOUP

The oniony flavour of this soup is surprisingly delicate and mild due to the use of spring onions (scallions) in addition to an ordinary onion. This is a versatile dish that can be served either warm or chilled.

SERVES 4–6

INGREDIENTS
25g/1oz/2 tbsp butter
1 small onion, chopped
150g/5oz/1¾ cups spring onions (scallions), chopped
225g/8oz potatoes, peeled and chopped
600ml/1 pint/2½ cups vegetable stock
350ml/12fl oz/1½ cups single (light) cream
30ml/2 tbsp lemon juice
salt and freshly ground white pepper
chopped spring onion (scallion) greens or fresh chives, to garnish

1 Melt the butter in a pan and add all the onions. Cover and cook over very low heat for about 10 minutes or until soft.

2 Add the potatoes and the stock. Bring to the boil, then cover again and simmer over moderately low heat for about 30 minutes. Cool slightly.

3 Purée the soup in a food processor or blender until the mixture has an even, smooth consistency.

4 If serving the soup hot, pour it back into the pan. Add the cream and season with salt and pepper. Reheat gently, stirring occasionally. Add the lemon juice.

5 If serving the soup cold, pour it into a bowl. Stir in the cream and lemon juice and season with salt and pepper. Cover the bowl and chill for at least 1 hour.

6 Lightly sprinkle the surface of the soup with the chopped spring onion greens or chives before serving.

CREAMY CORN SOUP

This tasty soup is simple to prepare yet full of flavour. It is sometimes made with sour cream and cream cheese. Poblano chillies may be added if you can find them, but these tend to be rather difficult to locate outside Mexico.

SERVES 4

INGREDIENTS
30ml/2 tbsp corn oil
1 onion, finely chopped
1 red (bell) pepper, seeded and chopped
450g/1lb/2⅔ cups corn kernels, thawed if frozen
750ml/1¼ pints/3 cups chicken stock
250ml/8fl oz/1 cup single (light) cream
salt and freshly ground black pepper
½ red (bell) pepper, seeded and finely diced, to garnish

1 Heat the corn oil in a frying pan and sauté the onion and red pepper for about 5 minutes, until soft. Add the corn kernels and sauté for 2 minutes.

2 Carefully tip the contents of the pan into a food processor or blender. Process until smooth, scraping down the sides of the blender and adding a little of the stock, if necessary.

3 Transfer the mixture to a pan and stir in the stock. Season to taste with salt and pepper, bring to a simmer and cook for 5 minutes.

4 Gently stir in the cream. Serve the soup hot or chilled, sprinkled with the diced red pepper. If serving hot, reheat gently after adding the cream, but do not allow the soup to boil.

VARIATIONS
Use 1 leek or 4 spring onions (scallions) in place of the onion. Use 1 yellow or orange (bell) pepper in place of the red (bell) pepper. Use well-flavoured vegetable stock in place of chicken stock.

YOGURT SOUP

This bright yellow Indian soup has yogurt as its main ingredient, and it is thickened with gram flour (besan) – a yellow, earthy type of gluten-free flour made from ground chickpeas. Some communities in India add sugar to this soup.

SERVES 4–6

INGREDIENTS

450ml/³⁄₄ pint/scant 2 cups natural (plain) yogurt, beaten
25g/1oz/¼ cup gram flour (besan)
2.5ml/½ tsp chilli powder
2.5ml/½ tsp turmeric salt, to taste
2–3 fresh green chillies, finely chopped
60ml/4 tbsp vegetable oil
1 whole dried red chilli
5ml/1 tsp cumin seeds
3–4 curry leaves
3 garlic cloves, crushed
5cm/2in piece fresh root ginger, peeled and crushed
30ml/2 tbsp chopped fresh coriander (cilantro)

1 Mix together the yogurt, gram flour, chilli powder and turmeric salt, and pass through a strainer into a pan. Add the green chillies and cook gently for about 10 minutes, stirring occasionally. Be careful not to let the soup boil over.

2 Heat the oil in a frying pan and fry the remaining spices with the garlic and ginger until the dried chilli turns black. Stir in 15ml/1 tbsp of the chopped fresh coriander.

3 Pour the spices over the yogurt soup, cover the pan and leave to rest for 5 minutes. Mix well and gently reheat for 5 minutes more. Serve hot, garnished with the remaining chopped coriander.

MUSHROOM & TARRAGON SOUP

This is a light soup made with brown cap (cremini) mushrooms. These have a more pronounced taste and a meatier texture than button (white) mushrooms. When subtly flavoured with tarragon, their taste is superb.

SERVES 6

INGREDIENTS
15g/½oz/1 tbsp butter or margarine
4 shallots, finely chopped
450g/16oz/6 cups brown cap (cremini) mushrooms, finely chopped
300ml/½ pint/1¼ cups vegetable stock
300ml/½ pint/1¼ cups semi-skimmed (low-fat) milk
15–30ml/1–2 tbsp chopped fresh tarragon
30ml/2 tbsp dry sherry (optional)
salt and freshly ground black pepper
sprigs of fresh tarragon, to garnish

1 Melt the butter or margarine in a large pan, add the shallots and cook gently for 5 minutes, stirring occasionally. Add the mushrooms and cook gently for 3 minutes, stirring. Add the stock and milk.

2 Bring to the boil, then cover and simmer gently for about 20 minutes until the vegetables are soft. Stir in the chopped tarragon and season to taste with salt and freshly ground black pepper.

3 Allow the soup to cool slightly, then purée in a food processor or blender, in batches if necessary, until smooth. Return to the rinsed-out pan and reheat.

4 Stir in the sherry, if using, then ladle the soup into warmed soup bowls and serve garnished with sprigs of tarragon.

VARIATION
If you prefer, use a mixture of wild and button (white) mushrooms instead of the brown cap (cremino) variety.

CREAM OF MUSHROOM SOUP

A good mushroom soup makes the most of the subtle flavour of mushrooms. Button (white) mushrooms are used here for their pale colour. Brown cap (cremini) or, better still, field (portabello) mushrooms give a fuller flavour but turn the soup brown.

SERVES 4

INGREDIENTS
275g/10oz button (white) mushrooms
15ml/1 tbsp sunflower oil
40g/1½oz/3 tbsp butter
1 small onion, finely chopped
15ml/1 tbsp plain (all-purpose) flour
450ml/¾ pint/scant 2 cups vegetable stock
450ml/¾ pint/scant 2 cups milk
a pinch of dried basil
30–45ml/2–3 tbsp single (light) cream (optional)
salt and freshly ground black pepper
fresh basil leaves, to garnish

COOK'S TIP
Choose button (white) or closed-cup white mushrooms that are firm with no dark or damp patches or dry stalk ends.

1 Separate the mushroom caps from the stalks. Finely slice the caps and finely chop the stalks.

2 Heat the oil and half the butter in a heavy-based pan and add the onion, mushroom stalks and about three-quarters of the sliced mushroom caps. Fry for about 1–2 minutes, stirring frequently, then cover and sweat over a gentle heat for 6–7 minutes, stirring from time to time.

3 Stir in the flour and cook for about 1 minute. Gradually add the stock and milk, to make a smooth, thin sauce. Add the dried basil, and season to taste. Bring to the boil and simmer, partly covered, for 15 minutes.

4 Cool the soup slightly and then pour into a food processor or blender and process until smooth. Melt the rest of the butter in a frying pan and fry the remaining mushroom caps gently for 3–4 minutes until they are just tender.

5 Pour the soup into a clean pan and stir in the fried mushrooms. Heat until very hot and adjust the seasoning. Add the cream, if using. Serve sprinkled with fresh basil leaves.

VARIATIONS
Use mixed fresh wild mushrooms or closed-cup white or brown cap (cremini) mushrooms in place of button (white) mushrooms. Use single (light) cream in place of half the milk.

CARROT & CORIANDER SOUP

Use a good home-made chicken stock for this soup – it adds a far greater depth of flavour than stock made from shop-bought cubes.

SERVES 4

INGREDIENTS
50g/2oz/4 tbsp butter
3 leeks, sliced
450g/1lb carrots, sliced
15ml/1 tbsp ground coriander
1.2 litres/2 pints/5 cups chicken stock
150ml/¼ pint/⅔ cup Greek yogurt (US strained plain)
salt and freshly ground black pepper
30–45ml/2–3 tbsp chopped fresh coriander (cilantro), to garnish

1 Melt the butter in a large pan. Add the leeks and carrots and stir well. Cover and cook for 10 minutes, until the vegetables are beginning to soften.

2 Stir in the ground coriander and cook for about 1 minute. Pour in the stock and add seasoning to taste. Bring to the boil, cover and simmer for about 20 minutes, until the leeks and carrots are tender.

3 Leave to cool slightly, then purée the soup in a food processor or blender until smooth. Return the soup to the pan and add 30ml/2 tbsp of the yogurt, then taste the soup and adjust the seasoning. Reheat gently, but do not boil.

4 Ladle the soup into bowls and put a spoonful of the remaining yogurt in the centre of each. Scatter over the chopped coriander and serve.

CARROT SOUP WITH GINGER

This bright orange soup has a wonderfully rich and creamy texture. The zing of fresh ginger is an ideal complement to the sweetness of cooked carrots.

SERVES 6

INGREDIENTS
25g/1oz/2 tbsp butter or margarine
1 onion, chopped
1 celery stick, chopped
1 medium potato, chopped
675g/1½lb carrots, chopped
10ml/2 tsp minced fresh root ginger
1.2 litres/2 pints/5 cups chicken stock
105ml/7 tbsp whipping cream
a good pinch of freshly grated nutmeg
salt and freshly ground black pepper

1 Combine the butter or margarine, onion and celery and cook for about 5 minutes until softened.

2 Stir in the potato, carrots, ginger and stock. Bring to the boil. Reduce the heat to low, cover and simmer for about 20 minutes.

3 Pour the soup into a food processor or blender and process until smooth. Alternatively, use a vegetable mill to purée the soup. Return the soup to the pan. Stir in the cream and nutmeg, and add salt and pepper to taste. Reheat gently before serving.

COOK'S TIP
To save a little time, use ready-prepared minced or chopped fresh root ginger, which is readily available, instead of preparing your own.

CREAMY COURGETTE & DOLCELATTE SOUP

The beauty of this soup is its delicate colour, its creamy texture and its subtle taste. If you prefer a more pronounced cheese flavour, use Gorgonzola instead of Dolcelatte.

SERVES 4–6

INGREDIENTS
30ml/2 tbsp olive oil
15g/½oz/1 tbsp butter
1 medium onion, roughly chopped
900g/2lb courgettes (zucchini), trimmed and sliced
5ml/1 tsp dried oregano
about 600ml/1 pint/2½ cups vegetable stock
115g/4oz Dolcelatte cheese, rind removed, diced
300ml/½ pint/1¼ cups single (light) cream
salt and freshly ground black pepper

TO GARNISH
sprigs of fresh oregano
extra Dolcelatte cheese

COOK'S TIP
Choose firm courgettes (zucchini) with unbroken skin and without soft or brown patches.

---

1 Heat the oil and butter in a large pan until foaming. Add the onion and cook gently for about 5 minutes, stirring frequently, until softened but not brown.

2 Add the courgettes and oregano, with salt and pepper to taste. Cook over a medium heat for 10 minutes, stirring frequently.

3 Pour in the stock and bring to the boil, stirring frequently. Lower the heat, half-cover the pan and simmer gently, stirring occasionally, for about 30 minutes. Stir in the diced Dolcelatte until it is melted.

4 Process the soup in a food processor or blender until smooth, then press through a sieve (strainer) into a clean pan.

5 Add two-thirds of the cream and stir over a low heat until hot, but not boiling. Check the consistency and add more stock if the soup is too thick. Taste and adjust the seasoning if necessary.

6 Pour into heated bowls. Swirl in the remaining cream, garnish with fresh oregano and extra Dolcelatte cheese, crumbled, and serve.

VARIATIONS
Use other blue cheeses such as Gorgonzola or Cambazola in place of Dolcelatte. Use dried marjoram in place of oregano. Use milk in place of cream. When in season, use baby courgettes (zucchini) in place of standard courgettes.

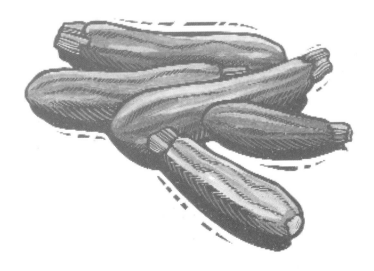

PUMPKIN & COCONUT SOUP

Rich and sweet flavours are married beautifully with sharpness and heat in this creamy South-east Asian-influenced soup.

SERVES 4–6

INGREDIENTS
2 garlic cloves, crushed
4 shallots, finely crushed
2.5ml/½ tsp shrimp paste
15ml/1 tbsp dried shrimp, soaked for 10 minutes and drained
1 lemon grass stalk, chopped
2 fresh green chillies, seeded
600ml/1 pint/2½ cups chicken stock
450g/1lb pumpkin, cut into 2cm/¾ in thick chunks
600ml/1 pint/2½ cups coconut cream
30ml/2 tbsp fish sauce
5ml/1 tsp sugar
115g/4oz small cooked peeled prawns (shrimp)
salt and freshly ground black pepper

TO GARNISH
2 fresh red chillies, seeded and finely sliced
10–12 fresh basil leaves

COOK'S TIP
Fresh lemon grass stalks are readily available in many supermarkets and green grocers, and Chinese supermarkets.

1 Using a pestle and mortar, grind the garlic, shallots, shrimp paste, dried shrimp, lemon grass, green chillies and a pinch of salt into a paste.

2 In a large pan, bring the chicken stock to the boil, add the paste and stir until it is dissolved.

3 Lower the heat, add the pumpkin, and simmer for about 10–15 minutes or until the pumpkin is tender.

4 Stir in the coconut cream, then bring back to a simmer. Add the fish sauce, sugar and freshly ground black pepper to taste.

5 Add the prawns and cook until they are heated through. Serve garnished with the sliced red chillies and basil leaves.

VARIATIONS
Use fresh red chillies if green chillies are not available. Use a well-flavoured vegetable stock in place of chicken stock.

SQUASH SOUP WITH HORSERADISH CREAM

The combination of cream, curry powder and horseradish makes a wonderful topping for this beautiful golden soup.

SERVES 6

INGREDIENTS
1 butternut squash
1 cooking apple
25g/1oz/2 tbsp butter
1 onion, finely chopped
5–10ml/1–2 tsp curry powder, plus extra to garnish
900ml/1½ pints/3¾ cups vegetable stock
5ml/1 tsp chopped fresh sage
150ml/¼ pint/⅔ cup apple juice
salt and freshly ground black pepper
lime shreds, to garnish (optional)

FOR THE HORSERADISH CREAM
60ml/4 tbsp double (heavy) cream
10ml/2 tsp horseradish sauce
2.5ml/½ tsp curry powder

COOK'S TIPS
Curry powders vary in strength of flavour from mild to strong – choose a curry powder to suit your palate. Use a citrus zester to make thin strips or shreds of lime rind for the garnish.

---

1 Peel the butternut squash, remove the seeds and chop the flesh. Peel, core and chop the apple.

2 Heat the butter in a large pan. Add the onion and cook, stirring occasionally, for 5 minutes until soft. Stir in the curry powder. Cook to bring out the flavour, stirring constantly, for 2 minutes.

3 Add the stock, squash, apple and sage. Bring to the boil, lower the heat, cover and simmer for 20 minutes until the squash and apple are soft.

4 Meanwhile, make the horseradish cream. Whip the cream in a bowl until stiff, then stir in the horseradish sauce and curry powder. Cover and chill until required.

5 Purée the soup in a food processor or blender. Return to the clean pan and add the apple juice, with salt and pepper to taste. Reheat gently, without boiling.

6 Serve the soup in bowls topped with a spoonful of horseradish cream and a dusting of curry powder. Garnish with a few lime shreds, if you like.

VARIATIONS
When in season, use 1 small pumpkin in place of the squash. Use 2 tablespoons sunflower oil in place of butter. Use 2 small leeks or 4 shallots in place of the onion. Use chopped fresh thyme or rosemary in place of sage.

SPICED PARSNIP SOUP

This pale, creamy-textured winter soup is given a special touch with an aromatic, spiced garlic and coriander garnish.

SERVES 4–6

INGREDIENTS

40g/1½oz/3 tbsp butter
1 onion, chopped
675g/1½lb parsnips, diced
5ml/1 tsp ground coriander
2.5ml/½ tsp ground cumin
2.5ml/½ tsp ground turmeric
1.5ml/¼ tsp chilli powder
1.2 litres/2 pints/5 cups chicken stock
150ml/¼ pint/⅔ cup single (light) cream
15ml/1 tbsp sunflower oil
1 garlic clove, cut into julienne strips
10ml/2 tsp yellow mustard seeds
salt and freshly ground black pepper

1 Melt the butter in a large pan, add the onion and parsnips and fry gently for about 3 minutes.

2 Stir in the spices and cook for 1 minute more. Add the stock, season with salt and pepper and bring to the boil.

3 Reduce the heat, cover and simmer for about 45 minutes, until the parsnips are tender. Cool slightly, then purée in a food processor or blender until smooth. Return the soup to the pan, add the cream and heat through gently over a low heat.

4 Heat the oil in a small pan, add the julienne strips of garlic and the yellow mustard seeds and fry quickly until the garlic is beginning to brown and the mustard seeds start to pop and splutter. Remove from the heat.

5 Ladle the soup into warmed soup bowls and pour a little of the hot spice mixture over each one. Serve immediately.

Fresh Pea Soup St Germain

This delicious green soup takes its name from a suburb of Paris where peas were formerly cultivated in market gardens.

Serves 2–3

Ingredients
a small knob (pat) of butter
2 or 3 shallots, finely chopped
400g/14oz/3 cups shelled fresh peas (from about 1.5 kg/3lb garden peas)
500ml/17fl oz/2¼ cups water
45–60ml/3–4 tbsp whipping cream (optional)
salt and freshly ground black pepper
croûtons, to garnish

1 Melt the butter in a heavy pan or flameproof casserole. Add the shallots and cook for about 3 minutes, stirring them occasionally.

2 Add the peas and water, and season with salt and a little pepper. Cover and simmer for about 12 minutes for young peas and up to 18 minutes for large or older peas, stirring occasionally.

3 When the peas are tender, ladle them into a food processor or blender with a little of the cooking liquid and process until smooth.

4 Strain the soup into the pan or casserole, stir in the cream, if using, and heat through without boiling. Add the seasoning and serve hot, garnished with a few croûtons.

Cook's Tip
If fresh peas are not available, use frozen peas, but thaw and rinse them before use.

Green Bean & Parmesan Soup

Fresh green beans and Parmesan cheese make a simple but delicious combination of flavours. The cheese adds both colour and flavour to the dish – and extra nutrition.

Serves 4

Ingredients

25g/1oz/2 tbsp butter or margarine
225g/8oz green beans, trimmed
1 garlic clove, crushed
450ml/¾ pint/scant 2 cups vegetable stock
40g/1½oz/½ cup grated Parmesan cheese
50ml/2fl oz/¼ cup single (light) cream
salt and freshly ground black pepper
30ml/2 tbsp chopped fresh parsley, to garnish

1 Melt the butter or margarine in a medium pan. Add the green beans and garlic and cook for 2–3 minutes over a medium heat, stirring frequently.

2 Stir in the stock and season with salt and pepper. Bring to the boil, then simmer, uncovered, for 10–15 minutes until the beans are tender.

3 Pour the soup into a food processor or blender and process until smooth. Alternatively, purée the soup in a food mill. Return to the pan and reheat the mixture gently.

4 Stir in the Parmesan cheese and cream. Pour into bowls, sprinkle with the parsley and serve.

Cook's Tip
To save a little time, use ready-prepared minced or chopped fresh garlic, which is widely available, instead of preparing your own. Tubs of finely grated fresh Parmesan cheese are also readily available to buy in supermarkets, to save you a little time.

BALINESE VEGETABLE SOUP

Any seasonal vegetables can be used in this tasty vegetable soup, which is known in its native Indonesia as Sayur Oelih.

SERVES 8

INGREDIENTS
225g/8oz green beans
1.2 litres/2 pints/5 cups boiling water
400ml/14floz/1⅔ cups coconut milk
1 garlic clove
2 macadamia nuts or 4 almonds
1cm/½ in cube shrimp paste
10–15ml/2–3 tsp coriander seeds, dry-fried and ground
oil for frying
1 onion, finely sliced
2 duan salam or bay leaves
225g/8oz beansprouts
30ml/2 tbsp lemon juice
salt

1 Top and tail the green beans and cut into small pieces. Cook the beans in the salted, boiling water for 3–4 minutes. Drain the beans and reserve the cooking water.

2 Spoon off 45–60ml/3–4 tbsp of the cream from the top of the coconut milk and set aside.

3 Grind the garlic, nuts, shrimp paste and ground coriander to a paste in a food processor or with a pestle and mortar.

4 Heat the oil in a wok or pan and fry the onion until transparent. Remove from the pan and reserve. Fry the paste for 2 minutes without browning. Pour in the reserved bean cooking water and coconut milk. Bring to the boil and add the duan salam or bay leaves. Cook, uncovered, for 15–20 minutes.

5 Just before serving, add the beans, fried onion, beansprouts, reserved coconut cream and lemon juice, and stir. Taste and adjust the seasoning, if necessary. Serve immediately.

Shrimp & Corn Bisque

A bisque is a thick, creamy soup made with shellfish. In this recipe, hot pepper sauce brings a welcome touch of spice to the mildly flavoured soup.

Serves 4

Ingredients

30ml/2 tbsp olive oil

1 onion, finely minced

50g/2oz/4 tbsp butter or margarine

25g/1oz/¼ cup plain (all-purpose) flour

750ml/1¼ pints/3 cups fish stock

250ml/8fl oz/1 cup milk

115g/4oz/1 cup peeled cooked small shrimp, deveined if necessary

225g/8oz/1½ cups corn kernels

2.5ml/½ tsp chopped fresh dill or thyme

hot pepper sauce

120ml/4fl oz/½ cup single (light) cream

salt

sprigs of fresh dill, to garnish

Cook's Tips
Use canned (drained) or frozen (defrosted) corn kernels. Serve the soup in warmed deep soup bowls, so that it retains its heat once served.

1 Heat the olive oil in a large heavy pan. Add the onion and cook over a low heat for 8–10 minutes until softened.

2 Meanwhile, melt the butter or margarine in a medium-size pan. Add the flour and cook for 1–2 minutes, stirring. Stir in the stock and milk, bring to the boil and cook for 5–8 minutes, stirring frequently.

3 Cut each shrimp into two or three pieces and add to the onion with the corn and dill or thyme. Cook for 2–3 minutes, then remove from the heat.

4 Add the sauce mixture to the shrimp and corn mixture, and mix well. Remove 750ml/1¼ pints/3 cups of the soup and purée in a food processor or blender. Return it to the rest of the soup in the pan and stir well. Season with salt and hot pepper sauce to taste.

5 Add the cream and stir to blend evenly. Heat the soup almost to boiling point, stirring frequently.

6 Divide the mixture into individual soup bowls and serve hot, garnished with sprigs of dill.

VARIATIONS
Use 4 shallots in place of the onion. For extra flavour and heat, sauté 1 finely chopped seeded fresh red or green chilli with the onion. Use frozen (defrosted) peas or petit pois (baby peas) in place of corn kernels.

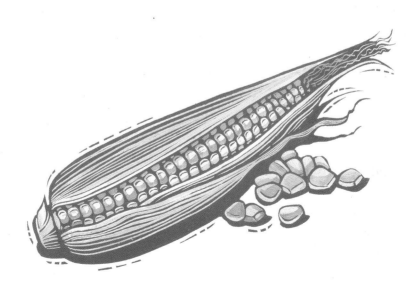

PRAWN BISQUE

The classic French method for making a bisque requires pushing the shellfish through a tamis, *or drum sieve (strainer). This recipe is simpler, but the result is just as smooth.*

SERVES 6-8

INGREDIENTS
675g/1½lb small or medium cooked prawns (shrimp) in their shells
25ml/1½ tbsp vegetable oil
2 onions, halved and sliced
1 large carrot, sliced
2 celery sticks, sliced
2 litres/3½ pints/9 cups water
a few drops of lemon juice
30ml/2 tbsp tomato purée (paste)
bouquet garni
50g/2oz/4 tbsp butter
50g/2oz/⅓ cup plain (all-purpose) flour
45-60ml/3-4 tbsp brandy
150ml/¼ pint/⅔ cup whipping cream

COOK'S TIP
If you prefer, you may leave the brandy out of this dish – it will still taste delicious.

1 Remove the heads from the prawns and peel away the shells. Reserve the heads and shells for the stock. Place the prawns in a covered bowl in the refrigerator.

2 Heat the oil in a large pan, add the heads and shells and cook over a high heat, stirring, until they start to brown. Reduce the heat to medium, add the vegetables and fry, stirring occasionally, for 5 minutes until the onions soften.

3 Add the water, lemon juice, tomato purée and bouquet garni. Bring the stock to the boil, then reduce the heat, cover and simmer gently for 25 minutes. Press the stock through a sieve (strainer).

4 Melt the butter in a heavy pan over a medium heat. Stir in the flour and cook until just golden, stirring occasionally.

5 Add the brandy. Gradually pour in half the prawn stock, whisking vigorously until smooth, then whisk in the remaining liquid. Season if necessary. Reduce the heat, cover and simmer for 5 minutes, stirring frequently.

6 Strain the soup into a clean pan. Add the cream and a little extra lemon juice to taste, then stir in most of the reserved prawns and cook over a medium heat, stirring frequently, until hot. Serve immediately, garnished with the remaining reserved prawns.

COCONUT & SEAFOOD SOUP

This long list of ingredients could mislead you into thinking that this soup is complicated and very time-consuming to prepare. In fact, it is extremely easy to put together, and the marriage of flavours works beautifully.

SERVES 4

INGREDIENTS
600ml/1 pint/2½ cups fish stock
5 thin slices fresh galangal or fresh root ginger
2 lemon grass stalks, chopped
3 kaffir lime leaves, shredded
bunch garlic chives, about 25g/1oz
small bunch fresh coriander (cilantro), about 15g/½oz
15ml/1 tbsp vegetable oil
4 shallots, chopped
400ml/14fl oz can coconut milk
30–45ml/2–3 tbsp Thai fish sauce
45–60ml/3–4 tbsp Thai green curry paste
450g/1lb raw large prawns (shrimp), peeled and deveined
450g/1lb prepared squid
a little fresh lime juice (optional)
salt and freshly ground black pepper
60ml/4 tbsp crisp fried shallot slices, to serve

VARIATIONS
- Instead of squid, you could add 400g/14oz firm white fish, such as monkfish, cut into small pieces.
- You could also replace the squid with mussels. Steam 675g/1½lb live mussels in a tightly covered pan for 3–4 minutes, or until they have opened. Discard any that remain shut, then remove them from their shells and add to the soup.

1 Pour the fish stock into a large pan and add the slices of galangal or ginger, the lemon grass and half the shredded kaffir lime leaves.

2 Reserve a few garlic chives for the garnish, then chop the remainder. Add half the chopped garlic chives to the pan. Strip the coriander leaves from the stalks and set the leaves aside. Add the stalks to the pan. Bring to the boil, reduce the heat to low and cover the pan, then simmer gently for 20 minutes. Strain the stock into a bowl.

3 Rinse and dry the pan. Add the oil and shallots. Cook over a medium heat for 5–10 minutes, until the shallots are just beginning to brown.

4 Stir in the strained stock, coconut milk, the remaining kaffir lime leaves and 30ml/2 tbsp of the fish sauce. Heat gently until simmering and cook over a low heat for 5–10 minutes.

5 Stir in the curry paste and prawns, then cook for 3 minutes. Add the squid and cook for a further 2 minutes. Add the lime juice, if using, and season, adding more fish sauce to taste. Stir in the remaining chives and the reserved coriander leaves. Serve in bowls and sprinkle each portion with fried shallots and whole garlic chives.

Fish & Sweet Potato Soup

The subtle sweetness of the potato, combined with the white fish and the aromatic flavour of oregano, makes this a truly appetizing soup.

SERVES 4

INGREDIENTS
½ onion, chopped
175g/6oz sweet potato, peeled and diced
175g/6oz boneless white fish fillet, skinned
50g/2oz carrot, chopped
5ml/1 tsp chopped fresh oregano or 2.5ml/½ tsp dried oregano
2.5ml/½ tsp ground cinnamon
1.5 litres/2½ pints/6¼ cups fish stock
75ml/5 tbsp single (light) cream
chopped fresh parsley, to garnish

1 Put the chopped onion, diced sweet potato, white fish, chopped carrot, oregano, cinnamon and half of the fish stock in a pan. Bring to the boil, then simmer for 20 minutes or until the potato is cooked.

2 Allow to cool, then pour into a food processor or blender and process the mixture until it is smooth.

3 Return the soup to the pan, then add the remaining fish stock and gently bring to the boil. Reduce the heat to low and add the single cream, then gently heat through without boiling, stirring occasionally.

4 Serve hot in warmed soup bowls, garnished lightly with a few sprigs of chopped fresh parsley.

COOK'S TIP
This soup works equally well garnished with chopped fresh tarragon instead of parsley.

CHICKEN & ALMOND SOUP

This soup makes an excellent lunch or supper dish when served with naan bread.
The ground almonds give the soup a rich, nutty flavour.

SERVES 4

INGREDIENTS
75g/3oz/6 tbsp unsalted butter
1 medium leek, chopped
2.5ml/½ tsp shredded fresh root ginger
75g/3oz/¾ cup ground almonds
5ml/1 tsp salt
2.5ml/½ tsp crushed black peppercorns
1 fresh green chilli, chopped
1 medium carrot, sliced
50g/2oz/½ cup frozen peas
115g/4oz/1 cup chicken, skinned, boned and cubed
30ml/2 tbsp chopped fresh coriander (cilantro)
450ml/¾ pint/scant 2 cups water
250ml/8fl oz/1 cup single (light) cream
4 sprigs of fresh coriander (cilantro)

1 Melt the unsalted butter in a deep, round-bottomed frying pan, and sauté the chopped leek and the root ginger until soft but only just turning brown.

2 Lower the heat and add the ground almonds, salt, peppercorns, chilli, carrot, peas and chicken. Fry for about 10 minutes or until the chicken is completely cooked, stirring constantly. Add the chopped fresh coriander.

3 Remove from the heat and allow to cool slightly. Transfer the mixture to a food processor or blender and process for about 1½ minutes. Pour in the water and blend for a further 30 seconds.

4 Pour back into the pan and bring to the boil, stirring occasionally. Once it has boiled, lower the heat and gradually stir in the cream. Cook gently for a further 2 minutes, stirring from time to time. Serve garnished with the sprigs of fresh coriander.

SPICY CHICKEN & MUSHROOM SOUP

This creamy chicken and mushroom soup makes a hearty meal. It is especially delicious served piping hot with fresh garlic bread.

SERVES 4

INGREDIENTS

75g/3oz/6 tbsp unsalted butter
2.5ml/½ tsp crushed garlic
5ml/1 tsp garam masala
5ml/1 tsp crushed black peppercorns
5ml/1 tsp salt
1.5ml/¼ tsp freshly grated nutmeg
225g/8oz chicken, skinned and boned
1 medium leek, sliced
75g/3oz/generous 1 cup mushrooms, sliced
50g/2oz/⅓ cup corn kernels
300ml/½ pint/1¼ cups water
250ml/8fl oz/1 cup single (light) cream
30ml/2 tbsp chopped fresh coriander (cilantro)
5ml/1 tsp crushed dried red chillies, to garnish (optional)

VARIATIONS
Use turkey or lean, tender pork in place of chicken. Use 1 onion in place of the leek. Use frozen (defrosted) peas in place of corn kernels. Use vegetable or chicken stock in place of water. Use milk or crème fraiche in place of cream. Use 15–30ml/1–2 tbsp chopped fresh tarragon in place of coriander (cilantro).

1 Melt the butter in a medium pan. Lower the heat slightly and add the garlic and garam masala. Lower the heat even further and add the black peppercorns, salt and nutmeg.

2 Cut the chicken pieces into very fine strips and add to the pan with the leek, mushrooms and corn. Cook for 5–7 minutes until the chicken is cooked thoroughly, stirring constantly.

3 Remove from the heat and allow to cool slightly. Transfer three-quarters of the mixture into a food processor or blender. Add the water and process for about 1 minute.

4 Pour the resulting purée back into the pan with the rest of the mixture and bring to the boil over a medium heat. Lower the heat and stir in the cream.

5 Add the fresh coriander. Taste and adjust the seasoning. Serve hot, garnished with crushed red chillies, if liked.

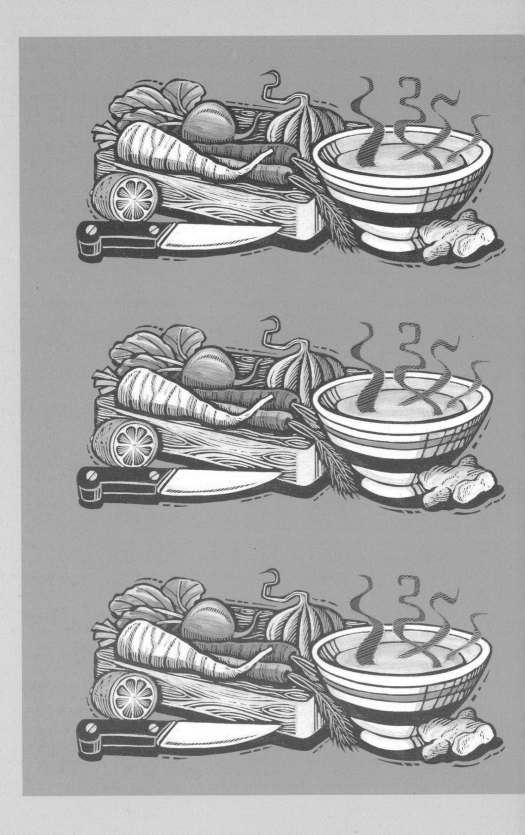

WINTER WARMING SOUPS

Winter is the time of year when it is hard to beat coming home to a bowl of delicious, steaming hot, home-made soup, after a long walk in the cold frosty air. Served with warm fresh bread, winter soups provide a substantial lunch or supper dish for all the family to enjoy. There is a good variety of warming winter soups in this chapter, which is bound to appeal to you on those chilly or damp wintry days. Choose from traditional recipes such as Borscht, French Onion Soup or Pumpkin Soup, or try more innovative recipes such as Roasted Garlic & Squash Soup, Curried Carrot & Apple Soup, Spicy Peanut Soup or Smoked Mackerel & Tomato Soup.

BORSCHT

A simply stunning bright red colour, this classic Russian soup is the perfect dish to serve when you want to offer something a little different.

SERVES 6

INGREDIENTS
1 onion, chopped
450g/1lb raw beetroot (beet), peeled and chopped
2 celery sticks, chopped
½ red (bell) pepper, chopped
115g/4oz mushrooms, chopped
1 large cooking apple, chopped
25g/1oz/2 tbsp butter
30ml/2 tbsp sunflower oil
2 litres/3½ pints/9 cups stock or water
5ml/1 tsp cumin seeds
a pinch of dried thyme
1 large bay leaf
fresh lemon juice
salt and freshly ground black pepper

FOR THE GARNISH
150ml/¼ pint/⅔ cup sour cream
a few sprigs of fresh dill

COOK'S TIP
The flavour of this marvellous soup matures and improves if it is made the day before it is needed.

1 Place the chopped vegetables and apple in a large pan with the butter, oil and 45ml/3 tbsp of the stock or water. Cover and cook gently for about 15 minutes, shaking the pan occasionally.

2 Stir in the cumin seeds and cook for 1 minute, then add the remaining stock or water, the thyme, bay leaf, lemon juice and seasoning to taste.

3 Bring the mixture to the boil, then cover the pan and turn down the heat to a gentle simmer. Cook for about 30 minutes.

4 Strain the vegetables and reserve the liquid. Process the vegetables in a food processor or blender until they are smooth and creamy.

5 Return the vegetables to the pan, add the reserved stock and reheat. Check the seasoning and adjust if necessary.

6 Divide into individual serving bowls. Garnish with swirls of sour cream in each bowl and top with a few sprigs of fresh dill.

CURRIED CELERY SOUP

An unusual but stimulating combination of vegetable flavours – onion, leek and celery – this warming soup is an excellent way to transform a green shoot vegetable that is more usually associated with salads. The soup is well-complemented by warm wholemeal bread rolls.

SERVES 4–6

INGREDIENTS
10ml/2 tsp olive oil
1 onion, chopped
1 leek, sliced
675g/1½lb celery, chopped
15ml/1 tbsp medium or hot curry powder
225g/8oz unpeeled potatoes, washed and diced
900ml/1½ pints/3¾ cups vegetable stock
1 bouquet garni
30ml/2 tbsp chopped fresh mixed herbs
salt
celery seeds and leaves, to garnish

> VARIATIONS
> Use 4 shallots in place of the onion. Use celeriac and sweet potatoes in place of celery and standard potatoes.

1 Heat the oil in a large pan. Add the onion, leek and celery, cover and cook gently for about 10 minutes, stirring occasionally.

2 Add the curry powder and cook gently for about 2 minutes, stirring from time to time.

3 Add the potatoes, stock and bouquet garni, cover and bring to the boil. Simmer for about 20 minutes, until the vegetables are tender, but not too soft.

4 Remove and discard the bouquet garni and set the soup aside to cool slightly before processing.

5 Transfer the soup to a food processor or blender and process in batches until the mixture is smooth.

6 Add the mixed herbs, season to taste and process briefly again. Return to the pan and reheat gently until piping hot. Ladle into bowls and garnish each one with a sprinkling of celery seeds and a few celery leaves before serving.

COOK'S TIPS
- *Choose a mixture of fresh herbs such as parsley, thyme, oregano and chives, for this recipe. Remember when using mixed herbs, to use stronger-flavoured herbs such as rosemary, thyme and tarragon, sparingly so they don't dominate the overall flavour.*
- *Dried bouquet garni is readily available, or you could make up your own fresh bouquet garni. For a typical bouquet garni, simply select 3 sprigs of fresh parsley, 2 sprigs of fresh thyme and 1 bay leaf and tie them together in a bundle with a celery stick or section of leek. Add other flavourings to the mixed herbs such as a thinly pared strip of orange, lemon or lime rind, or add other herbs such as rosemary or tarragon, to add extra flavour to dishes, depending on what other ingredients and flavourings are included in the recipe.*

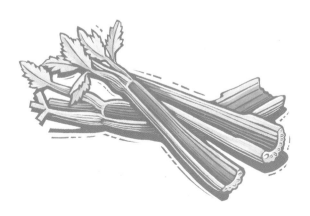

NETTLE SOUP

This is a country-style variation of the classic Irish potato soup. Use wild nettles if you can find them, or a washed head of round (butterhead) lettuce if you prefer.

SERVES 4

INGREDIENTS
115g/4oz/½ cup butter
450g/1lb onions, sliced
450g/1lb potatoes, cut into chunks
750ml/1¼ pints/3 cups chicken stock
25g/1oz nettle leaves
a small bunch of chives, snipped
salt and freshly ground black pepper
double (heavy) cream, to serve

1 Melt the butter in a large pan and add the sliced onions. Cover and cook for about 5 minutes until just softened. Add the potatoes to the pan with the chicken stock. Cover and cook for 25 minutes.

2 Wearing rubber gloves, remove the nettle leaves from their stalks. Wash the leaves under cold running water, then dry on kitchen paper. Add to the pan and cook for a further 5 minutes.

3 Ladle the soup into a food processor or blender and process until smooth. Return to a clean pan and season well. Stir in the chives and serve with a swirl of cream and a sprinkling of pepper.

COOK'S TIP
If you prefer, cut the vegetables finely and leave the cooked soup chunky rather than puréeing it.

BROCCOLI & BREAD SOUP

Broccoli grows abundantly around Rome and is traditionally served in this Italian soup, accompanied by garlic toasts.

SERVES 6

INGREDIENTS
675g/1½lb broccoli spears
1.75 litres/3 pints/7½ cups chicken or vegetable stock
15ml/1 tbsp lemon juice
salt and freshly ground black pepper

TO SERVE
6 slices white bread
1 large garlic clove, cut in half
grated Parmesan cheese (optional)

1 Using a small, sharp knife, peel the broccoli stems, starting from the base and pulling gently up towards the florets. (The peel should come off easily.) Chop the broccoli into small chunks.

2 Bring the stock to the boil in a large pan. Add the broccoli and simmer for about 10 minutes until soft.

3 Purée about half of the soup and mix into the rest of the soup. Season with salt, pepper and lemon juice.

4 Reheat the soup. Toast the bread, rub with garlic and cut into quarters. Place 3 or 4 pieces of toast in the bottom of each soup plate. Ladle on the soup. Serve at once, with Parmesan if liked.

FRENCH ONION SOUP

In France, this standard bistro fare is served so frequently that it is simply referred to as gratinée *rather than the Anglicized name French onion soup.*

SERVES 6–8

INGREDIENTS
15g/½oz/1 tbsp butter
30ml/2 tbsp olive oil
4 large onions, finely sliced
2–5 garlic cloves
5ml/1 tsp sugar
2.5ml/½ tsp dried thyme
30ml/2 tbsp plain (all-purpose) flour
120ml/4fl oz/½ cup dry white wine
2 litres/3½ pints/9 cups beef stock
30ml/2 tbsp brandy (optional)
6–8 thick slices French bread, toasted
350g/12oz/3 cups Gruyère or Emmenthal cheese, grated

1 In a large, heavy pan or flameproof casserole, heat the butter and oil over a medium-high heat. Add the onions and cook for 10–12 minutes until they are softened and beginning to brown.

2 Putting one garlic clove aside, finely chop the rest and add to the onions. Add the sugar and fresh thyme and continue cooking over a medium heat for 30–35 minutes until the onions are well browned, stirring frequently.

3 Sprinkle over the flour and stir until well blended. Stir in the wine and stock and bring to the boil. Skim off any foam that rises to the surface, then reduce the heat and simmer gently for 45 minutes. Stir in the brandy, if using.

4 Preheat the grill. Rub each slice of toasted French bread with the remaining garlic clove. Place six or eight ovenproof soup bowls on a baking sheet and fill about three-quarters full with the onion soup. Float a piece of toast in each bowl. Top with grated cheese, dividing it evenly, and grill about 15cm/6in from the heat for about 3–4 minutes until the cheese begins to melt and bubble. Serve piping hot.

SPANISH GARLIC SOUP

This is a simple and satisfying soup made with garlic, which is one of the most popular ingredients in the quick cook's kitchen.

SERVES 4

INGREDIENTS
30ml/2 tbsp olive oil
4 large garlic cloves, peeled
4 slices French bread, about 5 mm/¼ in thick
15ml/1 tbsp paprika
1 litre/1¾ pints/4 cups beef stock
1.5ml/¼ tsp ground cumin
a pinch of saffron strands
4 eggs
salt and freshly ground black pepper
chopped fresh parsley, to garnish

1 Preheat the oven to 230°C/450°F/Gas 8. Heat the oil in a large pan. Add the whole garlic cloves and cook until golden. Remove and set aside. Fry the bread in the oil until golden, then set aside.

2 Add the paprika to the pan, and fry for a few seconds. Stir in the beef stock, cumin and saffron, then add the reserved garlic, crushing the cloves with the back of a wooden spoon. Season with salt and pepper to taste, then cook for about 5 minutes.

3 Ladle the soup into four ovenproof bowls and break an egg into each one. Place a slice of fried bread on top of each egg, then put the bowls in the oven for about 3–4 minutes, until the eggs are set. Sprinkle each portion with parsley and serve at once.

COOK'S TIP
When you switch on the oven, put a baking sheet in at the same time. Stand the soup bowls on the hot baking sheet when you put them in the oven, and you will be able to remove them easily when the eggs are set.

Spicy Tomato & Coriander Soup

Although soups are not often eaten in India or Pakistan, tomato soup seems to be favoured in these countries. Deliciously spicy, this is also the perfect soup to prepare for a cold winter's day.

SERVES 4

INGREDIENTS
675g/1½lb tomatoes
30ml/2 tbsp vegetable oil
1 bay leaf
4 spring onions (scallions), chopped
5ml/1 tsp salt
2.5ml/½ tsp crushed garlic
5ml/1 tsp crushed black peppercorns
30ml/2 tbsp chopped fresh coriander (cilantro)
750ml/1¼ pints/3 cups water
15ml/1 tbsp cornflour (cornstarch)

FOR THE GARNISH
1 spring onion (scallion), chopped
30ml/2 tbsp single (light) cream

COOK'S TIP
If the only fresh tomatoes available are rather pale and under-ripe, add 15ml/1 tbsp tomato purée (paste) to the pan with the chopped tomatoes. This will enhance the colour and flavour of the soup.

1 To peel the tomatoes, plunge them into very hot water, then lift them out more or less straight away using a slotted spoon. The skin should peel off quickly and easily. Once this is done, chop the tomatoes roughly.

2 In a medium-size pan, heat the oil and fry the chopped tomatoes, bay leaf and chopped spring onions for a few minutes until soft and translucent, but not browned.

3 Gradually add the salt, garlic, peppercorns and fresh coriander to the tomato mixture, finally adding the water.

4 Bring to the boil, lower the heat and simmer for 15–20 minutes. Meanwhile, dissolve the cornflour in a little cold water, and set aside.

5 Remove the pan of soup from the heat and press the liquid through a sieve (strainer) placed over a bowl.

6 Return to the pan, add the cornflour mixture and stir over a gentle heat for about 3 minutes until thickened.

7 Pour into individual soup bowls and garnish with the chopped spring onion and a swirl of cream. Serve piping hot.

Tomato & Vermicelli Soup

Individual nests of fine vermicelli pasta are lightly fried in a pan of hot oil before being simmered in this tasty tomato soup.

Serves 4

Ingredients
30ml/2 tbsp olive or corn oil
50g/2oz/⅓ cup vermicelli
1 onion, roughly chopped
1 garlic clove, chopped
450g/1lb tomatoes, peeled, seeded and roughly chopped
1 litre/1¾ pints/4 cups chicken stock
1.5ml/¼ tsp sugar
15ml/1 tbsp finely chopped fresh coriander (cilantro), plus extra to garnish
salt and freshly ground black pepper
25g/1oz/⅓ cup grated Parmesan cheese, to serve

1 Heat the oil in a frying pan and sauté the vermicelli over a moderate heat until golden brown. Take care not to let the strands burn.

2 Remove the pan from the heat. Lift out the vermicelli with a slotted spoon, drain on kitchen paper and set aside.

3 Purée the onion, garlic and tomatoes in a food processor or blender until smooth. Return the frying pan to the heat. When the oil is hot, add the purée. Cook, stirring constantly, for about 5 minutes or until thick.

4 Transfer the purée to a pan. Add the vermicelli and pour in the stock. Season with sugar, salt and pepper. Stir in 15ml/1 tbsp coriander, bring to the boil, then lower the heat, cover the pan and simmer the soup until the vermicelli is tender.

5 Serve in heated bowls, sprinkle with chopped fresh coriander, and offer the Parmesan separately.

TOMATO & BREAD SOUP

This colourful Florentine recipe was created to use up stale bread. It can be made with very ripe fresh or canned plum tomatoes.

SERVES 4

INGREDIENTS
90ml/6 tbsp olive oil
small piece dried chilli, crumbled (optional)
175g/6oz/1½ cups stale bread, cut into 2.5cm/1in cubes
1 medium onion, finely chopped
2 garlic cloves, finely chopped
675g/1½lb ripe tomatoes, peeled and chopped, or 2 × 400g/14oz cans peeled plum tomatoes, chopped
45ml/3 tbsp chopped fresh basil
1.5 litres/2½ pints/6¼ cups light meat stock or water, or a combination of both
salt and freshly ground black pepper
extra virgin olive oil, to serve (optional)

1 Heat 60ml/4 tbsp of the oil in a large pan. Add the chilli, if using, and stir for 1–2 minutes. Add the bread cubes and cook until golden, then remove to a plate and drain on kitchen paper.

2 Add the remaining oil, the onion and garlic to the pan and cook until the onion softens. Stir in the tomatoes, basil and the reserved bread cubes. Season with salt. Cook over a moderate heat, stirring occasionally, for about 15 minutes.

3 Meanwhile, heat the stock or water to simmering. Add it to the tomato mixture and stir well. Bring to the boil. Lower the heat slightly and simmer for 20 minutes.

4 Remove the soup from the heat. Use a fork to mash together the tomatoes and bread. Season with pepper, and more salt if necessary. Allow to stand for 10 minutes. Just before serving, swirl in a little extra virgin olive oil, if liked.

Mushroom & Herb Potage

Do not worry if this soup is not completely smooth – it is actually especially nice when it has a slightly nutty, textured consistency.

SERVES 4

INGREDIENTS
50g/2oz smoked streaky (fatty) bacon
1 onion, chopped
15ml/1 tbsp sunflower oil
350g/12oz open field (portobello) mushrooms or a mixture of wild and
brown cap (cremini) mushrooms
600ml/1 pint/2½ cups good meat stock
30ml/2 tbsp sweet sherry
30ml/2 tbsp chopped fresh mixed herbs, such as sage, rosemary, thyme and
marjoram, or 10ml/2 tsp dried herbs
salt and freshly ground black pepper
a few sprigs of sage or marjoram, to garnish
60ml/4 tbsp thick Greek yogurt (US strained plain) or crème fraîche, to serve

1 Roughly chop the bacon and place in a large pan. Cook gently until all the fat comes out of the bacon.

2 Add the onion and soften, adding oil if necessary. Wipe the mushrooms clean, roughly chop and add to the pan. Cover and sweat until they have completely softened and their liquid has run out.

3 Add the stock, sherry, herbs and seasoning, cover the pan and simmer for 10–12 minutes. Process the soup in a food processor or blender until smooth, but don't worry if you still have a slightly textured result.

4 Check the seasoning and heat through. Serve with a dollop of yogurt or crème fraîche and a sprig of fresh sage or marjoram in each bowl.

MUSHROOM, CELERY & GARLIC SOUP

This is a robust soup in which the dominant flavour of mushrooms is enhanced with garlic, while celery introduces a contrasting note.

SERVES 4

INGREDIENTS
350g/12oz/4½ cups chopped mushrooms
4 celery sticks, chopped
3 garlic cloves
45ml/3 tbsp dry sherry or white wine
750ml/1¼ pints/3 cups chicken stock
30ml/2 tbsp Worcestershire sauce
5ml/1 tsp freshly grated nutmeg
salt and freshly ground black pepper
celery leaves, to garnish

1 Place the mushrooms, celery and garlic in a pan and stir in the sherry or wine. Cover and cook over a low heat for 30–40 minutes until the vegetables are tender.

2 Add half the stock and purée in a food processor or blender until smooth. Return the mixture to the pan and add the remaining stock, the Worcestershire sauce and nutmeg.

3 Bring to the boil and season to taste with salt and pepper. Serve hot, garnished with celery leaves.

COOK'S TIP
Always grate nutmeg freshly from a whole nutmeg, since the ready-ground spice loses its flavour quickly. Use a specialist nutmeg mill or grater. The nutmeg grater has very fine perforations and a curved surface, both of which reduce the risk of grated fingertips.

Roasted Garlic & Squash Soup

This is a wonderful, richly flavoured dish. A spoonful of hot and spicy tomato salsa gives bite to this sweet-tasting garlic and butternut squash soup.

Serves 4–5

Ingredients

2 garlic bulbs, outer papery skin removed
75ml/5 tbsp olive oil
a few fresh thyme sprigs
1 large butternut squash, halved and seeded
2 onions, chopped
5ml/1 tsp ground coriander
1.2 litres/2 pints/5 cups vegetable or chicken stock
30–45ml/2–3 tbsp chopped fresh oregano or marjoram
sea salt and freshly ground black pepper

For the salsa

4 large ripe tomatoes, halved and seeded
1 red (bell) pepper, halved and seeded
1 large fresh red chilli, halved and seeded
30–45ml/2–3 tbsp extra virgin olive oil
15ml/1 tbsp balsamic vinegar

1 Preheat the oven to 220°C/425°F/Gas 7. Place the garlic bulbs on a piece of foil and pour over half the olive oil. Add the thyme sprigs, then fold the foil around the garlic bulbs to enclose them completely. Place the foil parcel on a baking sheet with the butternut squash and brush the squash with 15ml/1 tbsp of the remaining olive oil. Add the halved and seeded tomatoes, red pepper and fresh chilli for the salsa.

2 Roast the vegetables for 25 minutes, then remove the tomatoes, pepper and chilli. Reduce the temperature to 190°C/375°F/Gas 5 and cook the squash and garlic for 20–25 minutes more, or until the squash is tender.

3 Heat the remaining oil in a large, heavy pan and cook the onions and ground coriander gently for about 10 minutes, or until softened.

4 Skin the pepper and chilli and process in a food processor or blender with the tomatoes and 30ml/2 tbsp olive oil. Stir in the vinegar and seasoning to taste. Add the remaining oil if you think the salsa needs it.

5 Squeeze the roasted garlic out of its papery skin into the onions. Scoop the squash out of its skin and add it to the pan. Add the vegetable or chicken stock, 2.5ml/½ tsp sea salt and plenty of freshly ground black pepper. Bring to the boil and simmer for 10 minutes.

6 Stir in half the chopped fresh oregano or marjoram and allow the soup to cool slightly, then process it in batches if necessary, in a food processor or blender until smooth. Alternatively, press the soup through a fine sieve (strainer).

7 Reheat the soup in a clean pan without allowing it to boil, then taste for seasoning before ladling it into individual warmed bowls. Top each with a spoonful of the tomato salsa and sprinkle over the remaining chopped fresh oregano or marjoram. Serve immediately.

PUMPKIN SOUP

The sweet flavour of pumpkin is excellent in soups, teaming well with other savoury ingredients such as onions and potatoes to make a warm and comforting dish.

SERVES 4–6

INGREDIENTS
15ml/1 tbsp sunflower oil
25g/1oz/2 tbsp butter
1 large onion, sliced
675g/1½lb pumpkin, cut into large chunks
450g/1 1b potatoes, sliced
600ml/1 pint/2½ cups vegetable stock
a good pinch of freshly grated nutmeg
5ml/1 tsp chopped fresh tarragon
600ml/1 pint/2½ cups milk
about 5–10ml/1–2 tsp lemon juice
salt and freshly ground black pepper

1 Heat the oil and butter in a heavy-based pan and fry the onion for 4–5 minutes over a gentle heat until soft but not browned, stirring frequently.

2 Add the pumpkin and sliced potatoes, stir well, then cover and sweat over a low heat for about 10 minutes until the vegetables are almost tender, stirring occasionally to stop them sticking to the pan.

3 Stir in the stock, nutmeg, tarragon and seasoning. Bring to the boil and then simmer for about 10 minutes until the vegetables are completely tender.

4 Allow to cool slightly, then pour into a food processor or blender and process until smooth. Pour back into a clean pan and add the milk. Heat gently and then taste, adding the lemon juice and extra seasoning, if necessary. Serve immediately, while piping hot.

VARIATION
For added flavour, try roasting the pumpkin chunks instead before adding to the soup with the stock.

ROOT VEGETABLE SOUP

Simmer a selection of popular winter root vegetables together for a warming and satisfying soup. Its creamy taste comes from adding crème fraîche just before serving.

SERVES 6

INGREDIENTS
3 medium carrots, chopped
1 large potato, chopped
1 large parsnip, chopped
1 large turnip or small swede (rutabaga), chopped
1 onion, chopped
30ml/2 tbsp sunflower oil
25g/1oz/2 tbsp butter
1.5 litres/2½ pints/6¼ cups water
1 piece fresh root ginger, peeled and grated
300ml/½ pint/1¼ cups milk
45ml/3 tbsp crème fraîche
30ml/2 tbsp chopped fresh dill
15ml/1 tbsp lemon juice
salt and freshly ground black pepper
sprigs of fresh dill, to garnish

1 Put the carrots, potato, parsnip, turnip or swede and onion into a large pan with the oil and butter. Fry lightly, then cover and sweat the vegetables on a low heat for 15 minutes, shaking the pan occasionally.

2 Pour in the water, bring to the boil and season well. Cover and simmer for 20 minutes until the vegetables are soft.

3 Strain the vegetables, reserving the stock, add the ginger and vegetables to a food processor or blender and purée until smooth. Return the puréed mixture and stock to the pan. Add the milk and stir while the soup gently reheats.

4 Remove from the heat and stir in the crème fraîche, dill and lemon juice. Season if necessary. Reheat the soup but do not allow it to boil or it may curdle. Serve garnished with sprigs of dill.

CURRIED CARROT & APPLE SOUP

The combination of mild curry powder with crunchy carrot and apple is a highly successful one. Curried fruit is delicious, and the soup has a vivid orange colour.

SERVES 4

INGREDIENTS
10ml/2 tsp sunflower oil
15ml/1 tbsp mild Korma curry powder
500g/1¼lb carrots, chopped
1 large onion, chopped
1 Bramley cooking apple, chopped
750ml/1¼ pints/3 cups chicken stock
salt and freshly ground black pepper
natural (plain) yogurt and carrot curls, to garnish

1 Heat the oil in a large, heavy-based pan and gently fry the Korma curry powder for 2–3 minutes.

2 Add the chopped carrots and onion and the cooking apple, stir well until coated with the curry powder, then cover the pan.

3 Cook over a low heat for about 15 minutes, shaking the pan occasionally, until softened. Spoon the vegetable mixture into a food processor or blender, then add half the stock and process until smooth.

4 Return to the pan and pour in the remaining stock. Bring the soup to the boil and adjust the seasoning before serving in bowls, garnished with a swirl of yogurt and a few curls of raw carrot.

VARIATIONS
Use parsnips, celeriac or swede (rutabaga) in place of carrots. Use 2 leeks in place of onion. Use a well-flavoured vegetable stock in place of chicken stock.

SPICY CARROT SOUP WITH GARLIC CROÛTONS

Carrot soup is given a touch of spice with ground coriander, cumin and chilli powder. The garlic croûtons provide a delicious contrasting texture and flavour.

SERVES 6

INGREDIENTS
15ml/l tbsp olive oil
1 large onion, chopped
675g/1½lb/3¾ cups carrots, sliced
5ml/1 tsp each ground coriander, ground cumin and hot chilli powder
900ml/1½ pints/3¾ cups vegetable stock
salt and freshly ground black pepper
sprigs of fresh coriander (cilantro), to garnish

FOR THE GARLIC CROÛTONS
a little olive oil
2 garlic cloves, crushed
4 slices bread, crusts removed, cut into 1cm/½in cubes

1 To make the soup, heat the oil in a large pan, add the onion and carrots and cook gently for 5 minutes, stirring occasionally. Add the ground spices and cook gently for 1 minute, continuing to stir.

2 Stir in the stock, bring to the boil, then cover and cook gently for about 45 minutes until the carrots are tender.

3 Meanwhile, make the garlic croûtons. Heat the oil in a frying pan, add the garlic and cook gently for 30 seconds, stirring. Add the bread cubes, turn them over in the oil and fry over a medium heat for a few minutes until crisp and golden brown all over, turning frequently. Drain on kitchen paper and keep warm.

4 Purée the soup in a food processor or blender until smooth, then season to taste with salt and pepper. Return the soup to the rinsed-out pan and reheat gently. Serve hot, sprinkled with garlic croûtons and garnished with coriander sprigs.

LEEK & THYME SOUP

This is a filling, heart-warming soup, which can be liquidized to a smooth purée or served as it is here, in its original peasant style.

SERVES 4

INGREDIENTS
900g/2lb leeks
450g/1lb potatoes
115g/4oz/½ cup butter
1 large sprig of fresh thyme, plus extra to garnish (optional)
300ml/½ pint/1¼ cups milk
salt and freshly ground black pepper
60ml/4 tbsp double (heavy) cream, to serve

1 Top and tail the leeks. If you are using big winter leeks, strip away all the coarse outer leaves, then cut the leeks into thick slices. Wash thoroughly under cold running water.

2 Cut the potatoes into rough dice, about 2.5cm/1in, and leave them to dry on kitchen paper.

3 Melt the butter in a large pan and add the leeks and a sprig of thyme. Cover and cook for 4–5 minutes until softened. Add the potato pieces and just enough cold water to cover the vegetables. Re-cover and cook over a low heat for 30 minutes.

4 Pour in the milk and season with salt and pepper. Cover and simmer for a further 30 minutes. You will find that some of the potato breaks up, leaving you with a semi-puréed and rather lumpy soup.

5 Remove the sprig of thyme (the leaves will have fallen into the soup) and serve, adding 15ml/1 tbsp cream and a garnish of thyme to each portion, if using.

LEEK, PARSNIP & GINGER SOUP

This soup is a flavoursome winter warmer. The added spiciness of fresh ginger gives it a hot, yet refreshing, taste.

SERVES 4–6

INGREDIENTS
30ml/2 tbsp olive oil
225g/8oz/2 cups leeks, sliced
25g/1oz fresh root ginger, peeled and finely chopped
675g/1½lb/5 cups parsnips, roughly chopped
300ml/½ pint/1¼ cups dry white wine
1.2 litres/2 pints/5 cups vegetable stock or water
salt and freshly ground black pepper
fromage blanc and paprika, to garnish

1 Heat the oil in a large pan and add the leeks and ginger. Cook the mixture gently for 2–3 minutes until the leeks start to soften.

2 Add the parsnips and cook for a further 7–8 minutes until they are beginning to soften.

3 Pour in the wine and stock or water and bring to the boil. Reduce the heat and simmer for 20–30 minutes or until the parsnips are tender.

4 Purée in a food processor or blender until smooth. Season to taste. Reheat and garnish with a swirl of fromage blanc and a light dusting of paprika.

COOK'S TIP
If you don't have time to make your own vegetable stock, or you don't have any to hand, choose a good-quality vegetable stock or bouillon powder and add water to make the stock.

Sweet Potato & Parsnip Soup

The sweetness of the two root vegetables comes through strongly in this delicious soup. The sweet potatoes give it a wonderfully appetizing orange colour.

Serves 6

INGREDIENTS
15ml/1 tbsp sunflower oil
1 large leek, sliced
2 celery sticks, chopped
450g/1lb sweet potatoes, diced
225g/8oz/1½ cups parsnips, diced
900ml/1½ pints/3¾ cups vegetable stock
salt and freshly ground black pepper

FOR THE GARNISH
15ml/1 tbsp chopped fresh parsley
roasted strips of sweet potatoes and parsnips

1 Heat the oil in a large pan and add the leek, celery, sweet potatoes and parsnips. Cook gently for about 5 minutes, stirring to prevent them browning or sticking to the pan.

2 Stir in the vegetable stock and bring to the boil, then cover and simmer gently for about 25 minutes, or until the vegetables are tender, stirring occasionally. Season to taste. Remove the pan from the heat and allow the soup to cool slightly.

3 Purée the soup in a food processor or blender until smooth, then return the soup to the pan and reheat gently. Ladle into warmed soup bowls to serve and sprinkle over the garnish of chopped fresh parsley and roasted strips of sweet potatoes and parsnips.

> VARIATIONS
> *Use 1 large onion in place of the leek. Use carrots in place of parsnips. Use chopped fresh coriander (cilantro) in place of parsley.*

GREEN PEA SOUP WITH SPINACH

This tasty green soup was invented by the wife of a 17th-century British Member of Parliament, and it has stood the test of time.

SERVES 6

INGREDIENTS
450g/1lb/generous 3 cups podded fresh or frozen peas
1 leek, finely sliced
2 garlic cloves, crushed
2 rindless back (lean) bacon rashers (strips), finely diced
1.2 litres/2 pints/5 cups ham or chicken stock
30ml/2 tbsp olive oil
50g/2oz fresh spinach, shredded
40g/1½oz/⅓ cup white cabbage, finely shredded
½ small lettuce, finely shredded
1 celery stick, finely chopped
a large handful of parsley, finely chopped
½ carton mustard and cress
20ml/4 tsp chopped fresh mint
a pinch of ground mace
salt and freshly ground black pepper

1 Put the peas, leek, garlic and bacon in a large pan. Add the stock, bring to the boil, then lower the heat and simmer for 20 minutes.

2 About 5 minutes before the pea mixture is ready, heat the olive oil in a deep frying pan.

3 Add the spinach, cabbage, lettuce, celery and herbs to the frying pan. Cover and sweat the mixture over a low heat until soft.

4 Transfer the pea mixture to a food processor or blender and process until smooth. Return to the clean pan, add the sweated vegetables and herbs and heat through. Season with mace, salt and pepper and serve.

Moroccan Vegetable Soup

Moroccans tend to eat soup as a supper dish or a meal in itself. This creamy parsnip and pumpkin soup is ideal for a main course, with its wonderfully rich texture.

SERVES 4

INGREDIENTS
15ml/1 tbsp olive or sunflower oil
15g/½oz/1 tbsp butter
1 onion, chopped
225g/8oz carrots, chopped
225g/8oz parsnips, chopped
225g/8oz pumpkin
about 900ml/1½ pints/3¾ cups vegetable or chicken stock
lemon juice, to taste
salt and freshly ground black pepper

FOR THE GARNISH
7.5ml/1½ tsp olive oil
½ garlic clove, finely chopped
45ml/3 tbsp chopped fresh parsley and coriander (cilantro), mixed
a good pinch of paprika

COOK'S TIP
Chop all the vegetables very finely and leave the soup chunky rather than puréeing it. Thicken the chunky soup with a little cornflour (cornstarch) blended with cold water towards the end of the cooking time, if desired.

1 Heat the oil and butter in a large pan and fry the onion for about 3 minutes until softened, stirring occasionally. Add the carrots and parsnips, stir well, cover and cook over a gentle heat for a further 5 minutes.

2 Cut the pumpkin into chunks, discarding the skin and pith, and stir into the pan. Cover and cook for a further 5 minutes, then add the stock and seasoning and slowly bring to the boil. Cover and simmer for 35–40 minutes until the vegetables are tender.

3 Allow the soup to cool slightly, then pour into a food processor or blender and purée until smooth, adding a little extra water if the soup seems too thick. Pour back into a clean pan and reheat gently.

4 To make the garnish, heat the oil in a small pan and fry the garlic and herbs for 1–2 minutes. Add the paprika and stir well.

5 Adjust the seasoning of the soup and stir in lemon juice to taste. Pour into bowls and spoon a little of the prepared garnish on top, which should then be swirled carefully into the soup.

VARIATIONS
Use turnip or swede (rutabaga) in place of carrots. Use celery or celeriac in place of parsnips. Use butternut squash in place of pumpkin.

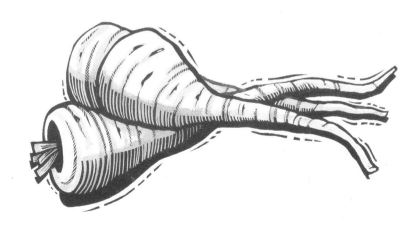

WHITE BEAN SOUP

This velvety dish is quite adaptable – you can use either haricot (navy) beans or butter beans. Instead of using dried beans, you could use a 400g/14oz can of cannellini beans.

SERVES 4

INGREDIENTS
175g/6oz/¾ cup dried white beans, soaked in cold water overnight
30–45ml/2–3 tbsp oil
2 large onions, chopped
4 celery sticks, chopped
1 parsnip, chopped
1 litre/1¾ pints/4 cups chicken stock
salt and freshly ground black pepper
chopped fresh coriander (cilantro) and paprika, to garnish

1 Drain the beans and boil rapidly in fresh water for 10 minutes. Drain, cover with more fresh water and simmer for 1–2 hours until soft. Reserve the liquid and discard any bean skins on the surface.

2 Heat the oil in a heavy pan and sauté the onions, celery and parsnip for 3 minutes.

3 Add the cooked beans and stock and continue cooking until the vegetables are tender. Allow the soup to cool slightly and, using a food processor or blender, blend the soup until it is velvety smooth.

4 Reheat the soup gently, gradually adding some of the bean liquid or a little water if it is too thick. Season to taste with salt and pepper.

5 To serve, transfer the soup into wide bowls. Garnish each bowl with fresh coriander and paprika.

SPICED LENTIL SOUP

A subtle blend of spices takes this warming soup to new heights. Serve it with crusty bread for a filling and satisfying lunch.

SERVES 6

INGREDIENTS
2 onions, finely chopped
2 garlic cloves, crushed
4 tomatoes, roughly chopped
2.5ml/½ tsp ground turmeric
5ml/1 tsp ground cumin
6 cardamom pods
½ cinnamon stick
225g/8oz/1 cup red lentils, rinsed and drained
900ml/1½ pints/3¾ cups water
400g/14oz can coconut milk
15ml/1 tbsp lime juice
salt and freshly ground black pepper
cumin seeds, to garnish

1 Put the onions, garlic, tomatoes, turmeric, cumin, cardamom pods, cinnamon, lentils and water into a pan. Bring to the boil, lower the heat, cover and simmer gently for 20 minutes or until the lentils are soft.

2 Remove the cardamom pods and cinnamon stick, then purée the mixture in a food processor or blender. Press the soup through a sieve (strainer), then return it to the clean pan.

3 Reserve a little of the coconut milk for the garnish and add the remainder to the pan with the lime juice. Stir well and season with salt and pepper. Reheat the soup gently without boiling. Swirl in the reserved coconut milk, garnish with cumin seeds and serve piping hot.

SPICY PEANUT SOUP

For anyone who loves peanuts, this thick and warming vegetable soup will become a favourite, with its crunchy, nutty texture flavoured with chilli.

SERVES 6

INGREDIENTS
30ml/2 tbsp oil
1 large onion, finely chopped
2 garlic cloves, crushed
5ml/1 tsp mild chilli powder
2 red (bell) peppers, seeded and finely chopped
225g/8oz carrots, finely chopped
225g/8oz potatoes, finely chopped
3 celery sticks, sliced
900ml/1½ pints/3¾ cups vegetable stock
90ml/6 tbsp crunchy peanut butter
115g/4oz/⅔ cup corn
salt and freshly ground black pepper
roughly chopped unsalted roasted peanuts, to garnish

1 Heat the oil in a large pan and cook the onion and garlic for about 3 minutes. Add the chilli powder and cook for a further 1 minute.

2 Add the red peppers, carrots, potatoes and celery. Stir well, then cook for a further 4 minutes, stirring occasionally.

3 Add the vegetable stock, followed by the peanut butter and corn. Stir until thoroughly combined.

4 Season well. Bring to the boil, cover and simmer for about 20 minutes until all the vegetables are tender. Adjust the seasoning before serving, sprinkled with the chopped peanuts.

WONTON SOUP

In China, wonton soup is traditionally served as a snack – or dim sum – rather than as a soup course during a large meal. It contains many complementary flavours.

SERVES 4

INGREDIENTS
175g/6oz pork, not too lean, roughly chopped
50g/2oz peeled prawns (shrimp), finely chopped
5ml/1 tsp light brown sugar
15ml/1 tbsp Chinese rice wine or dry sherry
15ml/1 tbsp light soy sauce
5ml/1 tsp finely chopped spring onions (scallions)
5ml/1 tsp finely chopped fresh root ginger
24 ready-made wonton skins
about 750ml/1¼ pints/3 cups stock
15ml/1 tbsp light soy sauce
finely chopped spring onions (scallions), to garnish

1 In a bowl, thoroughly mix the chopped pork and prawns with the sugar, rice wine or sherry, soy sauce, spring onions and ginger. Set aside for 25–30 minutes for the flavours to blend.

2 Place about 5ml/1 tsp of the pork and prawn mixture into the centre of each wonton skin.

3 Wet the edges of each filled wonton skin with a little water and press them together with your fingers to seal. Fold each wonton parcel over.

4 To cook, bring the stock to a rolling boil in a wok, add the wontons and cook for 4–5 minutes. Season with the soy sauce and add the spring onions. Transfer to individual soup bowls and serve.

Creamed Corn
& Crab Meat Soup

This soup originated in the USA but it has since been successfully introduced into China. You must use creamed corn in the recipe to achieve the right consistency.

SERVES 4

INGREDIENTS
115g/4oz crab meat
2.5ml/½ tsp finely chopped fresh root ginger
30ml/2 tbsp milk
15ml/1 tbsp cornflour (cornstarch)
2 egg whites
600ml/1 pint/2½ cups vegetable stock
225g/8oz can creamed corn
salt and freshly ground black pepper
chopped spring onions (scallions), to garnish

1 Flake the crab meat and mix with the ginger in a bowl. In another bowl, mix the milk and cornflour until smooth.

2 Beat the egg whites until frothy, add the milk and cornflour mixture and beat again until smooth. Blend with the crab meat.

3 In a wok or pan, bring the vegetable stock to the boil. Add the creamed corn and bring back to the boil once more.

4 Stir in the crab meat and egg white mixture, adjust the seasoning and stir gently until well blended. Serve garnished with chopped spring onions.

VARIATION
For a poultry version of this soup, you can use coarsely chopped chicken breast instead of crab meat.

SMOKED MACKEREL & TOMATO SOUP

All the ingredients for this unusual soup are cooked in a single pan, so it is not only quick and easy to prepare, but it reduces the amount of clearing up afterwards.

SERVES 4

INGREDIENTS

200g/7oz smoked mackerel fillets
4 tomatoes
1 litre/1¾ pints/4 cups vegetable stock
1 lemon grass stalk, finely chopped
5cm/2in piece fresh galangal, finely diced
4 shallots, finely chopped
2 garlic cloves, finely chopped
2.5ml/½ tsp dried chilli flakes
15ml/1 tbsp Thai fish sauce
5ml/1 tsp palm sugar or light muscovado (brown) sugar
45ml/3 tbsp thick tamarind juice, made by mixing tamarind paste with warm water
small bunch fresh chives or spring onions (scallions), to garnish

1 Prepare the smoked mackerel fillets. Remove and discard the skin, if necessary, then chop the flesh into large pieces. Remove any stray bones with your fingers or a pair of tweezers.

2 Cut the tomatoes in half, squeeze out most of the seeds with your fingers, then finely dice the flesh with a sharp knife. Set aside.

3 Pour the stock into a large pan and add the lemon grass, galangal, shallots and garlic. Bring to the boil, reduce the heat and simmer for 15 minutes.

4 Add the fish, tomatoes, chilli flakes, fish sauce, sugar and tamarind juice. Simmer for 4–5 minutes, until the fish and tomatoes are heated through. Serve garnished with chives or spring onions.

ONION & PANCETTA SOUP

This warming winter soup comes from Umbria in central Italy, where it is sometimes thickened with beaten eggs and plenty of grated Parmesan cheese. It is then served on top of hot toasted croûtes – rather like savoury scrambled eggs.

SERVES 4

INGREDIENTS

115g/4oz pancetta rashers (strips), rinds removed, roughly chopped
30ml/2 tbsp olive oil
15g/½oz/1 tbsp butter
675g/1½lb onions, finely sliced
10ml/2 tsp granulated sugar
about 1.2 litres/2 pints/5 cups chicken stock
350g/12oz ripe Italian plum tomatoes, peeled and roughly chopped
a few fresh basil leaves, shredded
salt and freshly ground black pepper
grated Parmesan cheese, to serve

COOK'S TIPS
• *Look for Vidalia onions to make this soup. They are available at large supermarkets, and have a sweet flavour and an attractive, yellowish flesh.*
• *Choose fresh basil leaves that have a good, fresh green colour. Avoid leaves that are limp or have dark patches or spots.*

1 Put the chopped pancetta in a large pan and heat gently, stirring constantly, until the fat runs. Increase the heat to medium, add the oil, butter, sliced onions and sugar and stir well to mix.

2 Half-cover the pan and cook the onions gently for about 20 minutes until golden. Stir frequently and lower the heat if necessary.

3 Add the stock, tomatoes and salt and pepper and bring to the boil, stirring. Lower the heat, half-cover the pan and simmer, stirring occasionally, for about 30 minutes.

4 Check the consistency of the soup and add a little more stock or water if it is too thick.

5 Just before serving, stir in most of the basil and adjust the seasoning to taste. Serve hot, garnished with the remaining shredded basil. Pass around the freshly grated Parmesan separately.

VARIATIONS
Use smoked streaky (fatty) or back (lean) bacon rashers (strips) or chorizo in place of pancetta. Use shallots or leeks in place of onions. Use vine-ripened tomatoes in place of plum tomatoes.

Chicken, Leek & Celery Soup

This dish makes a substantial main-course soup with fresh crusty bread. You will need nothing more than a salad and cheese, or just fresh fruit to follow.

Serves 4–6

Ingredients
1.4kg/3lb free-range chicken
1 small head of celery, trimmed
1 onion, coarsely chopped
1 fresh bay leaf
a few fresh parsley stalks
a few fresh tarragon sprigs
2.4 litres/4 pints/10 cups cold water
3 large leeks
65g/2½oz/5 tbsp butter
2 potatoes, cut into chunks
150ml/¼ pint/⅔ cup dry white wine
30–45ml/2–3 tbsp single (light) cream (optional)
salt and freshly ground black pepper
90g/3½oz pancetta, grilled until crisp, to garnish

1 Cut the breasts off the chicken and set aside. Chop the rest of the chicken carcass into 8–10 pieces and place in a large pan.

2 Chop 4–5 of the outer sticks of the celery and add them to the pan with the onion. Tie the bay leaf, parsley and tarragon together and add to the pan. Pour in the cold water to cover the ingredients and bring to the boil. Reduce the heat and cover the pan, then simmer for 1½ hours.

3 Remove the chicken and cut off and reserve the meat. Strain the stock, then return it to the pan and boil rapidly until it has reduced to about 1.5 litres/ 2½ pints/6¼ cups.

4 Meanwhile, set aside about 150g/5oz of the leeks. Slice the remaining leeks and the remaining celery, reserving any celery leaves. Chop the celery leaves and set aside to garnish the soup.

5 Melt half the butter in a large, heavy-based pan. Add the sliced leeks and celery, cover and cook over a low heat for about 10 minutes, or until softened but not browned. Add the potatoes, wine and 1.2 litres/2 pints/5 cups of the stock.

6 Season well with salt and pepper, bring to the boil and reduce the heat. Part-cover the pan and simmer the soup for 15–20 minutes, or until the potatoes are cooked.

7 Meanwhile, skin the reserved chicken breasts and cut the flesh into small pieces. Melt the remaining butter in a frying pan, add the chicken and fry for 5–7 minutes, until cooked.

8 Thickly slice the remaining leeks, add to the pan and cook, stirring occasionally, for a further 3–4 minutes, until just cooked.

9 Process the soup with the cooked chicken from the stock in a food processor or blender. Taste and adjust the seasoning as necessary, and add more stock if the soup is very thick.

10 Stir in the cream, if using, and the chicken and leek mixture. Reheat the soup gently. Serve in warmed bowls. Crumble the pancetta over the soup and sprinkle with the chopped celery leaves.

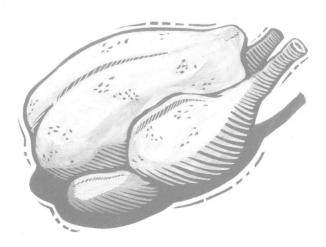

CHICKEN SOUP WITH KNAIDLACH

A bowl of chicken soup can heal the soul as well as the body, as anyone who has ever suffered from flu and been comforted in this way will know.

SERVES 6–8

INGREDIENTS
1–1.5kg/2¼–3¼lb chicken, cut into portions
2–3 onions
3–4 litres/5–7 pints/12–16 cups water
3–5 carrots, thickly sliced
3–5 celery sticks, thickly sliced
1 small parsnip, cut in half
30–45ml/2–3 tbsp roughly chopped fresh parsley
30–45ml/2–3 tbsp chopped fresh dill
1–2 pinches ground turmeric
2 chicken stock (bouillon) cubes
2 garlic cloves, finely chopped (optional)
salt and freshly ground black pepper

FOR THE KNAIDLACH
175g/6oz/¾ cup medium matzo meal
2 eggs, lightly beaten
45ml/3 tbsp vegetable oil or rendered chicken fat
1 garlic clove, finely chopped (optional)
30ml/2 tbsp chopped fresh parsley, plus extra to garnish
½ onion, finely grated
1–2 pinches of chicken stock (bouillon) cube or powder (optional)
about 90ml/6 tbsp water
salt and freshly ground black pepper

VARIATIONS
- Instead of knaidlach, this soup can be served over rice, noodles or kreplach.
- To make lighter knaidlach, separate the eggs and add the yolks to the matzo mixture. Whisk the whites until stiff, then fold into the mixture.

1 Put the chicken pieces into a very large pan. Keeping them whole, cut a large cross in the stem end of each onion and add to the pan with the water, carrots, celery, parsnip, parsley, half the fresh dill, the turmeric, and salt and black pepper.

2 Cover the pan and bring to the boil, then immediately lower the heat to a simmer. Skim and discard the scum that surfaces to the top. (Scum will continue to form but it is only the first scum that rises that will detract from the clarity and flavour of the soup.)

3 Add the crumbled stock cubes and simmer for 2–3 hours. When the soup is flavourful, skim off the fat. Alternatively, chill the soup and remove the layer of solid fat that forms.

4 To make the knaidlach, in a large bowl combine the matzo meal with the eggs, oil or fat, chopped garlic, if using, parsley, onion, salt and pepper. Add only a little chicken stock cube or powder, if using, as these are salty. Add the water and mix together until the mixture is of the consistency of a thick, soft paste.

5 Cover the matzo batter and chill for 30 minutes, during which time the mixture will become firm.

6 Bring a pan of water to the boil and have a bowl of water next to the stove. Dip two tablespoons into the water, then take a spoonful of the matzo batter. With wet hands, roll it into a ball, then slip it into the boiling water and reduce the heat so that the water simmers. Continue with the remaining matzo batter, working relatively quickly, then cover the pan and cook for 15–20 minutes.

7 Remove the knaidlach from the pan with a slotted spoon and transfer to a plate for about 20 minutes to firm up.

8 To serve, reheat the soup, adding the remaining dill and the garlic, if using. Put two to three knaidlach in each bowl, pour over the hot soup and garnish.

HEARTY LUNCH & SUPPER SOUPS

We often think of soups as typically being served as an appetizer or light snack, and while many soups do make great starters or snacks, some heartier, more substantial soups also make ideal lunch or supper dishes. Served with a good chunk of crusty fresh bread, you will find these soups really do provide a filling meal in themselves. Choose from tempting favourites such as Winter Vegetable Soup, Corn & Crab Bisque or Split Pea & Ham Soup, or flavourful filling soups such as Roasted Tomato & Pasta Soup, Chicken Minestrone or Beef Chilli Soup.

WINTER VEGETABLE SOUP

No fewer than eight varieties of vegetables are packed into this hearty and nutritious soup. The varied colours, flavours and textures make it a very satisfying winter meal.

SERVES 8

INGREDIENTS
1 medium Savoy cabbage, quartered and cored
30ml/2 tbsp corn oil
4 carrots, finely sliced
2 celery stalks, finely sliced
2 parsnips, diced
1.5 litres/2½ pints/6¼ cups chicken stock
3 medium potatoes, diced
2 courgettes (zucchini), sliced
1 small red (bell) pepper, seeded and diced
115g/4oz/2 cups cauliflower florets
2 tomatoes, seeded and diced
2.5ml/½ tsp fresh thyme leaves or ¼ tsp dried thyme
30ml/2 tbsp chopped fresh parsley
salt and freshly ground black pepper

1 Using a sharp knife, slice the Savoy cabbage quarters into thin strips, always cutting across the leaves.

2 Heat the corn oil in a large pan. Add the cabbage, carrots, celery and parsnips and cook for 10–15 minutes over medium heat, stirring frequently.

3 Stir the stock into the vegetables and bring to the boil, skimming off any foam that rises to the surface.

4 Add the potatoes, courgettes, red pepper, cauliflower and tomatoes with the herbs, and salt and pepper to taste. Bring back to the boil. Reduce the heat to low, cover the pan and simmer for 15–20 minutes until the vegetables are tender. Serve piping hot.

VEGETABLE SOUP WITH COCONUT

Coconut, marjoram, ginger, cinnamon and flaked almonds blend well to form a delicious flavour variation on a classic winter vegetable soup.

SERVES 4

INGREDIENTS

25g/1oz/2 tbsp butter or margarine
½ red onion, finely chopped
175g/6oz each, turnip, sweet potato and pumpkin, roughly diced
5ml/1 tsp dried marjoram
2.5ml/½ tsp ground ginger
1.5ml/¼ tsp ground cinnamon
15ml/1 tbsp chopped spring onions (scallions)
750ml/1¼ pints/3½ cups well-flavoured vegetable stock
30ml/2 tbsp flaked almonds
1 fresh chilli, seeded and chopped
5ml/1 tsp sugar
50ml/3¼ tbsp coconut milk
salt and freshly ground black pepper
chopped fresh coriander (cilantro), to garnish (optional)

1 Melt the butter or margarine in a large, non-stick pan. Fry the onion for 4–5 minutes. Add the diced vegetables and fry for 3–4 minutes.

2 Add the marjoram, ginger, cinnamon, spring onions and salt and pepper to taste. Fry over a low heat for about 10 minutes, stirring frequently.

3 Add the vegetable stock, flaked almonds, chilli and sugar and stir well to mix. Cover and simmer gently for 10–15 minutes until the vegetables are just tender.

4 Add the coconut milk to the soup and stir to mix. Spoon into warmed bowls, sprinkle with chopped coriander, if liked, and serve immediately.

Vegetable & Herb Chowder

A chowder is often made with clams, fish or bacon. In this version, however, a medley of fresh vegetables and herbs combines to make a delicious lunchtime soup.

SERVES 4

INGREDIENTS

25g/1oz/2 tbsp butter
1 onion, finely chopped
1 leek, finely sliced
1 celery stalk, diced
1 yellow or green (bell) pepper, seeded and diced
30ml/2 tbsp chopped fresh parsley
15ml/1 tbsp plain flour
1.2 litres/2 pints/5 cups vegetable stock
350g/12oz potatoes, diced
a few sprigs of fresh thyme or 2.5ml/½ tsp dried thyme
1 bay leaf
115g/4oz/1 cup young runner (green) beans, thinly sliced on the diagonal
120ml/4fl oz/½ cup milk
salt and freshly ground black pepper

> VARIATIONS
>
> *Use snipped fresh chives in place of parsley, or a mixture of fresh parsley and chives. Use sweet potatoes or new potatoes in place of standard potatoes. Use green beans or fresh (shelled) peas or baby broad (fava) beans in place of runner (green) beans. Use single (light) cream in place of milk.*

1 Melt the butter in a heavy pan or flameproof casserole and add the onion, leek, celery, yellow or green pepper and parsley. Cover and cook gently over low heat until the vegetables are soft.

2 Add the flour and stir until well blended. Slowly add the stock, stirring to combine. Bring to the boil, stirring frequently.

3 Add the potatoes, thyme and bay leaf. Simmer the mixture, uncovered, for about 10 minutes.

4 Add the beans and simmer for a further 10–15 minutes until all the vegetables are tender.

5 Stir in the milk. Season with salt and pepper. Heat through. Before serving, discard the thyme stalks and bay leaf. Serve hot.

YELLOW BROTH

This is one of many versions of this famous Northern Irish soup, which is both thickened with, and given its flavour by, oatmeal. The addition of spinach works well because the green leaves have a particular affinity with dairy products.

SERVES 4

INGREDIENTS
25g/1oz/2 tbsp butter
1 onion, finely chopped
1 celery stick, finely chopped
1 carrot, finely chopped
25g/1oz/¼ cup plain (all-purpose) flour
900ml/1½ pints/3¾ cups chicken stock
25g/1oz/¼ cup medium oatmeal
115g/4oz spinach, chopped
30ml/2 tbsp cream
salt and freshly ground black pepper
chopped fresh parsley, to garnish (optional)

1 Melt the butter in a large pan. Add the onion, celery and carrot and cook for about 2 minutes until the onion is beginning to soften.

2 Stir in the flour and cook gently for a further 1 minute, stirring constantly. Pour in the chicken stock, bring to the boil and cover. Reduce the heat and simmer for 30 minutes until the vegetables are tender.

3 Stir in the oatmeal and chopped spinach and cook for a further 15 minutes, stirring from time to time.

4 Stir in the cream and season well with salt and freshly ground black pepper. Serve garnished with chopped fresh parsley, if using.

Italian Rocket & Potato Soup

This filling and hearty soup is based on a traditional Italian peasant recipe. The peppery flavour of rocket (arugula) complements the potatoes perfectly. If rocket is unavailable, baby spinach leaves make an equally delicious alternative.

SERVES 4

INGREDIENTS
900g/2lb new potatoes
900ml/1½ pints/3¾ cups well-flavoured vegetable stock
1 medium carrot
115g/4oz rocket (arugula)
2.5ml/½ tsp cayenne pepper
½ loaf stale ciabatta bread, torn into chunks
4 garlic cloves, thinly sliced
60ml/4 tbsp olive oil
salt and freshly ground black pepper

1 Dice the potatoes, then place them in a pan with the stock and a little salt. Bring to the boil and simmer for 10 minutes.

2 Finely dice the carrot and add to the potatoes and stock, then tear the rocket leaves and drop into the pan. Simmer for a further 15 minutes, until the vegetables are tender.

3 Add the cayenne pepper, plus salt and black pepper to taste, then add the chunks of bread. Remove the pan from the heat, cover and leave to stand for about 10 minutes.

4 Meanwhile, sauté the garlic in the olive oil until golden brown. Pour the soup into bowls, add a little of the sautéed garlic to each bowl and serve.

Plantain & Corn Soup

Also known as cooking bananas, plantains have a coarser flesh and are larger and heavier than ordinary bananas. In this recipe the sweetness of the plantains and corn is offset by a little chilli to create an unusual soup.

SERVES 4

INGREDIENTS
25g/1oz/2 tbsp butter or margarine
1 onion, finely chopped
1 garlic clove, crushed
275g/10oz yellow plantains, peeled and sliced
1 large tomato, peeled and chopped
175g/6oz/1 cup corn kernels
5ml/1 tsp dried tarragon, crushed
900ml/1½ pints/3¾ cups vegetable or chicken stock
1 fresh green chilli, seeded and chopped
a pinch of freshly grated nutmeg
salt and freshly ground black pepper

1 Melt the butter or margarine in a pan over a moderate heat, add the onion and garlic and fry for a few minutes until the onion is soft.

2 Add the plantains, tomato and corn kernels, and cook the mixture for a further 5 minutes.

3 Add the tarragon, stock, green chilli and salt and freshly ground black pepper, then simmer for 10 minutes or until the plantain is tender. Stir in the grated nutmeg and serve at once.

COOK'S TIP
Plantain, often known as green banana, is a member of the banana family, but is bigger and coarser than the familiar dessert varieties. Ordinary sweet bananas quickly become too soft to be used in many recipes, whereas plantain contains more starch with less natural sugar and so is more suited to cooking.

GROUNDNUT SOUP

Groundnuts (or peanuts) are widely used in sauces in African cooking. You'll find groundnut paste in health food stores – it makes a wonderfully rich soup – but you could use peanut butter instead.

SERVES 4

INGREDIENTS
45ml/3 tbsp groundnut paste or peanut butter
1.5 litres/2½ pints/6¼ cups stock or water
30ml/2 tbsp tomato purée (paste)
1 onion, chopped
2 slices fresh root ginger
1.5ml/¼ tsp dried thyme
1 bay leaf
chilli powder
225g/8oz white yam, diced
10 small okra, trimmed (optional)
salt

1 Place the groundnut paste or peanut butter in a bowl, add 300ml/½ pint/ 1¼ cups of the stock or water and the tomato purée and blend together to make a smooth mixture.

2 Spoon the nut mixture into a pan and add the onion, ginger, thyme, bay leaf, chilli powder and salt to taste and the remaining stock.

3 Heat gently until simmering, then cook for 1 hour, whisking from time to time to prevent the nut mixture from sticking to the pan.

4 Add the white yam, cook for a further 10 minutes, then add the okra, if using, and simmer until both vegetables are tender. Serve immediately.

RIBOLLITA

Ribollita is rather like minestrone, but includes beans instead of pasta. In Italy it is traditionally served ladled over bread and a rich green vegetable, although you could omit these if you would prefer to eat a lighter version.

SERVES 6–8

INGREDIENTS
45ml/3 tbsp olive oil
2 onions, chopped
2 carrots, sliced
4 garlic cloves, crushed
2 celery sticks, finely sliced
1 fennel bulb, trimmed and chopped
2 large courgettes (zucchini), finely sliced
400g/14oz can chopped tomatoes
30ml/2 tbsp pesto, either home-made or ready-made
900ml/1½ pints/3¾ cups vegetable stock
400g/14oz can haricot (navy) or borlotti beans, drained
salt and freshly ground black pepper

TO SERVE
450g/1lb young spinach
15ml/1 tbsp extra virgin olive oil, plus extra for drizzling
6–8 slices white bread
Parmesan cheese shavings (optional)

1 Heat the oil in a large pan. Add the onions, carrots, garlic, celery and fennel and fry gently for 10 minutes. Add the courgette slices and fry for a further 2 minutes.

2 Add the chopped tomatoes, pesto, stock and beans and bring to the boil. Reduce the heat, cover and simmer gently for 25–30 minutes until all the vegetables are tender. Season with salt and freshly ground black pepper to taste.

3 To serve, fry the spinach in the oil for 2 minutes or until wilted. Spoon over the bread in soup bowls, then ladle the soup over the spinach. Serve with extra olive oil for drizzling on to the soup and Parmesan cheese to sprinkle on top, if liked.

PISTOU

This delicious vegetable soup originates from Nice in the south of France. It is the French equivalent of Italian pesto, and is served with a sun-dried tomato purée (paste) and fresh Parmesan cheese as tangy accompaniments.

SERVES 4

INGREDIENTS
1 courgette (zucchini), diced
1 small potato, diced
1 shallot, chopped
1 carrot, diced
225g/8oz can chopped tomatoes
1.2 litres/2 pints/5 cups vegetable stock
50g/2oz French (green) beans, cut into 1cm/½in lengths
50g/2oz/½ cup frozen petits pois (baby peas)
50g/2oz/½ cup small pasta shapes
60–90ml/4–6 tbsp pesto, either home-made or ready-made
15ml/1 tbsp sun-dried tomato purée (paste)
salt and freshly ground black pepper
grated Parmesan cheese, to serve

1 Place the courgette, potato, shallot, carrot and tomatoes in a large pan. Add the vegetable stock and season with salt and pepper. Bring to the boil, then cover and simmer for 20 minutes.

2 Add the French beans, petits pois and pasta shapes. Cook for a further 10 minutes, until the pasta is tender.

3 Taste the soup and adjust the seasoning as necessary. Ladle the soup into individual bowls. Mix together the pesto and sun-dried tomato purée, and stir a spoonful into each serving.

4 Pass around a bowl of freshly grated Parmesan cheese for sprinkling into each bowl.

Fresh Tomato & Bean Soup

This is a rich, chunky tomato and bean soup flavoured with coriander. It forms a hearty and satisfying meal when served with olive ciabatta.

SERVES 4

INGREDIENTS
900g/2lb ripe plum tomatoes
30ml/2 tbsp olive oil
275g/10oz onions, roughly chopped
2 garlic cloves, crushed
900ml/1½ pints/3¾ cups vegetable stock
30ml/2 tbsp sun-dried tomato purée (paste)
10ml/2 tsp paprika
15ml/1 tbsp cornflour (cornstarch)
425g/15oz can cannellini beans, rinsed and drained
30ml/2 tbsp chopped fresh coriander (cilantro)
salt and freshly ground black pepper
olive ciabatta, to serve

VARIATIONS
Use vine-ripened or beefsteak tomatoes in place of plum tomatoes. Use shallots in place of onions. Use standard tomato purée (paste) in place of sun-dried tomato purée (paste). Use canned haricot (navy) beans in place of cannellini beans. Use chopped fresh basil or flat leaf parsley in place of coriander (cilantro).

1 First peel the tomatoes. Using a sharp knife, make a small cross in each one and place in a bowl. Pour over boiling water to cover and leave to stand for 30–60 seconds.

2 Drain the tomatoes and, when they are cool enough to handle, peel off the skins. Quarter them and then cut each piece in half again.

3 Heat the oil in a large pan and cook the onions and garlic for 3 minutes or until just beginning to soften.

4 Add the tomatoes to the onions and stir in the stock, sun-dried tomato purée and paprika. Season with a little salt and pepper. Bring to the boil and simmer for 10 minutes.

5 Mix the cornflour to a paste with 30ml/2 tbsp water. Stir the beans into the soup with the cornflour paste. Cook for a further 5 minutes.

6 Adjust the seasoning and stir in the chopped coriander just before serving with olive ciabatta.

FRESH BROAD BEAN & ARBORIO RICE SOUP

This thick soup makes the most of fresh broad (fava) beans while they are in season. It works just as well with frozen beans for the rest of the year.

SERVES 4

INGREDIENTS
1 kg/2¼lb broad (fava) beans in their pods, or 400g/14oz shelled frozen broad (fava) beans, thawed
90ml/6 tbsp olive oil
1 medium onion, finely chopped
2 medium tomatoes, peeled and finely chopped
225g/8oz/1 cup arborio or other non-parboiled rice
25g/1oz/2 tbsp butter
1 litre/1¾ pints/4 cups boiling water
salt and freshly ground black pepper
grated Parmesan cheese, to serve (optional)

1 Shell the beans if they are fresh. To do this bring a large pan of water to the boil and blanch the beans, fresh or frozen, for 3–4 minutes. Rinse under cold water and peel off the skins.

2 Heat the oil in a large pan. Add the onion and cook over low to moderate heat until it softens. Stir in the beans and cook for about 5 minutes, stirring to coat them with the oil.

3 Season with salt and pepper. Add the tomatoes and cook for 5 minutes more, stirring often. Add the rice and cook for a further 1–2 minutes, stirring the mixture constantly.

4 Add the butter and stir until it melts. Pour in the water, a little at a time. Adjust the seasoning to taste. Continue cooking until the rice is tender. Serve with grated Parmesan, if liked.

CAULIFLOWER, FLAGEOLET & FENNEL SEED SOUP

The sweet, anise-liquorice flavour of the fennel seeds gives a delicious edge to this hearty cauliflower and bean soup. It is excellent served with warm French bread.

SERVES 4–6

INGREDIENTS
15ml/1 tbsp olive oil
1 garlic clove, crushed
1 onion, chopped
10ml/2 tsp fennel seeds
1 cauliflower, cut into small florets
2 × 400g/14oz cans flageolet (small cannellini) beans, drained and rinsed
1.2 litres/2 pints/5 cups vegetable stock or water
salt and freshly ground black pepper
chopped fresh parsley, to garnish
toasted slices of French bread, to serve

1 Heat the olive oil. Add the garlic, onion and fennel seeds and cook gently for 5 minutes or until softened.

2 Add the cauliflower florets, half the flageolet beans and the vegetable stock or water.

3 Bring the mixture to the boil. Reduce the heat and simmer for about 10 minutes or until the cauliflower is tender. Pour the soup into a food processor or blender and process until smooth.

4 Stir in the remaining beans and season to taste with salt and freshly ground black pepper. Reheat and pour into bowls. Sprinkle with chopped parsley and serve with toasted slices of French bread.

SPICY BEAN SOUP

This thick bean soup makes a very filling main dish. It is made with two kinds of beans – black and kidney – and is flavoured with ground cumin, which gives it a delicious, piquant flavour.

SERVES 6–8

INGREDIENTS
175g/6oz/1 cup dried black beans, soaked overnight and drained
175g/6oz/1 cup dried kidney beans, soaked overnight and drained
2 bay leaves
30ml/2 tbsp olive or vegetable oil
3 carrots, chopped
1 onion, chopped
1 celery stick
1 garlic clove, crushed
5ml/1 tsp ground cumin
1.5–2.5ml/¼–½ tsp cayenne pepper
2.5ml/½ tsp dried oregano
50ml/2fl oz/¼ cup red wine
1.2 litres/2 pints/5 cups beef stock
250ml/8fl oz/1 cup water
salt and freshly ground black pepper

FOR THE GARNISH
sour cream
chopped fresh coriander (cilantro)

1 Put the black beans and kidney beans into two separate pans with enough cold water to cover and a bay leaf in each. Boil rapidly for 10–15 minutes.

2 Reduce the heat and cover the pans. Simmer for 1 hour until the beans are tender, then drain.

3 Heat the oil in a large flameproof casserole. Add the carrots, onion, celery and garlic and cook over a low heat for 8–10 minutes, stirring, until softened. Stir in the cumin, cayenne, oregano and salt to taste.

4 Add the wine, beef stock and water and stir to mix all the ingredients together thoroughly. Remove the bay leaves from the cooked beans and add the beans to the casserole.

5 Bring to the boil, reduce the heat, then cover and simmer for about 20 minutes, stirring occasionally.

6 Transfer half the soup (including most of the solids) to a food processor or blender. Process until smooth. Return to the pan and stir to combine well.

7 Reheat the soup and adjust the seasoning to taste. Serve hot, garnished with sour cream and chopped coriander.

COOK'S TIP
It is important when preparing dried red kidney beans that you prepare them correctly. Raw kidney beans contain a substance that cannot be digested and which may cause food poisoning if the toxins are not extracted. It is therefore essential that you fast-boil red kidney beans for 15 minutes before use. It is then best to change the water, bring to the boil again and simmer the beans for a further 30 minutes at least (or according to the recipe) until the beans are tender enough to eat.

Split Pea & Pumpkin Soup

This creamy pea soup is a vegetarian version of a dish that is often made with salt beef. The pumpkin gives the soup a bright orange colour and a slightly honeyed flavour, which is perfectly complemented by the addition of coriander (cilantro).

SERVES 4

INGREDIENTS
225g/8oz/1 cup split peas
1.2 litres/2 pints/5 cups water
25g/1oz/2 tbsp butter
1 onion, finely chopped
225g/8oz pumpkin, chopped
3 tomatoes, peeled and chopped
5ml/1 tsp dried tarragon, crushed
15ml/1 tbsp chopped fresh coriander (cilantro)
2.5ml/½ tsp ground cumin
1 vegetable stock (bouillon) cube, crumbled
chilli powder, to taste
sprigs of fresh coriander (cilantro), to garnish

1 Soak the split peas overnight in enough water to cover them completely, then drain. Place the split peas in a large pan, add the water and boil for about 30 minutes until tender.

2 In a separate pan, melt the butter and sauté the onion until it is soft but not browned.

3 Add the pumpkin, tomatoes, tarragon, coriander, cumin, vegetable stock cube and chilli powder and, on a high heat, bring to the boil.

4 Stir the vegetable mixture into the cooked split peas and their liquid. Simmer gently for about 20 minutes or until the vegetables are tender. If the soup is too thick, add another 150ml/¼ pint/⅔ cup water. Serve hot, garnished with sprigs of fresh coriander.

GREEN LENTIL SOUP

Lentil soup is an eastern Mediterranean classic, varying in its spiciness according to the particular region where it is made. Red or Puy lentils make an equally good substitute for the green lentils used in this version.

SERVES 4–6

INGREDIENTS
225g/8oz/1 cup green lentils
75ml/5 tbsp olive oil
3 onions, finely chopped
2 garlic cloves, finely sliced
10ml/2 tsp cumin seeds, crushed
1.5ml/¼ tsp ground turmeric
600ml/1 pint/2½ cups vegetable stock
600ml/1 pint/2½ cups water
salt and freshly ground black pepper
30ml/2 tbsp roughly chopped fresh coriander (cilantro), to garnish
warm crusty bread, to serve

1 Put the lentils in a pan and cover with cold water. Bring to the boil and boil rapidly for 10 minutes. Drain.

2 Heat 30ml/2 tbsp of the oil in a pan and fry two of the onions with the garlic, cumin and turmeric for 3 minutes, stirring. Add the lentils, stock and water. Bring to the boil, reduce the heat, cover and simmer for 30 minutes until the lentils are soft.

3 Heat the remaining oil and fry the third onion until golden brown, stirring frequently.

4 Use a potato masher to lightly mash the lentils and make the soup pulpy in texture. Reheat gently and season with salt and freshly ground pepper to taste.

5 Pour the soup into bowls. Stir the fresh coriander in with the fried onion and scatter over the soup as a garnish. Serve with warm crusty bread.

Lentil & Pasta Soup

This rustic vegetarian soup makes a filling lunch or supper dish on its own, and also goes very well with granary or crusty Italian bread.

Serves 4–6

Ingredients
175g/6oz/¾ cup brown lentils
3 garlic cloves
1 litre/1¾ pints/4 cups water
45ml/3 tbsp olive oil
25g/1oz/2 tbsp butter
1 onion, finely chopped
2 celery sticks, finely chopped
30ml/2 tbsp sun-dried tomato purée (paste)
1.75 litres/3 pints/7½ cups vegetable stock
a few fresh marjoram leaves, plus extra to garnish
a few fresh basil leaves
leaves from 1 sprig of fresh thyme
50g/2oz/½ cup small pasta shapes, such as tubetti
salt and freshly ground black pepper

Cook's Tip
Use green lentils instead of brown, if you like, but the orange or red ones are not so good for this soup because they tend to go mushy.

1 Put the lentils into a large pan. Smash one of the garlic cloves (there's no need to peel it first) and add it to the lentils. Pour in the water and bring to the boil. Lower the heat to a gentle simmer and cook for about 20 minutes, stirring occasionally, until the lentils are just tender.

2 Tip the lentils into a sieve (strainer) to strain off the liquid, remove the cooked garlic clove and set it aside.

3 Rinse the lentils under the cold tap, then leave them to drain. Heat 30ml/2 tbsp of the oil with half of the butter in a large pan. Add the onion and celery and cook over a low heat, stirring frequently, for 5–7 minutes until softened.

4 Crush the remaining garlic and peel and mash the reserved cooked garlic clove. Add to the vegetables with the remaining oil, the tomato purée and lentils. Stir, then add the stock, herbs and salt and pepper to taste. Bring to the boil, stirring. Simmer for 30 minutes, stirring occasionally.

5 Add the pasta and bring to the boil, stirring. Simmer, stirring frequently, for 7–8 minutes or according to the instructions on the packet, until the pasta is *al dente*. Add the remaining butter and adjust the seasoning. Serve hot in warmed bowls, garnished with marjoram leaves.

LENTIL SOUP WITH ROSEMARY

A classic rustic Italian dish flavoured with rosemary, this lentil and bacon soup is delicious served with garlic bread. You can use green or brown lentils in the recipe.

SERVES 4

INGREDIENTS

225g/8oz/1 cup dried green or brown lentils
45ml/3 tbsp extra virgin olive oil
3 rindless streaky (fatty) bacon rashers (strips), cut into small dice
1 onion, finely chopped
2 celery sticks, finely chopped
2 carrots, finely chopped
2 sprigs of fresh rosemary, finely chopped
2 bay leaves
400g/14oz can plum tomatoes
1.75 litres/3 pints/7½ cups vegetable stock
salt and freshly ground black pepper
fresh bay leaves and sprigs of fresh rosemary, to garnish

COOK'S TIP
Look out for the small green lentils in Italian groceries or delicatessens.

1 Place the lentils in a bowl and cover with cold water. Leave to soak for at least 2 hours. Rinse and drain well.

2 Heat the oil in a large pan. Add the bacon and cook for about 3 minutes, then stir in the onion and cook for 5 minutes until softened. Stir in the celery, carrots, rosemary, bay leaves and lentils. Toss over the heat for 1 minute until thoroughly coated in the oil.

3 Tip in the tomatoes and stock, and bring to the boil. Lower the heat, half-cover the pan and simmer for about 1 hour until the lentils are perfectly tender.

4 Remove the bay leaves, add salt and freshly ground black pepper to taste and serve with a garnish of fresh bay leaves and sprigs of rosemary.

ROASTED TOMATO & PASTA SOUP

This vivid red soup has a wonderful smoky taste. The roasting process compensates for any lack of flavour in the tomatoes if they are not at the height of their season.

SERVES 4

INGREDIENTS
450g/1lb ripe Italian plum tomatoes, halved lengthways
1 large red (bell) pepper, quartered lengthways and seeded
1 large red onion, quartered lengthways
2 garlic cloves, unpeeled
15ml/1 tbsp olive oil
1.2 litres/2 pints/5 cups vegetable stock or water
a good pinch of granulated sugar
90g/3½oz/scant 1 cup small pasta shapes, such as tubetti or small macaroni
salt and freshly ground black pepper
fresh basil leaves, to garnish

1 Preheat the oven to 190°C/375°F/Gas 5. Spread out the tomatoes, red pepper, onion and garlic in a roasting pan and drizzle with the olive oil. Roast for 30–40 minutes until the vegetables are soft and charred, stirring and turning them halfway through cooking.

2 Tip the vegetables into a food processor or blender, add about 250ml/8fl oz/ 1 cup of the stock or water, and process until puréed. Scrape into a sieve (strainer) placed over a large pan and press the purée through into the pan.

3 Add the remaining stock or water, the sugar and salt and pepper to taste. Bring to the boil.

4 Add the pasta and simmer for 7–8 minutes (or according to the instructions on the packet), stirring frequently, until *al dente*. Taste and adjust the seasoning with salt and freshly ground black pepper. Serve hot in warmed bowls, garnished with the fresh basil leaves.

TINY PASTA IN BROTH

In Italy, this pasta soup is often served with bread for supper. You can use any type of soup pasta shapes, and there are hundreds to choose from: stellette are stars, anellini are rings, conchigliette are shells, farfallette are bows, tubetti are tubes. Alfabetini – alphabet shapes – are particularly popular with children.

SERVES 4

INGREDIENTS
1.2 litres/2 pints/5 cups beef stock
75g/3oz/¾ cup small soup pasta, such as stellette
2 pieces bottled roasted red (bell) pepper (about 50g/2oz)
salt and freshly ground black pepper
grated Parmesan cheese, to serve

1 Bring the beef stock to the boil in a large pan. Add salt and pepper to taste, then drop in the soup pasta. Stir well and bring the stock back to the boil.

2 Lower the heat to a simmer and cook for 7–8 minutes or according to the packet instructions, until the pasta is *al dente*. Stir often during cooking to prevent the pasta shapes sticking together.

3 Drain the pieces of bottled roasted pepper and dice them finely. Place them in the bottom of four warmed soup plates, and set them aside.

4 Taste the soup and adjust the seasoning. Ladle into the soup plates and serve immediately, with grated Parmesan handed around separately.

LITTLE STUFFED HATS IN BROTH

This soup is served in northern Italy on Santo Stefano (St Stephen's Day, on December 26th) and on New Year's Day. It makes a welcome change from all the special celebration food eaten the day before. It is traditionally made with the Christmas capon carcass, but chicken stock works equally well.

SERVES 4

INGREDIENTS
1.2 litres/2 pints/5 cups chicken stock
90–115g/3½–4oz/1 cup fresh or dried cappelletti
30ml/2 tbsp dry white wine (optional)
about 15ml/1 tbsp finely chopped fresh flat leaf parsley (optional)
salt and freshly ground black pepper
about 30ml/2 tbsp grated Parmesan cheese, to serve

1 Pour the chicken stock into a large pan and bring to the boil. Add a little salt and pepper to taste, then drop in the pasta.

2 Stir well and bring back to the boil. Lower the heat to a simmer and cook according to the instructions on the packet, until the pasta is *al dente*. Stir frequently during cooking to ensure that the pasta cooks evenly.

3 Swirl in the wine and parsley, if using, then taste and adjust the seasoning. Ladle into four warmed soup plates, then sprinkle each plate with grated Parmesan cheese. Serve immediately.

COOK'S TIP
Cappelletti is just another name for tortellini, a type of pasta that comes from Romagna. You can either buy it ready-made or make your own.

PASTA & CHICKPEA SOUP

This is a simple, country-style, filling soup. The shell shapes of the conchiglie pasta and the rounded chickpeas and beans complement one another beautifully.

SERVES 4–6

INGREDIENTS

60ml/4 tbsp olive oil
1 onion, finely chopped
2 carrots, finely chopped
2 celery sticks, finely chopped
400g/14oz can chickpeas, rinsed and drained
200g/7oz can cannellini beans, rinsed and drained
150ml/¹⁄₂ pint/²⁄₃ cup passata (bottled strained tomatoes)
120ml/4fl oz/¹⁄₂ cup water
1.5 litres/2¹⁄₂ pints/6¹⁄₄ cups vegetable or chicken stock
1 sprig of fresh rosemary, plus a few leaves to garnish
200g/7oz/scant 2 cups dried conchiglie
salt and freshly ground black pepper
shavings of Parmesan cheese, to serve

1 Heat the oil in a large pan, add the chopped vegetables and cook over a low heat, stirring frequently, for 5–7 minutes.

2 Add the chickpeas and cannellini beans, stir well to mix, then cook for 5 minutes. Stir in the passata and water. Cook, stirring, for 2–3 minutes.

3 Add 475ml/16fl oz/2 cups of the stock, the rosemary sprig and salt and freshly ground black pepper to taste. Bring to the boil, cover, then simmer gently, stirring occasionally, for 1 hour.

4 Pour in the remaining stock, add the pasta and bring to the boil. Lower the heat and simmer for 7–8 minutes (or according to the instructions on the packet), until the pasta is *al dente*. Remove the rosemary sprig. Serve the soup sprinkled with rosemary leaves and Parmesan shavings.

CHICKPEA & PARSLEY SOUP

The heartiness of chickpeas makes this a deliciously satisfying soup with a nutty, creamy flavour. Parsley and a hint of lemon bring freshness to the chickpeas.

SERVES 6

INGREDIENTS
225g/8oz/1⅓ cups chickpeas, soaked overnight
1 small onion
1 bunch of fresh parsley (about 40g/1½oz)
30ml/2 tbsp olive and sunflower oils, mixed
1.2 litres/2 pints/5 cups chicken stock
juice of ½ lemon
salt and freshly ground black pepper
lemon wedges and finely pared strips of rind, to garnish

1 Drain the chickpeas and rinse under cold water. Cook them in boiling water for 1–1½ hours until tender. Drain and peel.

2 Place the onion and parsley in a food processor or blender and process until finely chopped.

3 Heat the olive and sunflower oils in a pan or flameproof casserole and fry the onion mixture for about 4 minutes over a low heat until the onion is slightly softened.

4 Add the chickpeas, cook gently for 1–2 minutes then add the stock. Season well. Bring the soup to the boil, then cover and simmer for 20 minutes until the chickpeas are tender.

5 Allow the soup to cool a little and then mash the chickpeas with a fork until the soup is thick but still quite chunky.

6 Reheat the soup and add the lemon juice. Serve garnished with lemon wedges and strips of lemon rind.

Chickpea & Spinach Soup with Garlic

This tasty, thick and creamy soup is richly flavoured with garlic, cumin, ground coriander and cayenne pepper. It is a perfect choice for vegetarians.

Serves 4

Ingredients
30ml/2 tbsp olive oil
4 garlic cloves, crushed
1 onion, roughly chopped
10ml/2 tsp ground cumin
10ml/2 tsp ground coriander
1.2 litres/2 pints/5 cups vegetable stock
350g/12oz potatoes, finely chopped
425g/15oz can chickpeas, drained
15ml/1 tbsp cornflour (cornstarch)
150ml/¼ pint/⅔ cup double (heavy) cream
30ml/2 tbsp light tahini
200g/7oz spinach, shredded
cayenne pepper
salt and freshly ground black pepper

1 Heat the oil in a large pan and cook the garlic and onion for about 5 minutes or until the onion is softened and golden brown.

2 Stir in the ground cumin and coriander and cook for 1 minute. Add the stock and potatoes. Bring to the boil and simmer for 10 minutes.

3 Add the chickpeas and simmer for a further 5 minutes or until the potatoes are just tender.

4 Blend together the cornflour, cream, tahini and plenty of seasoning. Stir into the soup with the spinach. Bring to the boil, stirring, and simmer for a further 2 minutes. Adjust the seasoning with salt, pepper and cayenne pepper to taste. Serve sprinkled with a little extra cayenne pepper.

Eastern European Chickpea Soup

Chickpeas form part of the staple diet in the Balkans, where this soup originates. This dish is economical to make, and is a hearty and satisfying meal.

Serves 4–6

Ingredients
500g/1¼lb/5 cups chickpeas, soaked overnight
2 litres/3½ pints/9 cups vegetable stock
3 large waxy potatoes, cut into bite-size chunks
50ml/2fl oz/¼ cup olive oil
225g/8oz spinach leaves
salt and freshly ground black pepper

1 Drain the chickpeas and rinse under cold water. Place in a large pan with the vegetable stock. Bring to the boil, then reduce the heat and cook gently for about 1 hour.

2 Add the potatoes, olive oil and salt and pepper to taste. Cook for 20 minutes until the potatoes are tender.

3 Add the spinach 5 minutes before the end of cooking. Serve the soup in individual warmed soup bowls.

SPICED MUSSEL SOUP

Chunky and colourful, this Turkish fish soup is like a chowder in its consistency. It is flavoured with harissa sauce, which is more common in north African cookery.

SERVES 6

INGREDIENTS
1.5 kg/3–3½lb fresh mussels
150ml/¼ pint/⅔ cup white wine
30ml/2 tbsp olive oil
1 onion, finely chopped
2 garlic cloves, crushed
2 celery sticks, finely sliced
bunch of spring onions (scallions), finely sliced
1 potato, diced
7.5ml/1½ tsp harissa sauce
3 tomatoes, peeled and diced
45ml/3 tbsp chopped fresh parsley
freshly ground black pepper
thick natural (plain) yogurt, to serve (optional)

COOK'S TIPS
Harissa sauce or paste is a fiery chilli-based condiment that originates from North Africa. Most large supermarkets stock harissa sauce or paste, as do delicatessens and some large grocers.

1 Scrub the mussels, discarding any damaged ones or any open ones that do not close when tapped with a knife.

2 Bring the wine to the boil in a large pan. Add the mussels and cover with a lid. Cook for 4–5 minutes until the mussels have opened wide. Discard any mussels that remain closed. Drain the mussels, reserving the cooking liquid. Reserve a few mussels in their shells to use as a garnish and shell the rest.

3 Heat the oil in a pan and fry the onion, garlic, celery and spring onions for 5 minutes.

4 Add the shelled mussels, reserved liquid, potato, harissa sauce and tomatoes. Bring to the boil, reduce the heat and cover. Simmer gently for 25 minutes or until the potatoes are breaking up.

5 Stir in the parsley and pepper and add the reserved mussels in their shells. Heat through for 1 minute. Serve hot with a spoonful of yogurt, if liked.

VARIATIONS
Use 2 small carrots or parsnips in place of celery.
Use sweet potato in place of standard potato.

Corn & Scallop Chowder

Fresh corn is ideal for this chowder, although canned or frozen corn also works well. This soup is almost a meal in itself and makes a perfect lunch dish.

Serves 4–6

Ingredients

2 corn cobs or 200g/7oz/generous 1 cup frozen or canned corn
600ml/1 pint/2½ cups milk
15g/½oz butter or margarine
1 small leek or onion, chopped
40g/1½oz/¼ cup smoked streaky (fatty) bacon, finely chopped
1 small garlic clove, crushed
1 small green (bell) pepper, seeded and diced
1 celery stick, chopped
1 medium potato, diced
15ml/1 tbsp plain flour
300ml/½ pint/1¼ cups chicken or vegetable stock
4 scallops
115g/4oz cooked fresh mussels
a pinch of paprika
150ml/¼ pint/⅔ cup single (light) cream (optional)
salt and freshly ground black pepper

Cook's Tips

With scallops it is best to buy them on their shells, but if fresh scallops are not available use frozen (defrosted) ones. Keep fresh shellfish in the refrigerator and use as soon as possible after purchase. Shelled raw scallops, for example, should be kept in the refrigerator for no more than 24 hours.

1 Using a sharp knife, slice down the corn cobs to remove the kernels. Place half the kernels in a food processor or blender and process with a little of the milk. Set the other half aside.

2 Melt the butter or margarine in a large pan and gently fry the leek or onion, bacon and garlic for 4–5 minutes until the leek is soft but not browned. Add the green pepper, celery and potato and sweat over a gentle heat for a further 3–4 minutes, stirring frequently.

3 Stir in the flour and cook for about 1–2 minutes until golden and frothy. Stir in a little milk and the corn mixture, stock, the remaining milk and corn kernels and seasoning.

4 Bring to the boil, and then simmer, partially covered, for 15–20 minutes until the vegetables are tender.

5 Pull the corals away from the scallops and slice the white flesh into 5 mm/ ¼in slices. Stir the scallops into the soup, cook for 4 minutes and then stir in the corals, mussels and paprika. Heat through for a few minutes and then stir in the cream, if using. Check the seasoning and serve.

VARIATIONS
Use pancetta or chorizo in place of streaky (fatty) bacon. Use 1 small red or orange (bell) pepper in place of the green pepper. Use cooked fresh clams or prawns (shrimp) in place of mussels.

CORN & CRAB BISQUE

This is a Louisiana classic, which is certainly luxurious enough for a dinner party and is therefore well worth the extra time required to prepare the fresh crab. The crab shells, together with the corn cobs, from which the kernels are stripped, make a fine-flavoured stock. The bisque is excellent served with French bread.

SERVES 8

INGREDIENTS
4 large corn cobs
2 bay leaves
1 cooked crab (about 1kg/2¼lb)
25g/1oz/2 tbsp butter
30ml/2 tbsp plain (all-purpose) flour
300ml/½ pint/1¼ cups whipping cream
6 spring onions (scallions), shredded
a pinch of cayenne pepper
salt and freshly ground black and white pepper
hot French bread or grissini breadsticks, to serve

COOK'S TIPS
When buying fresh corn cobs, choose moist, bright husks with fresh silk threads and uniform, small, tightly packed kernels. Use a clean nylon hairbrush (or toothbrush) to remove the silk threads from corn cobs without damaging the kernels.

1 Pull away the husks and silk from the cobs of corn and strip off the kernels. Keep the kernels on one side.

2 Put the stripped cobs into a deep pan or flameproof casserole with 3 litres/ 5 pints/12½ cups cold water, the bay leaves and 10ml/2 tsp salt. Bring to the boil and leave to simmer while you prepare the crab.

3 Pull away the two flaps between the big claws of the crab, stand it on its "nose", where the flaps were, and bang down firmly with the heel of your hand on the rounded end. Separate the crab from its top shell, keeping the shell.

4 Push out the crab's mouth and its abdominal sac immediately below the mouth, and discard.

5 Pull away the feathery gills surrounding the central chamber and discard. Scrape out all the semi-liquid brown meat from the shell and set aside.

6 Crack the claws in as many places as necessary to extract all the white meat. Pick out the white meat from the fragile cavities in the central body of the crab. Set aside all the crab meat, brown and white.

7 Put the spidery legs, back shell and all the other pieces of shell into the pan with the corn cobs. Simmer for a further 15 minutes, then strain the stock into a clean pan and boil hard to reduce to 2 litres/3½ pints/9 cups.

8 Meanwhile, melt the butter in a small pan and sprinkle in the flour. Stir constantly over a low heat until the roux is the colour of rich cream.

9 Off the heat, slowly stir in 250ml/8fl oz/1 cup of the stock. Return to the heat and stir until it thickens, then stir this thickened mixture into the pan of strained stock. Add the corn kernels, return to the boil and simmer for 5 minutes.

10 Add the crab meat, cream and spring onions and season with cayenne, salt and pepper (preferably a mixture of black and white). Return to the boil and simmer for a further 2 minutes. Serve with hot French bread or grissini breadsticks.

VARIATION
If fresh crab meat is not available, use canned (drained) crabmeat instead.

CLAM CHOWDER

A traditional chowder from New England in the USA, the mixture of clams and pork, with potatoes and cream, is very rich and utterly delicious. Traditionally, the soup is served with savoury biscuits called saltine crackers, but it is equally well complemented by other types of biscuit.

SERVES 8

INGREDIENTS
48 clams, scrubbed
1.5 litres/2½ pints/6¼ cups water
40g/1½oz/¼ cup finely diced salt pork or bacon
3 medium onions, finely chopped
1 bay leaf
3 medium potatoes, diced
475ml/16fl oz/2 cups milk, warmed
250ml/8fl oz/1 cup single (light) cream
salt and freshly ground black pepper
chopped fresh parsley, to garnish

VARIATIONS
Use pancetta in place of salt pork or bacon. Use a dried, ready-prepared or fresh home-made bouquet garni in place of the bay leaf. Use sweet potatoes in place of standard potatoes, or a mixture of standard and sweet potatoes. Use crème fraiche in place of single (light) cream.

1 Rinse the clams well in cold water. Drain. Place them in a deep pan with the water and bring to the boil. Cover and steam for about 10 minutes until the shells open. Remove from the heat.

2 When the clams have cooled slightly, remove them from their shells. Discard any clams that have not opened. Chop the clams coarsely. Strain the cooking liquid through a sieve (strainer) lined with muslin (cheesecloth) and reserve.

3 In a large, heavy pan, fry the salt pork or bacon until it renders its fat and begins to brown. Add the onions and cook over a low heat for 8–10 minutes until softened.

4 Stir in the bay leaf, potatoes and clam cooking liquid. Bring to the boil and cook for 5–10 minutes.

5 Stir in the chopped clams. Continue to cook until the potatoes are tender, stirring from time to time. Season with salt and pepper.

6 Stir in the warmed milk and cream and heat very gently for a further 5 minutes. Discard the bay leaf, adjust the seasoning and serve sprinkled with chopped fresh parsley.

CREAMY COD CHOWDER

The sharp flavour of the smoked cod in this dish contrasts well with the creamy soup. Serve the chowder as a substantial appetizer before a light main course. Warm, crusty wholemeal bread is an excellent accompaniment to go with it.

SERVES 4–6

INGREDIENTS
350g/12oz smoked cod fillet
1 small onion, finely chopped
1 bay leaf
4 black peppercorns
900ml/1½ pints/3¾ cups milk
10ml/2 tsp cornflour (cornstarch)
10ml/2 tsp cold water
200g/7oz can corn kernels
15ml/1 tbsp chopped fresh parsley
crusty wholemeal bread, to serve

COOK'S TIPS
• A quick and easy way to chop parsley is to remove the stems, wash and dry the sprigs and place them in a jug or cup. Using a pair of clean kitchen scissors, simply snip the parsley into small pieces, then use as required.
• The flavour of this creamy cod chowder improves if it is made a day in advance. Chill in the refrigerator until required, then reheat gently to prevent the fish from disintegrating.

1 Skin the fish with a knife and put into a large pan with the onion, bay leaf, black peppercorns and milk.

2 Bring to the boil. Reduce the heat and simmer very gently for 12–15 minutes, or until the fish is just cooked. Do not overcook.

3 Using a slotted spoon, lift out the fish and flake into large chunks. Remove and discard the bay leaf and peppercorns.

4 Blend the cornflour with the water carefully until it forms a smooth paste, and add to the pan. Bring to the boil and simmer for 1 minute or until slightly thickened.

5 Drain the corn kernels and add to the pan together with the flaked fish and chopped fresh parsley.

6 Reheat the soup until piping hot, but do not boil, taking care that the fish does not disintegrate. Ladle into soup bowls and serve immediately with plenty of warm wholemeal bread.

Czech Fish Soup with Dumplings

Use a variety of whatever fish is available in this Czech soup, such as perch, catfish, cod or snapper. The basis of the dumplings is the same whether using semolina or flour.

SERVES 4–8

INGREDIENTS
3 rindless bacon rashers (strips), diced
675g/1½lb assorted fresh fish, skinned, boned and diced
15ml/1 tbsp paprika, plus extra to garnish
1.5 litres/2½ pints/6¼ cups fish stock or water
3 firm tomatoes, peeled and chopped
4 waxy potatoes, peeled and grated
5–10ml/1–2 tsp chopped fresh marjoram, plus extra to garnish

FOR THE DUMPLINGS
75g/3oz/½ cup semolina or flour
1 egg, beaten
45ml/3 tbsp milk or water
generous pinch of salt
15ml/1 tbsp chopped fresh parsly

1 Dry-fry the diced bacon in a large pan until pale golden brown, then add the pieces of assorted fish. Fry for 1–2 minutes, taking care not to break up the pieces of fish. Sprinkle in the paprika, pour in the fish stock or water, bring to the boil and simmer for 10 minutes.

2 Stir the tomatoes, grated potato and marjoram into the pan. Cook for 10 minutes, stirring occasionally.

3 Meanwhile, make the dumplings by mixing all the ingredients together, then leave to stand, covered with clear film (plastic wrap) for 5–10 minutes.

4 Drop spoonfuls of the dumpling mixture into the soup and cook for 10 minutes. Serve hot with a little marjoram and paprika.

Smoked Haddock & Potato Soup

The proper name for this traditional Scottish soup is cullen skink. *A cullen* is the sea town or port district of a town, while *skink* means stock or broth.

SERVES 6

INGREDIENTS
1 Finnan haddock, about 350g/12oz
1 onion, chopped
1 bouquet garni
900ml/1½ pints/3¾ cups water
500g/1¼lb potatoes, quartered
600ml/1 pint/2½ cups milk
40g/1½oz/3 tbsp butter
salt and freshly ground black pepper
snipped fresh chives, to garnish
crusty bread, to serve

1 Put the haddock, onion, bouquet garni and water into a large pan and bring to the boil. Skim the scum from the surface, then cover the pan. Reduce the heat and poach for 10–15 minutes, until the haddock flakes easily.

2 Lift the haddock from the pan, using a fish slice, and remove the skin and bones. Flake the flesh and reserve. Return the skin and bones to the pan and simmer, uncovered, for 30 minutes. Strain the stock through a sieve (strainer).

3 Return the stock to the pan, then add the potatoes and simmer for about 25 minutes, or until tender. Remove the potatoes from the pan using a slotted spoon. Add the milk to the pan and bring to the boil.

4 Meanwhile, mash the potatoes with the butter, then whisk into the liquid in the pan until thick and creamy. Add the flaked fish to the pan and adjust the seasoning. Sprinkle with chives and serve immediately with crusty bread.

FISH BALL SOUP

The Japanese name for this soup is Tsumire-jiru. Tsumire, *means, quite literally, sardine balls, and these are added to this delicious soup to impart their robust flavour.*

SERVES 4

INGREDIENTS
100ml/3½fl oz/generous ⅓ cup sake or dry white wine
1.2 litres/2 pints/5 cups instant dashi
60ml/4 tbsp white miso paste

FOR THE FISH BALLS
20g/¾oz fresh root ginger
800g/1¾lb fresh sardines, gutted and heads removed
30ml/2 tbsp white miso paste
15ml/1 tbsp sake or dry white wine
7.5ml/1½ tsp sugar
1 egg
30ml/2 tbsp cornflour (cornstarch)
150g/5oz shimeji mushrooms or 6 shiitake mushrooms
1 leek or large spring onion (scallion)

COOK'S TIP
Miso, a Japanese staple, is a fermented soya bean paste that is used widely in Japanese cooking. Many larger supermarkets stock a range of Japanese ingredients including miso paste, as well as other Japanese ingredients such as dashi and sake. Alternatively, try delicatessens, large grocers or specialist food stores for these products.

1 First make the fish balls. To do this, grate the ginger and squeeze it well to yield 5ml/1 tsp ginger juice.

2 Rinse the sardines under cold running water, then cut in half along the backbone. Remove all the bones. To skin a boned sardine, lay it skin-side down on a board, then run a sharp knife slowly along the skin from tail to head.

3 Coarsely chop the sardines and process with the ginger juice, miso, sake or wine, sugar and egg to a thick paste in a food processor or blender. Transfer to a bowl and mix in the cornflour until thoroughly blended.

4 Trim the shimeji mushrooms and either separate each stem or remove the stems from the shiitake mushrooms and shred them. Cut the leek or spring onion into 4cm/1½in strips.

5 Bring the ingredients for the soup to the boil. Use two wet spoons to shape small portions of the sardine mixture into bite-size balls and drop them into the soup. Add the prepared mushrooms and leek or spring onion.

6 Simmer the soup until the sardine balls float to the surface. Serve immediately, in individual, deep soup bowls.

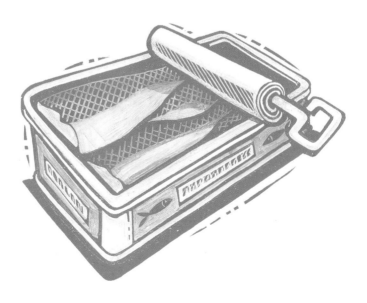

SALMON CHOWDER

Fresh salmon makes a delicious alternative to the more usual clam chowder. Dill is the perfect partner for the fish in this creamy soup.

SERVES 4

INGREDIENTS
20g/³⁄₄oz/1¹⁄₂ tbsp butter or margarine
1 onion, finely chopped
1 leek, finely chopped
1 small fennel bulb, finely chopped
25g/1oz/¹⁄₄ cup flour
1.75 litres/3 pints/7¹⁄₂ cups fish stock
2 medium potatoes, cut in 1cm/¹⁄₂in cubes
450g/1lb boneless, skinless salmon, cut in 2cm/³⁄₄in cubes
175ml/6fl oz/³⁄₄ cup milk
120ml/4fl oz/¹⁄₂ cup whipping cream
30g/2 tbsp chopped fresh dill
salt and freshly ground black pepper

1 Melt the butter or margarine in a large pan. Add the onion, leek and chopped fennel and cook over a medium heat for 5–8 minutes until softened, stirring from time to time.

2 Stir in the flour. Reduce the heat to low and cook for 3 minutes, stirring the mixture occasionally.

3 Add the fish stock and potatoes. Season with salt and freshly ground black pepper. Bring to the boil, then reduce the heat, cover and simmer for about 20 minutes or until the potatoes are tender.

4 Add the cubes of salmon and simmer gently for 3–5 minutes until it is just cooked.

5 Stir in the milk, cream, and dill. Cook until just warmed through, but do not boil. Adjust the seasoning and then serve.

THREE-DELICACY SOUP

This delicious Chinese-style soup combines the three complementary ingredients of chicken, ham and prawns (shrimp). It is very quick and simple to prepare.

SERVES 4

INGREDIENTS
115g/4oz chicken breast fillet
115g/4oz honey-roast ham
115g/4oz peeled prawns (shrimp)
700ml/1¼ pints/3 cups chicken stock
salt
chopped spring onions (scallions), to garnish

1 Thinly slice the chicken and ham into small pieces. If the prawns are large, cut them in half lengthways.

2 In a wok or pan, bring the stock to a rolling boil and add the chicken, ham and prawns. Bring back to the boil, add salt to taste and simmer for 1 minute.

3 Ladle into individual soup bowls. Serve hot, garnished with chopped spring onions.

COOK'S TIP
Fresh, uncooked prawns (shrimp) impart the best flavour in this dish. If these are not available, you can use ready-cooked prawns. They must be added towards the end of cooking, to prevent them from over-cooking.

CHICKEN MINESTRONE

An authentic minestrone is a thick Italian soup containing beans and pasta or rice, and does not usually contain meat. However, this version is a special minestrone made with fresh chicken. When served with crusty Italian bread, it makes a very hearty meal in itself.

SERVES 4–6

INGREDIENTS
15ml/1 tbsp olive oil
2 chicken thighs
3 rindless streaky bacon rashers (strips), chopped
1 onion, finely chopped
a few fresh basil leaves, shredded
a few fresh rosemary leaves, finely chopped
15ml/1 tbsp chopped fresh flat leaf parsley
2 potatoes, cut into 1cm/½in cubes
1 large carrot, cut into 1cm/½in cubes
2 small courgettes (zucchini), cut into 1cm/½in cubes
1–2 celery sticks, cut into 1cm/½in cubes
1 litre/1¾ pints/4 cups chicken stock
200g/7oz/1¾ cups frozen peas
90g/3½oz/scant 1 cup stellette or other small soup pasta
salt and freshly ground black pepper
Parmesan cheese shavings, to serve

VARIATIONS
Use pancetta or chorizo in place of bacon. Use 1 parsnip or sweet potato in place of carrot. Use canned (drained) or frozen corn kernels or fine green beans in place of peas. Use 1 red or green (bell) pepper, seeded and diced, in place of carrot or celery.

1 Heat the oil in a large frying pan, add the chicken thighs and fry for about 5 minutes on each side. Remove with a slotted spoon and set aside.

2 Add the bacon, onion and herbs to the pan and cook gently, stirring constantly, for about 5 minutes. Add the potatoes, carrot, courgettes and celery and cook for 5–7 minutes more.

3 Return the chicken thighs to the pan, add the stock and bring to the boil. Cover and cook over a low heat for 35–40 minutes, stirring the soup occasionally.

4 Remove the chicken thighs with a slotted spoon and place them on a board. Stir the peas and pasta into the soup and bring back to the boil. Simmer, stirring frequently, for 7–8 minutes or according to the instructions on the packet, until the pasta is just *al dente*.

5 Meanwhile, remove and discard the chicken skin, then remove the meat from the chicken bones and cut it into small (1cm/½in) pieces.

6 Return the meat to the soup, stir well and heat through. Taste and adjust the seasoning as necessary. Serve hot in warmed soup plates or bowls, topped with Parmesan cheese shavings.

PORK & VEGETABLE SOUP

This is an interesting Japanese soup made with a few unusual ingredients. Gobo is a thin, brown burdock root, konnyaku is a glutinous cake derived from the root of a kind of yam potato, and mooli (daikon) is a smooth-skinned, long, white radish. The stock is made from kombu, a type of seaweed, and bonito, a tropical tuna-like fish. All of these ingredients are available from specialist food stores.

SERVES 4

INGREDIENTS
50g/2oz gobo (optional)
5ml/1 tsp rice vinegar
½ black konnyaku (about 115g/4oz)
10ml/2 tsp oil
200g/7oz pork belly, cut into thin 3–4cm/1¼–½in long strips
115g/4oz mooli, peeled and thinly sliced
50g/2oz carrot, thinly sliced
1 medium potato, thinly sliced
4 shiitake mushrooms, stems removed and thinly sliced
800ml/scant 1½ pints/3½ cups kombu and bonito stock or instant dashi
15ml/1 tbsp sake or dry white wine
45ml/3 tbsp red or white miso paste

FOR THE GARNISH
2 spring onions (scallions), thinly sliced
seven spice flavour (shichimi)

VARIATIONS
Use parsnip or celeriac in place of mooli (daikon). Use swede (rutabaga) or turnip in place of carrot. Use sweet potato in place of standard potato. Use oyster mushrooms in place of shiitake mushrooms.

1 Scrub the skin off the gobo, if using, with a vegetable brush. Slice the vegetable into fine shavings. Soak the prepared gobo for 5 minutes in plenty of water with the vinegar added to remove any bitter taste, then drain.

2 Put the piece of konnyaku in a small pan and add enough water just to cover it. Bring to the boil over a moderate heat, then drain and allow to cool. This removes any bitter taste.

3 Using your hands, tear the konnyaku into 2cm/¾in lumps. Do not use a knife because a smooth cut surface will not absorb any flavour.

4 Heat the oil in a pan and quickly stir-fry the pork. Add the gobo, mooli, carrot, potato, shiitake mushrooms and konnyaku, then stir-fry for 1 minute. Pour in the stock and sake or wine.

5 Bring the soup to the boil, then skim it and simmer for 10 minutes, until the vegetables have softened.

6 Ladle a little of the soup into a small bowl and dissolve the miso paste in it. Pour the mixture back into the pan and bring to the boil once more. Do not continue to boil or the flavour will be lost.

7 Remove the pan from the heat, then pour into individual serving bowls. Sprinkle with the spring onions and seven spice flavour and serve immediately.

BUTTERNUT SQUASH, BACON & SWISS CHEESE SOUP

This is a lightly spiced soup full of large chunks of butternut squash and pieces of smoked bacon. The flavour is enriched with plenty of creamy melting cheese.

SERVES 4

INGREDIENTS
900g/2lb butternut squash
225g/8oz smoked back (lean) bacon
15ml/1 tbsp oil
225g/8oz onions, roughly chopped
2 garlic cloves, crushed
10ml/2 tsp ground cumin
15ml/1 tbsp ground coriander
275g/10oz potatoes, cut into small chunks
900ml/1½ pints/3¾ cups vegetable stock
10ml/2 tsp cornflour (cornstarch)
30ml/2 tbsp crème fraîche
Tabasco sauce, to taste
salt and freshly ground black pepper
175g/6oz/1½ cups Gruyère cheese, grated, to serve
crusty bread, to serve

VARIATION
Pumpkin can be used in this recipe instead of butternut squash, and is equally delicious.

1 Cut the butternut squash into large pieces. Using a sharp knife, carefully remove the skin, wasting as little flesh as possible.

2 Scoop out and discard the seeds. Chop the squash into small chunks. Remove all the fat from the bacon and roughly chop it into small pieces.

3 Heat the oil in a large pan and cook the onions and garlic for 3 minutes, or until beginning to soften.

4 Add the bacon and cook for about 3 minutes. Stir in the spices and cook on a low heat for a further 1 minute.

5 Add the chopped squash, potatoes and stock. Bring to the boil and simmer for 15 minutes, or until the squash and potatoes are tender.

6 Blend the cornflour with 30ml/2 tbsp water and add to the soup with the crème fraîche. Bring to the boil and simmer, uncovered, for 3 minutes. Adjust the seasoning and add Tabasco sauce to taste.

7 Ladle the soup into warm bowls and sprinkle the Gruyère cheese on top. Serve immediately, with crusty bread to scoop up the melted cheese.

Pasta Squares & Peas in Broth

This thick soup is from Lazio on the western side of Italy, where it is traditionally made with fresh home-made pasta and peas. In this modern version, ready-made pasta is used with frozen peas to save time.

Serves 4–6

Ingredients
25g/1oz/2 tbsp butter
50g/2oz/⅓ cup pancetta or rindless smoked streaky (fatty) bacon, roughly chopped
1 small onion, finely chopped
1 celery stick, finely chopped
400g/14oz/3½ cups frozen peas
5ml/1 tsp tomato purée (paste)
5–10ml/1–2 tsp finely chopped fresh flat leaf parsley
1 litre/1¾ pints/4 cups chicken stock
300g/11oz fresh lasagne sheets
about 50g/2oz/⅓ cup prosciutto or Parma ham, cut into cubes
salt and freshly ground black pepper
grated Parmesan cheese, to serve

1 Melt the butter in a large pan and add the pancetta or bacon, with the onion and celery. Cook over a low heat, stirring constantly, for 5 minutes.

2 Add the peas and cook, stirring, for 3–4 minutes. Stir in the tomato purée and parsley, then add the stock, with salt and pepper to taste. Bring to the boil. Cover the pan, lower the heat and simmer gently for 10 minutes. Meanwhile, cut the lasagne sheets into 2cm/¾in squares.

3 Taste the soup and adjust the seasoning. Drop in the pasta, stir and bring to the boil. Simmer for 2–3 minutes or until the pasta is *al dente*, then stir in the ham. Serve hot in warmed bowls, with grated Parmesan handed around separately.

Cook's Tip
Take care when adding salt because of the saltiness of the pancetta and the prosciutto.

SPLIT PEA & HAM SOUP

The main ingredient for this dish is bacon hock, which is the narrow piece of bone cut from a leg of ham. You could use a piece of pork belly instead, if you prefer, and remove it with the herbs before serving.

SERVES 4

INGREDIENTS
450g/1lb/2½ cups green split peas
4 rindless bacon rashers (strips)
1 onion, roughly chopped
2 carrots, sliced
1 celery stick, sliced
2.4 litres/4¼ pints/10½ cups cold water
1 sprig of fresh thyme
2 bay leaves
1 large potato, roughly diced
1 bacon hock
freshly ground black pepper

1 Put the split peas into a bowl, cover them with cold water and leave to soak overnight.

2 Cut the bacon into small pieces. In a large pan, dry-fry the bacon for 4–5 minutes, until crisp. Remove from the pan with a slotted spoon. Add the onion, carrots and celery to the fat in the pan and cook for 3–4 minutes until the onion is softened but not brown. Return the bacon to the pan with the water.

3 Drain the split peas and add to the pan with the thyme, bay leaves, potato and bacon hock. Bring to the boil, reduce the heat, cover and cook gently for 1 hour.

4 Remove the thyme, bay leaves and hock. Process the soup in a food processor or blender until smooth. Return to a clean pan.

5 Cut the meat from the hock and add to the soup and heat through gently. Season with plenty of freshly ground black pepper. Ladle into warm soup bowls and serve.

Brown Lentil, Bacon & Frankfurter Soup

This is a wonderfully hearty German soup, but it is possible to make a lighter version by omitting the frankfurters, if preferred.

SERVES 6

INGREDIENTS
225g/8oz/1 cup brown lentils
15ml/1 tbsp sunflower oil
1 onion, finely chopped
1 leek, finely chopped
1 carrot, finely diced
2 celery sticks, chopped
115g/4oz piece back (lean) bacon
2 bay leaves
1.5 litres/2½ pints/6¼ cups water
30ml/2 tbsp chopped fresh parsley, plus extra to garnish
225g/8oz frankfurters, sliced
salt and freshly ground black pepper

COOK'S TIP
Unlike most pulses, brown lentils do not need to be soaked before cooking.

1 Rinse the lentils thoroughly under cold running water until the water runs clear, then drain.

2 Heat the oil in a large pan and gently fry the onion for 5 minutes until soft. Add the leek, carrot, celery, bacon and bay leaves.

3 Add the lentils. Pour in the water, then slowly bring to the boil. Skim the surface, then simmer, half-covered, for about 45–50 minutes, or until the lentils are soft.

4 Remove the piece of bacon from the soup and cut into small cubes. Trim off any fat and discard.

5 Return the bacon to the soup with the parsley and sliced frankfurters, and season well with salt and freshly ground black pepper. Simmer for 2–3 minutes, then remove the bay leaves.

6 Transfer to individual soup bowls and serve garnished with chopped sprigs of fresh parsley.

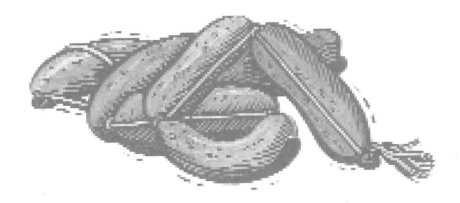

Pork & Noodle Broth with Prawns

This delicately flavoured soup from Vietnam is quick and easy to make, while tasting really special. The noodles make the soup into a satisfying and wholesome dish.

Serves 4–6

Ingredients
350g/12oz pork chops or fillet
225g/8oz raw prawn (shrimp) tails or cooked prawns (shrimp)
150g/5oz thin egg noodles
15ml/1 tbsp vegetable oil
10ml/2 tsp sesame oil
4 shallots or 1 medium onion, sliced
15ml/1 tbsp finely sliced fresh root ginger
1 garlic clove, crushed
5ml/l tsp sugar
1.5 litres/2½ pints/6¼ cups chicken stock
2 kaffir lime leaves
45ml/3 tbsp fish sauce
juice of ½ lime

For the garnish
4 sprigs of fresh coriander (cilantro)
2 spring onions (scallions), green parts only, chopped

Variation
This delicious recipe can be made with 200g/7oz boneless chicken breast instead of pork.

1 If you are using pork chops rather than fillet, remove any fat and the bones. Place the pork in the freezer for 30 minutes to firm, but not freeze, it. The cold makes the meat easier to slice thinly. Once sliced, set aside.

2 If using raw prawn tails, peel and devein the prawns. If using cooked prawns, no preparation in needed.

3 Bring a large pan of salted water to the boil and simmer the egg noodles according to the instructions on the packet. Drain and refresh under cold running water. Set the noodles to one side.

4 Preheat a wok. Add the vegetable and sesame oils and heat through. When the oil is hot, add the shallots or onion and stir-fry for 3–4 minutes, until evenly browned. Remove from the wok and set aside.

5 Add the ginger, garlic, sugar and chicken stock to the wok and bring to a simmer. Add the lime leaves, fish sauce and lime juice. Add the pork, then simmer for 15 minutes.

6 Add the prawns and noodles and simmer for 3–4 minutes, or longer if using raw prawns, to ensure that they are cooked.

7 Serve garnished with fresh coriander sprigs and the green parts of the chopped spring onion.

BULGARIAN SOUR LAMB SOUP

*This traditional Eastern European sour soup uses lamb as its principal ingredient,
though pork and poultry are popular alternatives.*

SERVES 4–5

INGREDIENTS
30ml/2 tbsp oil
450g/1lb lean lamb, trimmed and cubed
1 onion, diced
30ml/2 tbsp plain (all-purpose) flour
15ml/1 tbsp paprika
1 litre/1¾ pints/4 cups hot lamb stock
3 sprigs of fresh parsley
4 spring onions (scallions)
4 sprigs of fresh dill
25g/1oz/scant ¼ cup long grain rice
2 eggs, beaten
30–45ml/2–3 tbsp or more vinegar or lemon juice
salt and freshly ground black pepper

FOR THE GARNISH
25g/1oz/2 tbsp butter, melted
5ml/1 tsp paprika
a little fresh parsley or lovage and dill

1 Heat the oil in a large pan and fry the meat until brown. Add the onion and
cook until it has softened. Sprinkle in the flour and paprika. Stir well, add the
stock and cook for 10 minutes.

2 Tie the parsley, spring onions and dill together with string and add to the
large pan with the rice and seasoning. Bring to the boil, then simmer for about
30–40 minutes, or until the lamb is tender.

3 Remove the pan from the heat and stir in the eggs. Add the vinegar or lemon
juice. Discard the tied herbs and season to taste. For the garnish, melt the butter
in a pan and add the paprika. Ladle the soup into warmed serving bowls. Garnish
with the herbs and a little red paprika butter.

BEEF CHILLI SOUP

This is a hearty dish based on a traditional American chilli recipe. It is ideal served with fresh crusty bread as a warming start to any meal.

SERVES 4

INGREDIENTS
15ml/1 tbsp oil
1 onion, chopped
175g/6oz/³⁄₄ cup minced beef
2 garlic cloves, chopped
1 fresh red chilli, sliced
25g/1oz/¹⁄₄ cup plain (all-purpose) flour
400g/14oz can chopped tomatoes
600ml/1 pint/2¹⁄₂ cups beef stock
225g/8oz/2 cups canned kidney beans, drained
30ml/2 tbsp chopped fresh parsley
salt and freshly ground black pepper
crusty bread, to serve

1 Heat the oil in a large pan. Fry the onion and minced beef for 5 minutes until brown and sealed.

2 Add the garlic, chilli and flour. Cook for 1 minute. Add the tomatoes and pour in the stock. Bring to the boil.

3 Stir in the kidney beans into the mixture and add salt and pepper to taste. Cook for 20 minutes.

4 Add the chopped parsley, reserving a little to garnish the finished dish. Pour the soup into warm bowls, sprinkle with the reserved chopped parsley and serve with crusty bread.

COOK'S TIP
If you prefer a milder flavour, remove the seeds from the chilli after slicing it.

Clear Soup with Meatballs

This is a Chinese-style clear soup in which meatballs are combined with lightly cooked vegetables in a tasty beef or chicken stock.

SERVES 8

INGREDIENTS
4–6 Chinese mushrooms, soaked in warm water for 30 minutes
30ml/2 tbsp groundnut (peanut) oil
1 large onion, finely chopped
2 garlic cloves, finely crushed
1cm/½in piece fresh root ginger, bruised
2 litres/3½ pints/9 cups beef or chicken stock, including soaking liquid
  from the mushrooms
30ml/2 tbsp soy sauce
115g/4oz curly kale, spinach or Chinese leaves, shredded

FOR THE MEATBALLS
175g/6oz/¾ cup finely minced beef
1 small onion, finely chopped
1–2 garlic cloves, crushed
15ml/1 tbsp cornflour (cornstarch)
a little egg white, lightly beaten
salt and freshly ground black pepper

COOK'S TIP
A quick and easy way to bruise a piece of fresh root ginger is by placing the ginger on a board and hitting it with the flat base of a heavy pan. Once bruised, the flavour of the ginger will be quickly and easily infused into dishes, such as this soup.

1 First prepare the meatballs. Mix the beef with the onion, garlic, cornflour and seasoning in a food processor or blender and then bind with sufficient egg white to make a firm mixture. With wet hands, roll into tiny, bite-size balls and set aside.

2 Drain the mushrooms and reserve the soaking liquid. Trim off and discard the stalks. Slice the caps finely and set aside.

3 Heat a wok or large pan and add the oil. Fry the onion, garlic and ginger to bring out the flavour, but do not allow to brown.

4 When the onion is soft, pour in the stock. Bring to the boil, then stir in the soy sauce and mushroom slices and simmer for 10 minutes. Add the meatballs and cook for 10 minutes.

5 Just before serving, remove the ginger. Stir in the shredded curly kale, spinach or Chinese leaves. Heat through for 1 minute only – no longer or the leaves will be overcooked. Serve the soup immediately.

VARIATION
Use finely minced lamb, pork or chicken in place of beef.

MEATBALL & PASTA SOUP

This soup, which comes from sunny Sicily, is substantial enough for a hearty supper, whatever the weather. The addition of Parmesan cheese gives it a tangy bite.

SERVES 4

INGREDIENTS

2 × 300g/11oz cans condensed beef consommé
90g/3½oz/¾ cup very thin pasta, such as fidelini or spaghettini
chopped fresh flat leaf parsley, to garnish
grated Parmesan cheese, to serve

FOR THE MEATBALLS

1 very thick slice white bread, crusts removed
30ml/2 tbsp milk
225g/8oz/1 cup minced beef
1 garlic clove, crushed
30ml/2 tbsp grated Parmesan cheese
30–45ml/2–3 tbsp fresh flat leaf parsley leaves, coarsely chopped
1 egg
a generous pinch of freshly grated nutmeg
salt and freshly ground black pepper

> VARIATIONS
> *Use wholemeal or brown bread in place of white bread. Use single (light) or double (heavy) cream in place of milk. Use minced lamb, pork or chicken in place of minced beef. Use 15–30ml/1–2 tbsp chopped fresh mixed herbs, such as parsley, chives, basil and thyme, in place of parsley.*

1 Make the meatballs first. Break the bread into a small bowl, add the milk and set aside to soak. Meanwhile, put the minced beef, garlic, Parmesan cheese, parsley and egg into another large bowl. Grate the nutmeg liberally over the top and add salt and pepper to taste.

2 Squeeze the bread with your hands to remove as much milk as possible, then add the bread to the meatball mixture and mix everything together well with your hands. Wash your hands, rinse them under the cold tap, then form the mixture into tiny balls about the size of small marbles.

3 Tip both cans of consommé into a large pan, add water as directed on the labels, then add an extra can of water. Season to taste, bring to the boil and add the meatballs.

4 Break the pasta into small pieces and add it to the soup. Bring to the boil, stirring gently. Simmer, stirring frequently, for 7–8 minutes or according to the instructions on the packet, until the pasta is *al dente*. Taste and adjust the seasoning.

5 Serve hot in warmed bowls, garnished with chopped parsley and freshly grated Parmesan cheese.

ONE-POT-MEAL SOUPS

Delicious, wholesome soups are ideal served as one-pot-meals, the idea being that the soup is prepared and cooked in one pot or pan to create a hearty, flavourful meal. It saves on washing up too, which is sure to be a popular quality! This chapter draws on international cuisine and presents an eclectic selection of tasty soups. Enjoy the flavours of the Mediterranean with recipes for Tuscan Bean Soup, Chunky Pasta Soup or Genoese Minestrone, or choose soups from further afield such as Japanese Crushed Tofu Soup, Thai Chicken Soup or Chiang Mai Noodle Soup.

Tuscan Bean Soup

There are many versions of this wonderful soup. This one uses cannellini beans, leeks, cabbage and extra virgin olive oil – and it tastes even better when it is reheated.

Serves 4

Ingredients
45ml/3 tbsp extra virgin olive oil
1 onion, roughly chopped
2 leeks, roughly chopped
1 large potato, diced
2 garlic cloves, finely chopped
1.2 litres/2 pints/5 cups vegetable stock
400g/14oz can cannellini beans, drained and liquid reserved
175g/6oz Savoy cabbage, shredded
45ml/3 tbsp chopped fresh flat leaf parsley
30ml/2 tbsp chopped fresh oregano
75g/3oz/1 cup Parmesan cheese, shaved
salt and freshly ground black pepper

For the garlic toasts
30–45ml/2–3 tbsp extra virgin olive oil
6 thick slices country bread
1 garlic clove, peeled and bruised

Cook's Tip
Tubs of fresh Parmesan cheese shavings are readily available to buy in supermarkets, to save you a little time.

1 Heat the oil in a large pan and gently cook the onion, leeks, potato and garlic for 4–5 minutes until they are just beginning to soften.

2 Pour on the stock and the liquid from the beans. Cover and simmer for 15 minutes.

3 Stir in the cabbage, beans and half the herbs, season and cook for a further 10 minutes. Spoon about one-third of the soup into a food processor or blender and process until fairly smooth. Return to the soup in the pan, adjust the seasoning and heat through for 5 minutes.

4 Make the garlic toasts. Drizzle a little oil over the slices of bread, then rub both sides of each slice with the garlic. Toast until browned on both sides.

5 Ladle the soup into bowls. Sprinkle with the remaining herbs and the Parmesan shavings. Add a drizzle of olive oil and serve with the hot garlic toasts.

VARIATIONS
Use 1 red onion in place of standard onion. Use canned haricot (navy) or black-eyed beans in place of cannellini beans. Use green cabbage or curly kale if Savoy cabbage is not available. Use chopped fresh marjoram in place of oregano.

FARMHOUSE SOUP

Root vegetables form the basis of this chunky, minestrone-style main-meal soup.
You can vary the vegetables according to what you have at hand.

SERVES 4

INGREDIENTS
30ml/2 tbsp olive oil
1 onion, roughly chopped
3 carrots, cut into large chunks
175–200g/6–7oz turnips, cut into large chunks
about 175g/6oz swede (rutabaga), cut into large chunks
400g/14oz can chopped Italian tomatoes
15ml/1 tbsp tomato purée (paste)
5ml/1 tsp dried mixed herbs
5ml/1 tsp dried oregano
50g/2oz/½ cup dried (bell) peppers, finely sliced (optional)
1.5 litres/2½ pints/6¼ cups vegetable stock or water
50g/2oz/½ cup small macaroni or conchiglie
400g/14oz can red kidney beans, rinsed and drained
30ml/2 tbsp chopped fresh flat leaf parsley
salt and freshly ground black pepper
grated Parmesan cheese, to serve

1 Heat the oil in a large pan, add the onion and cook over a low heat for about 5 minutes until softened. Add the fresh vegetables, canned tomatoes, tomato purée, dried herbs and dried peppers, if using. Stir in salt and pepper to taste.

2 Pour in the stock or water and bring to the boil. Stir well, cover, lower the heat and simmer for 30 minutes, stirring occasionally.

3 Add the pasta and bring to the boil, stirring. Lower the heat and simmer, uncovered, for about 5 minutes or according to the instructions on the packet until the pasta is just *al dente*. Stir frequently during the cooking.

4 Stir in the beans. Heat through for 2–3 minutes, then remove from the heat and stir in the parsley. Taste and adjust the seasoning. Serve hot in warmed soup bowls and hand round the grated Parmesan separately.

Chunky Bean & Vegetable Soup

This is a substantial soup, not unlike minestrone, using a selection of vegetables and cannellini beans for extra protein and fibre. Serve with a hunk of wholegrain bread.

Serves 4

Ingredients
30ml/2 tbsp olive oil
2 celery sticks, chopped
2 leeks, sliced
3 carrots, sliced
2 garlic cloves, crushed
400g/14oz can chopped tomatoes with basil
1.2 litres/2 pints/5 cups vegetable stock
400g/14oz can cannellini beans (or mixed pulses), drained
15ml/1 tbsp pesto sauce
salt and freshly ground black pepper
Parmesan cheese shavings, to serve

1 Heat the olive oil in a large pan. Add the celery, leeks, carrots and garlic and cook gently for about 5 minutes until they have softened.

2 Stir in the tomatoes and stock. Bring to the boil, then cover and cook gently for 15 minutes.

3 Stir in the beans and pesto, with salt and freshly ground black pepper to taste. Heat through for a further 5 minutes. Serve in heated bowls, sprinkled with shavings of Parmesan cheese.

Cook's Tip
Extra vegetables can be added to the soup to make it even more substantial. For example, add some thinly sliced courgettes (zucchini) or finely shredded cabbage for the last 5 minutes of the cooking time. Or stir in some small wholewheat pasta shapes, if liked. Add them at the same time as the tomatoes, as they will take 10–15 minutes to cook.

PROVENÇAL VEGETABLE SOUP

This satisfying soup captures all the flavours of summer in Provence. The basil and garlic purée, pistou, gives it extra colour and a wonderful aroma – so don't leave it out.

SERVES 6–8

INGREDIENTS
275g/10oz/1½ cups shelled fresh broad (fava) beans or 175g/6oz/¾ cup dried haricot
    (navy) beans, soaked overnight
2.5ml/½ tsp dried herbes de Provence
2 garlic cloves, finely chopped
15ml/1 tbsp olive oil
1 onion, finely chopped
1 large leek, finely sliced
1 celery stick, finely sliced
2 carrots, finely diced
2 small potatoes, finely diced
115g/4oz French (green) beans
1.2 litres/2 pints/5 cups water
2 small courgettes (zucchini), finely chopped
3 medium tomatoes, peeled, seeded and finely chopped
115g/4oz/l cup shelled garden peas, fresh or frozen
a handful of spinach leaves, cut into thin ribbons
salt and freshly ground black pepper
sprigs of fresh basil, to garnish

FOR THE PISTOU
1 or 2 garlic cloves, finely chopped
15g/½oz/½ cup (packed) basil leaves
60ml/4 tbsp grated Parmesan cheese
60ml/4 tbsp extra virgin olive oil

COOK'S TIPS
Both the pistou and the soup can be made 1 or 2 days in advance and chilled in the refrigerator. To serve, reheat gently, stirring occasionally.

1 To make the pistou, put the garlic, basil and Parmesan cheese in a food processor or blender and process until smooth, scraping down the sides once. With the machine running, slowly add the olive oil through the feed tube. Alternatively, pound the garlic, basil and cheese in a mortar and pestle and stir in the oil.

2 To make the soup, if using dried haricot beans, drain them, place in a pan and cover with water. Boil vigorously for 10 minutes and drain.

3 Place the par-boiled beans, or fresh beans if using, in a pan with the herbes de Provence and one of the garlic cloves. Add water to cover by 2.5cm/1in. Bring to the boil, reduce the heat and simmer over a medium-low heat until tender, about 10 minutes for fresh beans or 1 hour for dried beans. Set aside in the cooking liquid.

4 Heat the olive oil in a large pan or flameproof casserole. Add the onion and leek and cook for 5 minutes, stirring occasionally, until they are beginning to soften.

5 Add the celery, carrots and the remaining garlic clove and cook, covered, for 10 minutes, stirring occasionally.

6 Add the potatoes, French beans and water, then season lightly with salt and pepper. Bring to the boil, skimming any foam that rises to the surface, then reduce the heat, cover and simmer gently for 10 minutes.

7 Add the courgettes, tomatoes and peas, together with the reserved beans and their cooking liquid, and simmer for about 25–30 minutes until all the vegetables are tender. Add the spinach and simmer for 5 minutes. Season the soup and swirl a spoonful of pistou into each bowl. Garnish with basil and serve.

CARIBBEAN VEGETABLE SOUP

This vegetable soup is refreshing and filling, and a good choice for a main lunch dish.
Yams are similar in size and colour to potatoes, but they have a nuttier flavour.

SERVES 4

INGREDIENTS
25g/1oz/2 tbsp butter or margarine
1 onion, chopped
1 garlic clove, crushed
2 carrots, sliced
1.5 litres/2½ pints/6¼ cups vegetable stock
2 bay leaves
2 sprigs of fresh thyme
1 celery stick, finely chopped
2 green bananas, peeled and cut into 4 pieces
175g/6oz white yam or eddoe, peeled and cubed
25g/1oz/2 tbsp red lentils
1 christophene, peeled and chopped
25g/1oz/2 tbsp macaroni (optional)
salt and freshly ground black pepper
chopped spring onions (scallions), to garnish

1 Melt the butter or margarine and fry the onion, garlic and carrots for a few minutes, stirring occasionally, until beginning to soften. Add the stock, bay leaves and thyme and bring to the boil.

2 Add the celery, green bananas, white yam or eddoe, lentils, christophene and macaroni, if using. Season and simmer for 25 minutes or until all the vegetables are cooked. Serve garnished with chopped spring onions.

COOK'S TIPS
You can use other root vegetables or potatoes if a yam or eddoes are not available. Add more stock if you want a thinner soup.

SUMMER MINESTRONE

This bright red, green and yellow fresh-tasting soup makes the most of summer vegetables. The grated Parmesan cheese on top adds a delicious bite to the flavour.

SERVES 4

INGREDIENTS
45ml/3 tbsp olive oil
1 large onion, finely chopped
15ml/1 tbsp sun-dried tomato purée (paste)
450g/1lb ripe Italian plum tomatoes, peeled and finely chopped
225g/8oz green courgettes (zucchini), trimmed and roughly chopped
225g/8oz yellow courgettes (zucchini), trimmed and roughly chopped
3 waxy new potatoes, diced
2 garlic cloves, crushed
about 1.2 litres/2 pints/5 cups vegetable stock or water
60ml/4 tbsp shredded fresh basil
50g/2oz/⅔ cup grated Parmesan cheese
salt and freshly ground black pepper

1 Heat the oil in a large pan, add the onion and cook gently for about 5 minutes, stirring constantly, until softened.

2 Stir in the sun-dried tomato purée, chopped tomatoes, different coloured courgettes, diced potatoes and garlic. Mix well and cook gently for 10 minutes, uncovered, shaking the pan frequently to stop the vegetables sticking to the base.

3 Pour in the stock or water. Bring to the boil, lower the heat, half-cover the pan and simmer gently for 15 minutes or until the vegetables are just tender. Add more stock if necessary.

4 Remove the pan from the heat and stir in the basil and half the cheese. Taste and adjust the seasoning. Serve hot, sprinkled with the remaining cheese.

CHUNKY PASTA SOUP

Mixed beans combine well with corn, broccoli and cauliflower to make a very hearty main-meal soup. Serve with tasty pesto-topped French bread croûtons.

SERVES 4

INGREDIENTS

115g/4oz/½ cup dried beans (a mixture of red kidney and haricot [navy] beans),
   soaked overnight
1.2 litres/2 pints/5 cups water
15ml/1 tbsp oil
1 onion, chopped
2 celery sticks, finely sliced
2–3 garlic cloves, crushed
2 leeks, finely sliced
1 vegetable stock (bouillon) cube
400g/14oz can or jar pimientos
45–60ml/3–4 tbsp tomato purée (paste)
115g/4oz pasta shapes
4 slices French bread
15ml/1 tbsp pesto sauce
115g/4oz/l cup baby corn, halved
50g/2oz each broccoli and cauliflower florets
a few drops of Tabasco sauce
salt and freshly ground black pepper

> COOK'S TIPS
> Use dried pasta such as short-cut macaroni or fusilli (pasta twists) for this recipe. Use ready-made green or red pesto sauce.

1 Drain the beans and place in a large pan with the water. Bring to the boil and simmer for about 1 hour, or until nearly tender.

2 When the beans are almost ready, heat the oil in a large pan and fry the vegetables for 2 minutes. Add the stock cube and the beans with about 600ml/1 pint/2½ cups of their liquid. Cover and simmer for 10 minutes.

3 Meanwhile, purée the pimientos with a little of their liquid and add to the pan. Stir in the tomato purée and pasta and cook for 15 minutes. Preheat the oven to 200°C/400°F/Gas 6.

4 Meanwhile, make the pesto croûtons. Spread the French bread with the pesto sauce and bake for 10 minutes or until crisp.

5 When the pasta is just cooked, add the corn, broccoli and cauliflower florets, Tabasco sauce and seasoning to taste. Heat through for 2–3 minutes and serve at once with the pesto croûtons.

VARIATIONS
Use 4 shallots in place of onion. Use sun-dried tomato purée (paste) in place of tomato purée (paste). Use French (green) beans or baby courgettes (zucchini) in place of baby corn.

GENOESE MINESTRONE

In Genoa they often make minestrone like this, with pesto stirred in towards the end of cooking. It is packed full of vegetables and has a strong, heady flavour, making it an excellent vegetarian supper dish when served with bread. There is Parmesan cheese in the pesto, so there is no need to serve any extra cheese with the soup.

SERVES 4–6

INGREDIENTS
45ml/3 tbsp olive oil
1 onion, finely chopped
2 celery sticks, finely chopped
1 large carrot, finely chopped
150g/5oz French (green) beans, cut into 5cm/2in pieces
1 courgette (zucchini), finely sliced
1 potato, cut into 1cm/½in cubes
¼ Savoy cabbage, shredded
1 small aubergine (eggplant), cut into 1cm/½in cubes
200g/7oz can cannellini beans, drained and rinsed
2 Italian plum tomatoes, chopped
1.2 litres/2 pints/5 cups vegetable stock
90g/3½oz spaghetti or vermicelli
salt and freshly ground black pepper

FOR THE PESTO
about 20 fresh basil leaves
1 garlic clove
10ml/2 tsp pine nuts
15ml/1 tbsp freshly grated Parmesan cheese
15ml/1 tbsp freshly grated pecorino cheese
30ml/2 tbsp olive oil

1 Heat the oil in a large pan, add the chopped onion, celery and carrot, and cook over a low heat, stirring frequently, for 5–7 minutes.

2 Mix in the French beans, courgette, potato and Savoy cabbage. Stir-fry over a medium heat for about 3 minutes. Add the aubergine, cannellini beans and plum tomatoes and stir-fry for 2–3 minutes.

3 Pour in the stock with salt and pepper to taste. Bring to the boil. Stir well, cover and lower the heat. Simmer for 40 minutes, stirring occasionally.

4 Meanwhile, process all the pesto ingredients in a food processor or blender until the mixture forms a smooth sauce, adding 15–45ml/1–3 tbsp water through the feeder tube if the sauce seems too thick.

5 Break the pasta into small pieces and add it to the soup. Simmer, stirring frequently, for 5 minutes. Add the pesto sauce and stir it in well, then simmer for 2–3 minutes more, or until the pasta is *al dente*. Check the seasoning and serve hot, in warmed soup plates or bowls.

VARIATIONS

Use 1 large parsnip or 1 turnip in place of the carrot. Use peeled celeriac (about 175g/6oz) in place of celery. Use fresh (shelled) peas or broad (fava) beans in place of French (green) beans. Use vine-ripened tomatoes in place of plum tomatoes. Use canned haricot (navy) beans or chickpeas in place of cannellini beans.

JAPANESE CRUSHED TOFU SOUP

The main ingredient for this Japanese one-pot-meal soup is crushed tofu, which is both nutritious and satisfying. You should be able to find all the ingredients in good delicatessens and supermarkets.

SERVES 4

INGREDIENTS
150g/5oz fresh tofu, weighed without water
2 dried shiitake mushrooms
50g/2oz gobo
5ml/1 tsp rice vinegar
½ black or white konnyaku (about 115g/4oz)
30 ml/2 tbsp sesame oil
115g/4oz mooli (daikon), finely sliced
50g/2oz carrot, finely sliced
750ml/1¼ pints/3 cups kombu and bonito stock or instant dashi
a pinch of salt
30ml/2 tbsp sake or dry white wine
7.5ml/1½ tsp mirin
45ml/3 tbsp white or red miso paste
a dash of soy sauce
6 mangetouts (snow peas), trimmed, boiled and finely sliced, to garnish

COOK'S TIP
Fresh plain and flavoured varieties of tofu are readily available in many supermarkets, delicatessens and health food stores.

1 Crush the tofu roughly by hand until it resembles lumpy scrambled egg in texture – do not crush it too finely.

2 Wrap the tofu in a clean tea towel and put it in a sieve (strainer), then pour over plenty of boiling water. Leave the tofu to drain for 10 minutes.

3 Soak the dried shiitake mushrooms in tepid water for 20 minutes, then drain them. Remove their stems and cut the caps into 4–6 pieces.

4 Use a vegetable brush to scrub the skin off the gobo and slice it into thin shavings. Soak the shavings for 5 minutes in plenty of cold water with the vinegar added to remove any bitter taste. Drain.

5 Put the konnyaku in a small pan and cover with water. Bring to the boil, then drain and cool. Tear the konnyaku into 2cm/¾in lumps: do not use a knife, as smooth cuts will prevent it from absorbing flavour.

6 Heat the sesame oil in a deep pan. Add all the shiitake mushrooms, gobo, mooli, carrot and konnyaku. Stir-fry for 1 minute, then add the tofu and stir well.

7 Pour in the stock/dashi and add the salt, sake or wine and mirin. Bring to the boil. Skim the broth and simmer it for 5 minutes.

8 In a small bowl, dissolve the miso paste in a little of the soup, then return it to the pan. Simmer the soup gently for 10 minutes, until the vegetables are soft. Add the soy sauce, then remove from the heat. Serve immediately in four bowls, garnished with the mangetouts.

VARIATIONS
Use turnip, swede (rutabaga) or celeriac in place of mooli (daikon). Use parsnip or celery in place of carrot. Use sugar-snap peas in place of mangetouts (snow peas), for the garnish.

SEAFOOD LAKSA

For a delicious and satisfying meal, serve creamy rice noodles in a spicy coconut-flavoured soup, topped with seafood. This recipe uses blachan, a South-east Asian flavouring made from fermented shrimp, sardines and other small salted fish.

SERVES 4

INGREDIENTS
4 fresh red chillies, seeded and roughly chopped
1 onion, roughly chopped
1 piece blachan, the size of a stock (bouillon) cube
1 lemon grass stalk, chopped
1 small piece fresh root ginger, peeled and roughly chopped
6 macadamia nuts or almonds
60ml/4 tbsp vegetable oil
5ml/1 tsp paprika
5ml/1 tsp ground turmeric
475ml/16fl oz/2 cups fish stock
600ml/1 pint/2½ cups coconut milk
a dash of fish sauce, to taste
12 king prawns (shrimp), peeled and deveined
8 scallops
225g/8oz prepared squid, cut into rings
350g/12oz rice vermicelli or rice noodles, soaked in warm water until soft
salt and freshly ground black pepper
lime halves, to serve

FOR THE GARNISH
¼ cucumber, cut into matchsticks
2 fresh red chillies, seeded and finely sliced
30ml/2 tbsp mint leaves
30ml/2 tbsp fried shallots or onions

VARIATIONS
Use 4 shallots in place of the onion. Use a well-flavoured vegetable stock in place of fish stock. Use fresh mussels in place of scallops.

1 Process the chillies, onion, blacan, lemon grass, ginger and nuts in a food processor or blender, until the mixture is smooth in texture.

2 Heat 45ml/3 tbsp of the oil in a large pan. Add the chilli paste and fry for 6 minutes. Stir in the paprika and turmeric and fry for about 2 minutes more.

3 Add the stock and the coconut milk to the pan. Bring to the boil, then simmer gently for 15–20 minutes. Season with fish sauce.

4 Season the seafood with salt and pepper. Fry quickly in the remaining oil for 2–3 minutes until cooked.

5 Add the noodles to the soup and heat through. Divide among individual serving bowls. Place the fried seafood on top, then garnish with the cucumber, chillies, mint and fried shallots or onions. Serve with the limes.

PRAWN CREOLE

Raw prawns (shrimp) are combined with chopped fresh vegetables and cayenne pepper to make this tasty one-pot soup.

SERVES 4

INGREDIENTS
675g/1½lb raw prawns (shrimp) in the shell, with heads, if available
475ml/16fl oz/2 cups water
45ml/3 tbsp olive or vegetable oil
175g/6oz/1½ cups onions, very finely chopped
75g/3oz/½ cup celery, very finely chopped
75g/3oz/½ cup green (bell) pepper, very finely chopped
25g/1oz/½ cup chopped fresh parsley
1 garlic clove, crushed
15ml/1 tbsp Worcestershire sauce
1.5ml/¼ tsp cayenne pepper
120ml/4fl oz/½ cup dry white wine
50g/2oz/1 cup chopped peeled plum tomatoes
5ml/1 tsp salt
1 bay leaf
5ml/1 tsp sugar
fresh parsley, to garnish
boiled rice, to serve

VARIATIONS
Use leeks, spring onions (scallions) or red onion in place of standard onions. Use peeled celeriac in place of celery. Use 15g/½oz chopped fresh chives or coriander (cilantro) in place of half the parsley. Use vine-ripened tomatoes in place of plum tomatoes.

1 Peel and devein the prawns, reserving the heads and shells. Keep the prawns in a covered bowl in the refrigerator while you make the sauce.

2 Put the prawn heads and shells in a pan with the water. Bring to the boil and simmer for 15 minutes. Strain and reserve 350ml/12fl oz/1½ cups of the stock.

3 Heat the oil in a heavy pan. Add the onions and cook over a low heat for 8–10 minutes until softened. Add the celery and green pepper and cook for 5 minutes further. Stir in the parsley, garlic, Worcestershire sauce and cayenne. Cook for another 5 minutes.

4 Raise the heat to medium. Stir in the wine and simmer for 3–4 minutes. Add the tomatoes, reserved prawn stock, salt, bay leaf and sugar and bring to the boil. Stir well, then reduce the heat to low and simmer for about 30 minutes until the tomatoes have fallen apart and the sauce has reduced slightly. Remove from the heat and cool slightly.

5 Discard the bay leaf. Pour the sauce into a food processor or blender and purée until quite smooth. Taste and adjust the seasoning as necessary.

6 Return the tomato sauce to the pan and bring to the boil. Add the prawns and simmer for 4–5 minutes until they turn pink. Ladle into individual soup bowls, garnish with fresh parsley and serve with rice.

BOUILLABAISSE

Perhaps the most famous of all Mediterranean fish soups, this recipe, originating from Marseilles, in the south of France, is a rich and colourful mixture of fish and shellfish, flavoured with tomatoes, saffron and orange.

SERVES 4–6

INGREDIENTS

1.5 kg/3–3½lb mixed fish and raw shellfish, such as red mullet, John Dory, monkfish, red snapper, whiting, large raw prawns (shrimp) and clams
225g/8oz well-flavoured tomatoes
a pinch of saffron strands
90ml/6 tbsp olive oil
1 onion, sliced
1 leek, sliced
1 celery stick, sliced
2 garlic cloves, crushed
1 bouquet garni
1 strip orange rind
2.5ml/½ tsp fennel seeds
15ml/1 tbsp tomato purée (paste)
10ml/2 tsp Pernod
salt and freshly ground black pepper
4–6 thick slices French bread and 45ml/3 tbsp chopped fresh parsley, to serve

COOK'S TIP
Saffron comes from the orange and red stigmas of a type of crocus, which must be harvested by hand and is therefore extremely expensive – the highest-priced spice in the world. However, its flavour is unique and cannot be replaced by any other spice. It is an essential ingredient in traditional bouillabaisse and should not be omitted.

1 Remove the heads, tails and fins from the fish and set the fish aside. Put the trimmings into a large pan with 1.2 litres/2 pints/5 cups water. Bring to the boil and simmer for 15 minutes. Strain and reserve the liquid.

2 Cut the fish into large chunks. Leave the shellfish in their shells. Scald the tomatoes, then drain and refresh in cold water. Peel them and chop roughly. Soak the saffron in 15–30ml/1–2 tbsp hot water.

3 Heat the oil in a large pan, add the onion, leek and celery and cook until softened. Add the garlic, bouquet garni, orange rind, fennel seeds and chopped tomatoes, then stir in the saffron and its soaking liquid and the reserved fish stock. Season with salt and pepper, then bring to the boil and simmer for 30–40 minutes.

4 Add the shellfish and boil for about 6 minutes. Add the fish and cook for 6–8 minutes more, until it flakes easily.

5 Using a slotted spoon, transfer the fish to a warmed serving platter. Keep the liquid boiling to allow the oil to emulsify with the broth. Add the tomato purée and Pernod, then check the seasoning.

6 Ladle the bouillabaisse into warm bowls, scatter with chopped parsley and serve with French bread.

Clam & Pasta Soup

This soup is a variation of the pasta dish spaghetti alle vongole, *using store-cupboard ingredients. Serve it with hot focaccia or ciabatta for an informal supper with friends.*

Serves 4

INGREDIENTS
30ml/2 tbsp olive oil
1 large onion, finely chopped
2 garlic cloves, crushed
400g/14oz can chopped tomatoes
15ml/1 tbsp sun-dried tomato purée (paste)
5ml/1 tsp granulated sugar
5ml/1 tsp dried mixed herbs
about 750ml/1¼ pints/3 cups fish or vegetable stock
150ml/¼ pint/⅔ cup red wine
50g/2oz/½ cup small pasta shapes
150g/5oz jar or can clams in natural juice
30ml/2 tbsp finely chopped fresh flat leaf parsley, plus a few whole leaves to garnish
salt and freshly ground black pepper

1 Heat the oil in a large pan. Cook the onion gently for 5 minutes, stirring frequently, until softened.

2 Add the garlic, tomatoes, tomato purée, sugar, herbs, stock and wine, with salt and pepper to taste. Bring to the boil. Lower the heat, half-cover the pan and simmer for 10 minutes, stirring occasionally.

3 Add the pasta and continue simmering, uncovered, for about 10 minutes or until *al dente*. Stir occasionally to prevent the pasta shapes sticking together.

4 Add the clams and their juice to the soup and heat through for 3–4 minutes, adding more stock if required. Do not allow the soup to boil, or the clams will become tough. Remove from the heat, stir in the chopped parsley and adjust the seasoning. Serve hot, sprinkled with coarsely ground black pepper and a few whole flat leaf parsley leaves.

CREAMY FISH CHOWDER

This is a traditional soup that never fails to please, whether it is made with milk or more luxuriously with a generous quantity of cream.

SERVES 4

INGREDIENTS
3 thick-cut bacon rashers (strips)
1 large onion
675g/1½ potatoes
1 litre/1¾ pints/4 cups fish stock
450g/1lb skinless haddock, cut into 2.5cm/1in cubes
30ml/2 tbsp chopped fresh parsley
15ml/1 tbsp snipped fresh chives
300ml/½ pint/1¼ cups whipping cream or full cream (whole) milk
salt and freshly ground black pepper

1 Remove the rind from the bacon and discard it, then cut the bacon into small pieces. Chop the onion and cut the potatoes into 2cm/¾in cubes.

2 Fry the bacon in a deep pan until the fat is rendered. Add the onion and potatoes and cook over low heat, without browning, for about 10 minutes. Season to taste .

3 Pour off excess bacon fat from the pan. Add the fish stock to the pan and bring to a boil. Simmer until the vegetables are tender, about 15–20 minutes.

4 Stir in the cubes of fish, the parsley and chives. Simmer until the fish is just cooked, 3–4 minutes.

5 Stir the cream or milk into the chowder and reheat gently, but do not bring to the boil. Season to taste and serve immediately.

VARIATION
Cod fillets would be equally good in this chowder, or you could try smoked fillets for a stronger taste.

Provençal Fish Soup with Pasta

This colourful fish soup has all the traditional flavours of the Mediterranean. Serve it as a main course for a deliciously filling lunch.

SERVES 4

INGREDIENTS
30ml/2 tbsp olive oil
1 onion, sliced
1 garlic clove, crushed
1 leek, sliced
1 litre/1¾ pints/4 cups water
225g/8oz canned chopped tomatoes
a pinch of Mediterranean herbs
1.5ml/¼ tsp saffron strands (optional)
115g/4oz small pasta
about 8 live mussels in the shell
450g/1lb white fish, such as cod, plaice or monkfish, filleted and skinned
salt and freshly ground black pepper

FOR THE ROUILLE
2 garlic cloves, crushed
1 canned pimiento, drained and chopped
15ml/1 tbsp fresh white breadcrumbs
60ml/4 tbsp mayonnaise
toasted French bread, to serve

COOK'S TIP
Use small soup pasta such as stellette, conchigliette or tubetti for this recipe.

1 Heat the oil in a large pan and add the onion, garlic and leek. Cover and cook gently for 5 minutes, stirring occasionally until the vegetables are soft.

2 Add the water, tomatoes, herbs, saffron, if using, and pasta. Season and cook for 15–20 minutes.

3 Scrub the mussels and pull off the "beards". Discard any that do not close when sharply tapped with a knife.

4 Cut the fish into bite-size chunks and add to the soup, placing the mussels on top. Simmer for 5–10 minutes until the mussels open and the fish is cooked. Discard any unopened mussels.

5 To make the rouille, pound together the garlic, canned pimiento and breadcrumbs in a pestle and mortar (or in a food processor or blender). Stir in the mayonnaise and season well. Spread the toasted French bread with the rouille and serve with the soup.

VARIATIONS
Instead of adding Mediterranean herbs, use chopped tomatoes with herbs already in the can. Use fresh brown or wholemeal breadcrumbs in place of white breadcrumbs for the rouille.

FISHERMAN'S SOUP

There is something truly delicious about the combined flavours of bacon and fish. In winter, when fresh tomatoes are lacking in flavour, you can substitute canned chopped tomatoes. The soup will taste slightly different but will still be successful.

SERVES 4

INGREDIENTS
6 streaky bacon rashers (strips), cut into thin lengths
15g/½oz/1 tbsp butter
1 large onion, chopped
1 garlic clove, finely chopped
30ml/2 tbsp chopped fresh parsley
5ml/1 tsp fresh thyme leaves or 2.5ml/½ tsp dried thyme
450g/1lb tomatoes, peeled, seeded and chopped
150ml/¼ pint/⅔ cup dry vermouth or white wine
450ml/¾ pint/scant 2 cups fish stock
300g/11oz potatoes, diced
675–900g/1½–2lb skinless white fish fillets, cut into large chunks
salt and freshly ground black pepper
fresh flat leaf parsley, to garnish

1 Fry the bacon in a large pan over moderate heat until lightly browned but not crisp. Remove from the pan and drain on kitchen paper.

2 Add the butter to the pan and cook the onion, stirring occasionally, for 3–5 minutes until soft. Add the garlic and herbs and continue cooking for 1 minute, stirring well. Add the tomatoes, vermouth or wine and stock and bring to the boil.

3 Reduce the heat, cover and simmer the stew for 15 minutes. Add the potatoes, cover again and simmer for a further 10–12 minutes or until the potatoes are almost tender.

4 Add the chunks of fish and the bacon strips. Simmer gently, uncovered, for 5 minutes or until the fish is just cooked and the potatoes are tender. Adjust the seasoning, garnish with flat leaf parsley and serve.

CHUNKY CHICKEN SOUP

Large cubes of pan-fried boneless chicken form the basis of this thick soup. When combined with long grain rice, the dish is particularly warm and satisfying. It is served with garlic-flavoured fried croûtons.

SERVES 4

INGREDIENTS
4 skinless, boneless chicken thighs
15g/½oz/1 tbsp butter
2 small leeks, finely sliced
25g/1oz/2 tbsp long grain rice
900ml/1½ pints/3¾ cups chicken stock
15ml/1 tbsp chopped mixed fresh parsley and mint
salt and freshly ground black pepper

FOR THE GARLIC CROÛTONS
30ml/2 tbsp olive oil
1 garlic clove, crushed
4 slices bread, cut into cubes

1 Cut the chicken into 1cm/½in cubes. Melt the butter in a pan, add the leeks and cook until tender. Add the rice and chicken and cook for 2 minutes.

2 Add the stock, then cover the pan and simmer the mixture gently for 15–20 minutes until tender.

3 To make the garlic croûtons, heat the oil in a large frying pan. Add the crushed garlic clove and bread cubes and cook until the bread is golden brown, stirring all the time to prevent burning. Drain on kitchen paper and sprinkle with a pinch of salt.

4 Add the parsley and mint to the soup and adjust the seasoning to taste. Serve with the garlic croûtons.

THAI CHICKEN SOUP

This soup makes full use of the characteristic Thai flavours of garlic, coconut, lemon, peanut butter, fresh coriander (cilantro) and chilli.

SERVES 4

INGREDIENTS
15ml/1 tbsp vegetable oil
1 garlic clove, finely chopped
2 skinless, boneless chicken breasts (175g/6oz each) chopped
2.5ml/½ tsp ground turmeric
1.5ml/¼ tsp hot chilli powder
105ml/7 tbsp coconut milk
750ml/1¼ pints/3 cups hot chicken stock
30ml/2 tbsp lemon or lime juice
30ml/2 tbsp crunchy peanut butter
50g/2oz/1 cup thread egg noodles, broken into small pieces
15ml/1 tbsp chopped spring onions (scallions)
15ml/1 tbsp chopped fresh coriander (cilantro)
salt and freshly ground black pepper
desiccated (dry unsweetened shredded) coconut and finely chopped
  fresh red chilli, to garnish

VARIATIONS
Use 2 small skinless, boneless turkey or duck breasts in place of chicken breasts. Use chopped fresh flat leaf parsley in place of coriander (cilantro). Garnish the soup with finely chopped peanuts in place of desiccated (dry unsweetened shredded) coconut.

1 Heat the oil in a large pan and fry the garlic for 1 minute until lightly golden. Add the chicken and spices. Stir-fry for 3–4 minutes.

2 Pour the coconut milk into the hot chicken stock and stir until blended. Pour on to the chicken breasts and add the lemon or lime juice, peanut butter and thread egg noodles.

3 Cover the pan and simmer for 15 minutes. Add the spring onions and fresh coriander, season well with salt and freshly ground black pepper and cook gently for a further 5 minutes.

4 Meanwhile, heat the desiccated coconut and chilli in a small frying pan for 2–3 minutes, stirring frequently, until the coconut is lightly browned.

5 Pour the soup into individual bowls and sprinkle each one with the dry-fried coconut and chilli before serving.

Corn Chowder with Conchigliette

Corn kernels combine with smoked turkey and pasta to make this satisfying and filling one-pot meal, perfect for a hungry family or for guests.

Serves 6–8

Ingredients
1 small green (bell) pepper
450g/1lb potatoes, diced
350g/12oz/2 cups canned or frozen corn kernels
1 onion, chopped
1 celery stick, chopped
1 bouquet garni
600ml/1 pint/2½ cups chicken stock
300ml/½ pint/1¼ cups skimmed milk
50g/2oz conchigliette
oil, for frying
150g/5oz smoked turkey rashers (strips), diced
salt and freshly ground black pepper
bread sticks, to serve

1 Seed the green pepper and cut into dice. Cover with boiling water and leave to stand for 2 minutes. Drain and rinse.

2 Put the potatoes into a pan with the corn, onion, celery, diced pepper, bouquet garni and stock. Bring to the boil, cover and simmer for 20 minutes until tender.

3 Add the milk and salt and pepper. Process half of the soup in a food processor or blender and return to the pan with the pasta. Simmer for 10 minutes or until the pasta is *al dente*.

4 Heat the oil in a non-stick frying pan and fry the turkey rashers quickly for 2–3 minutes. Stir into the soup. Serve the soup with bread sticks.

Chiang Mai Noodle Soup

A signature dish of the city of Chiang Mai, this delicious noodle soup has Burmese origins and is the Thai equivalent of the Malaysian laksa.

SERVES 4–6

INGREDIENTS

600ml/1 pint/2½ cups coconut milk
30ml/2 tbsp red curry paste
5ml/1 tsp ground turmeric
450g/1lb chicken thighs, boned and cut into bite-size chunks
600ml/1 pint/2½ cups chicken stock
60ml/4 tbsp fish sauce
15ml/1 tbsp dark soy sauce
juice of ½–1 lime
450g/1lb fresh egg noodles, blanched briefly in boiling water
salt and freshly ground black pepper

FOR THE GARNISH

3 spring onions (scallions), chopped
4 fresh red chillies, chopped
4 shallots, chopped
60ml/4 tbsp sliced pickled mustard leaves, rinsed
30ml/2 tbsp fried sliced garlic
fresh coriander (cilantro) leaves
4 fried noodle nests (optional)

1 Pour about one-third of the coconut milk into a large pan and bring to the boil, stirring often with a wooden spoon until it separates. Add the curry paste and ground turmeric, stir to mix together and cook until fragrant. Add the chicken and stir-fry for about 2 minutes, ensuring that all the chunks are coated with the paste.

2 Add the remaining coconut milk, chicken stock, fish sauce and soy sauce. Season to taste and simmer gently for 7–10 minutes. Remove from the heat and stir in the lime juice.

3 Reheat the noodles in boiling water, drain and divide between individual bowls. Ladle in the chicken and soup. Top with a few of the garnishes.

NOODLES IN SOUP

In China, noodles in soup (tang mein) *are far more popular than fried noodles* (chow mein). *This is a basic recipe for noodles in soup that you can adapt by using a range of different ingredients for the "dressing".*

SERVES 4

INGREDIENTS
225g/8oz chicken breast fillet, pork fillet or ready-cooked meat
3–4 shiitake mushrooms, soaked
115g/4oz canned sliced bamboo shoots, drained
115g/4oz spinach leaves, lettuce hearts, or Chinese leaves
2 spring onions (scallions)
350g/12oz dried egg noodles
600ml/1 pint/2½ cups chicken stock
30ml/2 tbsp vegetable oil
5ml/1 tsp salt
2.5ml/½ tsp soft light brown sugar
15ml/1 tbsp light soy sauce
10ml/2 tsp Chinese rice wine or dry sherry
a few drops of sesame oil
red chilli sauce, to serve

VARIATIONS
Use dried oyster mushrooms in place of shiitake mushrooms. Use 1 small leek in place of spring onions (scallions). Use vegetable stock instead of chicken stock. Use toasted sesame oil for a more pronounced flavour.

1 Thinly shred the meat. Squeeze dry the shiitake mushrooms and discard any hard stalks. Then thinly shred the mushrooms, bamboo shoots, greens and spring onions.

2 Cook the noodles in boiling water according to the instructions on the packet, then drain and rinse under cold water. Place in a serving bowl.

3 Bring the stock to the boil and pour over the noodles. Set aside and keep the liquid warm.

4 Heat the oil in a preheated wok, add about half of the spring onions and the meat, and stir-fry for about 1 minute.

5 Add the mushrooms, bamboo shoots and greens and stir-fry for 1 minute. Add the salt, sugar, soy sauce and rice wine or sherry and blend well.

6 Pour the "dressing" over the noodles, garnish with the remaining spring onions and sprinkle over a few drops of sesame oil. Divide into individual soup bowls and serve with hot red chilli sauce.

CHICKEN SOUP WITH VERMICELLI

In Morocco, the cook – who is almost always the most senior female of the household – would use a whole chicken for this nourishing soup, to serve to her large extended family. This is a slightly simplified version, using chicken portions.

SERVES 4–6

INGREDIENTS

30ml/2 tbsp sunflower oil
15g/½oz/1 tbsp butter
1 onion, chopped
2 chicken legs or breast pieces, halved or quartered
flour, for dusting
2 carrots, cut into 4cm/1½in pieces
1 parsnip, cut into 4cm/1½in pieces
1.5 litres/2½ pints/6½cups chicken stock
1 cinnamon stick
a good pinch of paprika
a pinch of saffron
2 egg yolks
juice of ½ lemon
30ml/2 tbsp chopped fresh coriander (cilantro)
30ml/2 tbsp chopped fresh parsley
150g/5oz vermicelli
salt and freshly ground black pepper

COOK'S TIPS
When buying onions, choose those that have dry skins with no discolouration. Avoid onions that are sprouting, feel soft or are showing signs of mould. Onions keep well if stored in a cool, dry, dark, airy place.

1 Heat the oil and butter in a pan or flameproof casserole, and fry the onion for 3–4 minutes until softened. Dust the chicken pieces in seasoned flour and fry gently until they are evenly browned.

2 Transfer the chicken to a plate and add the carrots and parsnip to the pan. Cook over a gentle heat for 3–4 minutes, stirring frequently, then return the chicken to the pan. Add the stock, cinnamon stick and paprika and season well with salt and pepper.

3 Bring the soup to the boil, cover and simmer for 1 hour until the vegetables are very tender.

4 Meanwhile, blend the saffron in 30ml/2 tbsp boiling water. Beat the egg yolks with the lemon juice in a separate bowl and add the coriander and parsley. When the saffron water has cooled, stir into the egg and lemon mixture.

5 When the vegetables are tender, transfer the chicken to a plate. Spoon away any excess fat from the soup, then increase the heat a little and stir in the noodles. Cook for 5–6 minutes until the noodles are tender. Meanwhile, remove the skin and bones from the chicken and chop the flesh into bite-size pieces.

6 When the vermicelli is cooked, stir in the chicken pieces and the egg, lemon and saffron mixture. Cook over a low heat for 1–2 minutes, stirring constantly. Adjust the seasoning and serve.

MULLIGATAWNY SOUP

Mulligatawny *(which literally means "pepper water")* was introduced into England
in the late 18th century by members of the colonial services returning home from
India. It is always richly endowed with meat and piquantly spiced.

SERVES 4

INGREDIENTS
50g/2oz/4 tbsp butter or 60ml/4 tbsp oil
2 large chicken joints (about 350g/12oz each)
1 onion, chopped
1 carrot, chopped
1 small turnip, chopped
about 15ml/1 tbsp curry powder, to taste
4 cloves
6 black peppercorns, lightly crushed
50g/2oz/¼ cup lentils
900ml/1½ pints/3¾ cups chicken stock
40g/1½oz/¼ cup sultanas (golden raisins)
salt and freshly ground black pepper

1 Melt the butter or heat the oil in a large pan, then brown the chicken over a brisk heat. Transfer the chicken to a plate and set aside.

2 Add the onion, carrot and turnip to the pan and cook, stirring occasionally, until lightly coloured. Stir in the curry powder, cloves and crushed peppercorns and cook for 1–2 minutes, then add the lentils.

3 Pour the stock into the pan, bring to the boil, then add the sultanas, the chicken and any juices from the plate. Cover and simmer gently for about 1¼ hours.

4 Remove the chicken from the pan and discard the skin and bones. Chop the flesh, return to the soup and reheat. Check the seasoning before serving the soup piping hot.

COCK-A-LEEKIE

This traditional Scottish soup recipe – known from as long ago as 1598 – originally included beef as well as chicken. In the olden days, it would have been made from an old cock bird, hence the name.

SERVES 4

INGREDIENTS
2 chicken portions, (about 275g/10oz each)
1.2 litres/2 pints/5 cups chicken stock
1 bouquet garni
4 leeks
8–12 prunes, soaked
salt and freshly ground black pepper

1 Put the chicken portions into a pan with the stock and bouquet garni. Bring to the boil and simmer gently for 40 minutes.

2 Cut the white part of the leeks into 2.5cm/1in slices and finely slice a little of the green part.

3 Add the white part of the leeks and the prunes to the pan and cook gently for 20 minutes, then add the green part of the leeks and cook for a further 10–15 minutes.

4 Remove the bouquet garni and discard. Take the chicken out of the pan, discard the skin and bones, and chop the flesh. Return the chopped flesh to the pan and season the soup.

5 Heat the soup through gently. Ladle into warm soup bowls and serve hot with bread.

BEAN & PASTA SOUP

This hearty main-meal soup sometimes goes by the simpler name of pasta e fagioli, *while some Italians refer to it as* minestrone di pasta e fagioli. *Traditional recipes use dried beans and a ham bone as the main ingredients.*

SERVES 4–6

INGREDIENTS
30ml/2 tbsp olive oil
115g/4oz/⅔ cup pancetta or rindless smoked streaky (fatty) bacon, diced
1 onion
1 carrot
1 celery stick
1.75 litres/3 pints/7½ cups beef stock
1 cinnamon stick or a good pinch of ground cinnamon
90g/3½oz/scant 1 cup small pasta shapes, such as conchiglie or coralini
400g/14oz can borlotti beans, rinsed and drained
1 thick slice cooked ham (about 225g/8oz) diced
salt and freshly ground black pepper
Parmesan cheese shavings, to serve

1 Heat the oil in a large pan, add the pancetta or bacon and cook, stirring, until lightly coloured. Finely chop the vegetables, add to the pan and cook for about 10 minutes, stirring frequently, until lightly coloured. Pour in the stock, add the cinnamon with salt and pepper to taste and bring to the boil. Cover and simmer gently for 15–20 minutes.

2 Add the pasta shapes. Bring back to the boil, stirring all the time. Lower the heat and simmer, stirring frequently, for 5 minutes. Add the borlotti beans and diced ham and simmer for 2–3 minutes, or according to the instructions on the packet, until the pasta is *al dente*.

3 Remove the cinnamon stick, if used, taste the soup and adjust the seasoning. Serve hot in warmed bowls, sprinkled with Parmesan shavings.

BACON & LENTIL SOUP

Lentils are ideal for thickening soups – they cook in 20 minutes and eventually disintegrate into a thick paste. They have a particular affinity with bacon. For an even heartier meal, serve this substantial soup with chunks of warm, crusty bread.

SERVES 4

INGREDIENTS
450g/1lb thick-sliced bacon, cubed
1 onion, roughly chopped
1 small turnip, roughly chopped
1 celery stick, chopped
1 potato, roughly chopped
1 carrot, sliced
75g/3oz/scant ½ cup lentils
1 bouquet garni
freshly ground black pepper
fresh flat leaf parsley, to garnish

1 Heat a large pan and add the bacon. Cook for a few minutes, allowing the fat to run out.

2 Add the chopped onion, turnip, celery and potato and the sliced carrot. Cook for 4 minutes, stirring from time to time.

3 Add the lentils, bouquet garni, seasoning and enough water to cover. Bring to the boil and simmer for 1 hour or until the lentils are tender. Pour the soup into warmed bowls and serve garnished with flat leaf parsley.

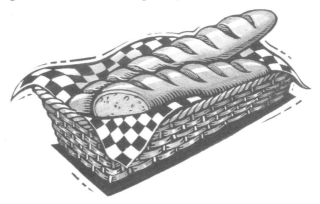

Seafood & Sausage Gumbo

Originating in southern Louisiana in the United States, gumbo is a thick, robust soup, often thickened with okra, as here. Although it is a soup, gumbo is often served over rice as a main course. The addition of sausages makes it very satisfying.

Serves 10–12

Ingredients

1.5 kg/3 lbs raw prawns (shrimp) in shell

1.5 litres/2½ pints/6¼ cups water

4 medium onions, 2 of them quartered

4 bay leaves

175ml/6fl oz/¾ cup vegetable oil

115g/4oz/1 cup flour

60ml/5 tbsp margarine or butter

2 green (bell) peppers, seeded and finely chopped

4 celery sticks, finely chopped

675g/1½lb Polish or andouille sausage, cut into 1cm/½in slices

450g/1lb fresh okra, cut into 1cm/½in slices

3 garlic cloves, crushed

2.5ml/½ tsp fresh or dried thyme leaves

10ml/2 tsp salt

2.5ml/½ tsp freshly ground black pepper

2.5ml/½ tsp white pepper

5ml/1 tsp cayenne pepper

30ml/2 tbsp hot pepper sauce (optional)

175g/6oz/2 cups chopped, peeled, fresh or canned plum tomatoes

450g/1lb fresh crab meat

boiled rice, to serve

1 Peel and devein the prawns; reserve the heads and shells. Cover and chill the prawns while you make the sauce.

2 Place the prawn heads and shells in a pan with the water, quartered onion and 1 bay leaf. Bring to the boil, then partly cover and simmer for 20 minutes. Strain and set aside.

3 To make a Cajun roux, heat the oil in a heavy-based frying pan. When the oil is hot, add the flour, a little at a time, and blend to a smooth paste.

4 Cook over a medium-low heat, stirring constantly for 25–40 minutes until the roux reaches the colour of peanut butter. Remove the pan from the heat and continue stirring until the roux has cooled and stopped cooking.

5 Melt the margarine or butter in a large, heavy-based pan or flameproof casserole. Finely chop the remaining onions and add to the pan with the peppers and celery. Cook over a medium-low heat for 6–8 minutes, until the onions are softened, stirring occasionally.

6 Add the sausage and mix well. Cook for 5 minutes more. Add the okra and garlic, stir, and cook until the okra stops producing white "threads".

7 Add the remaining bay leaves, the thyme, salt, black and white peppers, cayenne pepper, and hot pepper sauce to taste, if using. Mix well. Stir in 1.35 litres/2¼ pints/6 cups of the prawn stock and the tomatoes. Bring to the boil, partly cover the pan, lower the heat and simmer for about 20 minutes.

8 Whisk in the Cajun roux. Raise the heat and bring to the boil, whisking well. Lower the heat again and simmer, uncovered, for a further 40–45 minutes, stirring occasionally.

9 Gently stir in the prawns and crab meat. Cook for 3–4 minutes until the prawns turn pink.

10 To serve, put a mound of hot boiled rice in each serving bowl and ladle on the gumbo, making sure each person gets some prawns, some crab meat and some sausage.

Green Herb Gumbo

Traditionally served at the end of Lent, this is a joyful, sweetly spiced and revitalizing dish, even if you haven't been fasting. The variety of green ingredients is important, so buy substitutes if you cannot find all of them.

SERVES 6–8

INGREDIENTS
350g/12oz piece raw smoked gammon
30ml/2 tbsp lard or cooking oil
1 large Spanish onion, roughly chopped
2–3 garlic cloves, crushed
5ml/1 tsp dried oregano
5ml/1 tsp dried thyme
2 bay leaves
2 cloves
2 celery sticks, finely sliced
1 green (bell) pepper, seeded and chopped
½ medium green cabbage, stalked and finely shredded
2 litres/3½ pints/9 cups light stock or water
200g/7oz spring greens (collards) or kale, finely shredded
200g/7oz Chinese mustard cabbage, finely shredded
200g/7oz spinach, shredded
1 bunch of watercress, shredded
6 spring onions (scallions), finely shredded
25g/1oz/½ cup chopped fresh parsley
2.5ml/½ tsp ground allspice
¼ nutmeg, grated
a pinch of cayenne pepper
salt and freshly ground black pepper

COOK'S TIP
When buying greens such as spring greens (collards) and spinach, always choose leaves that look fresh and bright in colour. Avoid any with thick woody stems and limp or discoloured leaves that have brown or damaged patches.

1 Dice the ham quite small, keeping any fat and rind in one separate piece. Put the fat piece with the lard or oil into a deep pan and heat until it sizzles. Stir in the diced ham, onion, garlic, oregano and thyme and cook over a medium heat for 5 minutes, stirring occasionally.

2 Add the bay leaves, cloves, celery and green pepper and stir over a medium heat for another 2–3 minutes, then add the cabbage and stock or water. Bring to the boil and simmer gently for 5 minutes.

3 Add the spring greens or kale and mustard cabbage, boil for a further 2 minutes, then add the spinach, watercress and spring onions. Return to the boil, then lower the heat and simmer for 1 minute. Add the parsley, allspice and nutmeg, salt, black pepper and cayenne to taste.

4 Remove the piece of ham fat and, if you can find them, the cloves. Ladle into individual soup bowls and serve immediately, with warm French bread or garlic bread.

VARIATION
Use dried marjoram in place of oregano. Use Savoy cabbage in place of green cabbage. Use rocket (arugula) leaves in place of watercress.

GALICIAN BROTH

This delicious main-meal soup is very similar to the warming, chunky meat and potato broths of cooler climates. For extra colour, a few onion skins can be added when cooking the gammon, but remember to remove them before serving.

SERVES 4

INGREDIENTS
450g/1lb piece gammon
2 bay leaves
2 onions, sliced
1.5 litres/2½ pints/6¼ cups cold water
10ml/2 tsp paprika
675g/1½lb potatoes, cut into large chunks
225g/8oz spring greens (collards)
400g/14oz can haricot (navy) or cannellini beans, drained
salt and freshly ground black pepper

1 Soak the gammon overnight in cold water. Drain and put in a large pan with the bay leaves and onions. Pour the water on top.

2 Bring to the boil, then reduce the heat and simmer gently for about 1½ hours until the meat is tender. Keep an eye on the pan to make sure that it doesn't boil over.

3 Drain the meat, reserving the cooking liquid, and leave to cool slightly. Discard the skin and any excess fat from the meat and cut into small chunks. Return to the pan with the paprika and potatoes. Cover and simmer gently for 20 minutes.

4 Cut away the cores from the greens. Roll up the leaves and cut into thin shreds. Add to the pan with the beans and simmer for about 10 minutes. Season with salt and freshly ground black pepper to taste and serve piping hot.

COOK'S TIP
Bacon knuckles can be used instead of the gammon.
The bones will give the juices a delicious flavour.

SCOTCH BROTH

Sustaining and warming, this soup makes a delicious one-pot meal. It is a traditional dish from Scotland, and is always a thick soup made with either beef or mutton with vegetables and pearl barley.

SERVES 6

INGREDIENTS
900g/2lb lean neck of lamb, cut into large, even-size chunks
1.75 litres/3 pints/7½ cups water
1 large onion, chopped
50g/2oz/¼ cup pearl barley
1 bouquet garni
1 large carrot, chopped
1 turnip, chopped
3 leeks, chopped
½ small white cabbage, shredded
salt and freshly ground black pepper
chopped fresh parsley, to garnish (optional)

1 Put the lamb and water into a large pan and bring to the boil. Skim off the scum, then stir in the onion, barley and bouquet garni.

2 Bring the soup back to the boil, then partly cover the pan and simmer gently for 1 hour. Add the remaining vegetables and the seasoning, bring back to the boil, partly cover again and simmer for about 35 minutes until all of the vegetables are tender.

3 Remove the surplus fat from the top of the liquid. Serve the soup hot, sprinkled with chopped parsley, if you like.

Lamb, Bean & Pumpkin Soup

This is a hearty one-pot soup to warm the cockles of the heart in even the chilliest weather. The inclusion of pumpkin gives the soup a vivid orange colour, and banana makes the texture thick and sweet.

Serves 4

INGREDIENTS

115g/4oz/⅔ cup split black-eyed beans, soaked for 1–2 hours or overnight
675g/1½lb neck of lamb, cut into medium-size chunks
5ml/1 tsp chopped fresh thyme or 2.5ml/½ tsp dried thyme
2 bay leaves
1.2 litres/2 pints/5 cups stock or water
1 onion, sliced
225g/8oz pumpkin, diced
2 black cardamom pods
7.5ml/1½ tsp ground turmeric
15ml/1 tbsp chopped fresh coriander (cilantro)
2.5ml/½ tsp caraway seeds
1 fresh green chilli, seeded and chopped
2 green bananas
1 carrot
salt and freshly ground black pepper

VARIATIONS
Use 2 leeks in place of the onion. Use butternut squash in place of pumpkin. Use plantain in place of green bananas. Use 1 parsnip or 1 turnip in place of carrot.

1 Drain the black-eyed beans thoroughly, then place them in a pan and cover with fresh cold water.

2 Bring the beans to the boil, boil rapidly for 10 minutes and then reduce the heat and simmer, covered, for about 40–50 minutes until tender, adding more water if necessary. Remove the pan from the heat and set aside to cool.

3 Meanwhile, put the lamb in a large pan, add the thyme, bay leaves and stock or water and bring to the boil. Cover and simmer over a moderate heat for 1 hour until tender.

4 Add the onion, pumpkin, cardamoms, turmeric, coriander, caraway, chilli and seasoning and stir. Bring back to a simmer and cook, uncovered, for 15 minutes, stirring occasionally, until the pumpkin is tender.

5 When the beans are cool, spoon into a food processor or blender with their liquid and blend to a smooth paste.

6 Peel the bananas and cut into medium slices. Cut the carrot into thin slices. Stir into the soup with the beans and cook for 10–12 minutes, until the carrot is tender. Adjust the seasoning and serve.

Spinach & Lemon Soup with Meatballs

This spinach-based soup, known as aarshe saak, *is almost standard fare in many parts of the Middle East. In Greece, it is normally made without the meatballs and is simply called* avgolemono. *It can be served hot or cold.*

Serves 6

Ingredients
2 large onions
45ml/3 tbsp oil
15ml/1 tbsp ground turmeric
115g/4oz/½ cup yellow split peas
1.2 litres/2 pints/5 cups water
225g/8oz minced lamb
450g/1lb spinach, chopped
50g/2oz/½ cup rice flour
juice of 2 lemons
1–2 garlic cloves, finely chopped
30ml/2 tbsp chopped fresh mint
4 eggs, beaten
salt and freshly ground black pepper
sprigs of fresh mint, to garnish

Variations
Use minced beef or pork in place of lamb. Use spring greens (collards) in place of spinach. Use chopped fresh coriander (cilantro) in place of mint.

1 Chop one of the onions and fry in 30ml/2 tbsp of the oil in a large pan until golden. Add the turmeric, peas and water and bring to the boil. Simmer for 20 minutes.

2 Grate the other onion into a bowl, add the lamb and seasoning and mix well. Using your hands, form the mixture into small balls, about the size of walnuts. Carefully add to the pan and simmer for 10 minutes, then add the spinach, cover and simmer for 20 minutes.

3 Mix the flour with about 250ml/8fl oz/1 cup cold water to make a smooth paste, then slowly add to the pan, stirring all the time. Add the lemon juice, season and cook over a gentle heat for 20 minutes.

4 Meanwhile, heat the remaining oil in a small pan and fry the garlic briefly until golden. Stir in the mint and remove the pan from the heat.

5 Remove the soup from the heat and stir in the beaten eggs. Sprinkle the prepared garlic and mint mixture over the soup, garnish with mint sprigs and serve immediately.

Moroccan Harira

In Morocco, this substantial meat and vegetable soup is traditionally eaten during the month of Ramadan, when the Muslim population fasts between sunrise and sunset.

Serves 4

Ingredients
25g/1oz/2 tbsp butter
225g/8oz lamb, cut into 1cm/¹⁄₂in pieces
1 onion, chopped
450g/1lb well-flavoured tomatoes
60ml/4 tbsp chopped fresh coriander (cilantro)
30ml/2 tbsp chopped fresh parsley
2.5ml/¹⁄₂ tsp ground turmeric
2.5ml/¹⁄₂ tsp ground cinnamon
50g/2oz/¹⁄₄ cup red lentils
75g/3oz/¹⁄₂ cup chickpeas, soaked overnight
600ml/1 pint/2¹⁄₂ cups water
4 baby onions or small shallots, peeled
25g/1oz/¹⁄₄ cup soup noodles
salt and freshly ground black pepper

For the garnish
chopped fresh coriander (cilantro)
lemon slices
ground cinnamon

> ### Variations
> *Use 30ml/2 tbsp olive or sunflower oil in place of butter. Use lean pork or beef in place of lamb. Use green or Puy lentils in place of red lentils. Use small soup pasta in place of soup noodles.*

1 Heat the butter in a large pan or flameproof casserole and fry the lamb and onion for 5 minutes, stirring frequently.

2 Peel the tomatoes, if you wish, by plunging them into boiling water to loosen the skins. Wait for them to cool a little before peeling off the skins. Then cut them into quarters and add to the lamb with the herbs and spices.

3 Rinse the lentils under cold running water and drain the chickpeas. Add both to the pan with the water. Season with salt and pepper. Bring to the boil, cover and simmer gently for 1½ hours.

4 Add the baby onions or small shallots and cook for a further 30 minutes. Add the noodles 5 minutes before the end of the cooking time. Serve the soup when the noodles are tender, garnished with the coriander, lemon slices and cinnamon.

BEEF NOODLE SOUP

Offer your fortunate friends or family a steaming bowl of this beefy soup, packed with many delicious flavours of the Orient.

SERVES 4

INGREDIENTS
10g/¼oz dried porcini mushrooms
150ml/¼ pint/⅔ cup boiling water
6 spring onions (scallions)
115g/4oz carrots
350g/12oz rump (round) steak
about 30ml/2 tbsp oil
1 garlic clove, crushed
2.5cm/1in piece fresh root ginger, peeled and finely chopped
1.2 litres/2 pints/5 cups beef stock
45ml/3 tbsp light soy sauce
60ml/4 tbsp dry sherry
75g/3oz thin egg noodles
75g/3oz spinach, shredded
salt and freshly ground black pepper

COOK'S TIP
Dried porcini mushrooms are now widely available in supermarkets. They may seem expensive, but are full of flavour, so a small quantity goes a long way and really gives a lift to a soup like this one.

1 Break the mushrooms into small pieces, place in a bowl and pour over the boiling water. Leave to soak for 15 minutes.

2 Shred the spring onions and carrots into 5cm/2in long, fine strips. Trim any fat off the meat and slice into thin strips.

3 Heat the oil in a large pan and cook the beef in batches until browned, adding a little more oil if necessary. Remove the beef with a slotted spoon and drain on kitchen paper.

4 Add the garlic, ginger, spring onions and carrots to the pan and stir-fry for 3 minutes.

5 Add the beef stock, the mushrooms and their soaking liquid, soy sauce and sherry. Season generously with salt and freshly ground black pepper. Bring to the boil and simmer, covered, for 10 minutes.

6 Break up the noodles slightly and add to the pan with the shredded spinach. Simmer gently for 5 minutes until the beef is tender. Adjust the seasoning to taste before serving.

Vegetable Broth with Minced Beef

This is a veritable cornucopia of flavours, combining to produce a rich and satisfying broth. The addition of ground nuts makes the soup very thick and smooth.

Serves 6

Ingredients

30ml/2 tbsp groundnut (peanut) oil
115g/4oz finely minced beef
1 large onion, grated or finely chopped
1 garlic clove, crushed
1–2 fresh chillies, seeded and chopped
1cm/½in cube shrimp paste, prepared
3 macadamia nuts or 6 almonds, finely ground
1 carrot, finely grated
5ml/1 tsp brown sugar
1 litre/1¾ pints/4 cups chicken stock
50g/2oz dried shrimp, soaked in warm water for 10 minutes
225g/8oz spinach, finely shredded
8 baby corn, sliced, or 200g/7oz canned corn kernels
1 large tomato, chopped
juice of ½ lemon
salt

> **Cook's Tip**
> To make this broth very hot and spicy, add the seeds from the chillies.

1 Heat the oil in a pan. Add the beef, onion and garlic and cook, stirring, until the meat changes colour.

2 Add the chillies, shrimp paste, macadamia nuts or almonds, carrot, sugar and salt to taste.

3 Add the stock and bring gently to the boil. Reduce the heat to a simmer and then add the soaked shrimp, with its soaking liquid. Simmer for about 10 minutes.

4 A few minutes before serving, add the spinach, corn, tomato and lemon juice. Simmer for 1–2 minutes, to heat through. Do not overcook at this stage because this will spoil both the appearance and the taste of the end result. Serve the soup immediately.

SPECIAL OCCASION SOUPS

Enjoy some of the more unusual and exotic flavours and combinations of this selection of soups, all of which are ideal for serving for a special occasion, such as a special family gathering, a celebratory meal or a dinner party with friends. Choose from tempting soups such as Melon & Basil Soup, Hungarian Sour Cherry Soup or Saffron Mussel Soup, or try delicious recipes such as Wild Mushroom Soup, Hot-&-Sour Soup, Lobster Bisque or Indian Beef & Summer Berry Soup.

Melon & Basil Soup

This is a deliciously refreshing, chilled fruit soup, just right for a hot summer's day. Melons are ready for eating when their skin is fairly easy to depress.

SERVES 4–6

INGREDIENTS
2 Charentais or rock melons
75g/3oz/scant ½ cup caster (superfine) sugar
175ml/6fl oz/¾ cup water
finely grated rind and juice of 1 lime
45ml/3 tbsp shredded fresh basil, plus whole leaves, to garnish

1 Cut the melons in half across the middle. Scrape out the seeds and discard. Using a melon baller, scoop out 20–24 balls and set aside for the garnish. Scoop out the remaining flesh and place in a food processor or blender.

2 Place the sugar, water and lime rind in a small pan over a low heat. Stir until dissolved, bring to the boil and simmer for 2–3 minutes. Remove from the heat and leave to cool slightly. Pour half the mixture into the food processor or blender with the melon flesh. Blend until smooth, adding the remaining syrup and lime juice to taste.

3 Pour the mixture into a bowl, stir in the shredded basil and chill. Serve garnished with whole basil leaves and the reserved melon balls.

COOK'S TIP
Add the syrup in two stages, as the amount of sugar needed will depend on the sweetness of the melon.

PEAR & WATERCRESS SOUP

This unusual soup combines sweet pears with slightly sharp watercress. A more traditional partner, Stilton (blue) cheese, appears in the form of crisp croûtons.

SERVES 6

INGREDIENTS
1 bunch of watercress
4 medium pears, sliced
900ml/1½ pints/3¾ cups chicken stock, preferably home-made
120ml/4fl oz/½ cup double (heavy) cream
juice of 1 lime
salt and freshly ground black pepper

FOR THE STILTON CROÛTONS
25g/1oz/2 tbsp butter
15ml/1 tbsp olive oil
200g/7oz/3 cups cubed stale bread
115g/4oz/1 cup Stilton (blue) cheese, chopped

1 Place two-thirds of the watercress leaves and all the stalks in a pan with the pears, stock and a little seasoning. Simmer for about 15–20 minutes.

2 Reserving some of the watercress leaves for the garnish, add the rest to the soup and immediately process in a food processor or blender until smooth.

3 Put the mixture into a bowl and stir in the cream and the lime juice to mix the flavours thoroughly. Season again to taste. Pour all the soup back into the pan and reheat, stirring gently, until warmed through.

4 To make the Stilton croûtons, melt the butter and oil and fry the cubes of bread until golden brown. Drain on kitchen paper. Put the cheese on top and heat under a hot grill until bubbling.

5 Pour the soup into warmed bowls. Divide the croûtons and reserved watercress among the bowls and serve.

APPLE SOUP

You may not normally think of apples as being an ingredient for soup, but they are perfect for puréeing and cooking. This delicious soup makes the most of freshly-picked apples. You need to add sugar to counterbalance the tartness of the green apples.

SERVES 6

INGREDIENTS
45ml/3 tbsp oil
1 kohlrabi, diced
3 carrots, diced
2 celery sticks, diced
1 green (bell) pepper, seeded and diced
2 tomatoes, diced
2 litres/3½ pints/9 cups chicken stock
6 large green apples
45ml/3 tbsp plain (all-purpose) flour
150ml/¼ pint/⅔ cup double (heavy) cream
15ml/1 tbsp granulated sugar
30–45ml/2–3 tbsp lemon juice
salt and freshly ground black pepper
lemon wedges and crusty bread, to serve

1 Heat the oil in a large pan. Add the kohlrabi, carrots, celery, green pepper and tomatoes and fry for 5–6 minutes until just softened.

2 Pour in the chicken stock, bring to the boil, then reduce the heat and simmer for about 45 minutes.

3 Meanwhile, peel and core the apples, then chop into small cubes. Add to the pan and simmer for a further 15 minutes.

4 In a bowl, mix together the flour and cream, then pour slowly into the soup, stirring well, and bring to the boil. Add the sugar and lemon juice before seasoning. Serve immediately with lemon wedges and crusty bread.

HUNGARIAN SOUR CHERRY SOUP

Particularly popular in summer, this fruit soup is typical of Hungarian cooking. The recipe makes good use of plump, sour cherries. Fruit soups are thickened with flour, and a touch of salt is added to help bring out the flavour of the cold soup.

SERVES 4

INGREDIENTS
15ml/1 tbsp plain (all-purpose) flour
120ml/4fl oz/½ cup sour cream
a generous pinch of salt
5ml/1 tsp caster (superfine) sugar
225g/8oz/1½ cups fresh sour or morello cherries, stoned
900ml/1½ pints/3¾ cups water
50g/2oz/¼ cup granulated sugar

1 In a bowl, blend the flour with the sour cream until smooth, then add the salt and caster sugar.

2 Put the cherries in a pan with the water and granulated sugar. Gently poach for about 10 minutes.

3 Remove from the heat and set aside 30ml/2 tbsp of the cooking liquid as a garnish. Stir another 30ml/2 tbsp of the cherry liquid into the flour and sour cream mixture, then pour this on to the cherries.

4 Return to the heat. Bring to the boil, then simmer gently for 5–6 minutes. Remove from the heat, cover with clear film (plastic wrap) and leave to cool. Add extra salt if necessary. Serve with the reserved cooking liquid swirled in.

Beetroot Soup with Ravioli

Beetroot and pasta make an unusual combination, but this soup is no less good for that. It has a radiant red colour and is delicious with fresh crusty bread.

Serves 4–6

Ingredients
1 quantity of basic pasta dough
1 egg white, beaten, for brushing
flour, for dusting
1 small onion or shallot, finely chopped
2 garlic cloves, crushed
5ml/1 tsp fennel seeds
600ml/1 pint/2½ cups chicken or vegetable stock
225g/8oz cooked beetroot (beet)
30ml/2 tbsp fresh orange juice
fresh fennel or dill leaves, to garnish
crusty bread, to serve

For the filling
115g/4oz mushrooms, finely chopped
1 shallot or small onion, finely chopped
1–2 garlic cloves, crushed
5ml/1 tsp chopped fresh thyme
15ml/1 tbsp chopped fresh parsley
90ml/6 tbsp fresh white breadcrumbs
salt and freshly ground black pepper
a large pinch of freshly grated nutmeg

Cook's Tip
When using a garlic press, leave the peel on the garlic clove. The soft garlic flesh will still be pushed through the mesh and the peel will be left behind. The garlic press will be much easier to clean after using.

1 Put all the ingredients for the filling in a food processor or blender and process them to a paste.

2 Roll the pasta into thin sheets. Lay one piece over a ravioli tray and put 5ml/ 1 tsp of the filling into each depression. Brush around the edges of each ravioli with egg white. Cover with another sheet of pasta and press the edges together well to seal. Transfer to a floured dishtowel and rest for 1 hour before cooking.

3 Cook the ravioli in boiling, salted water for 2 minutes. (Cook in batches to prevent them from sticking together.) Remove the ravioli and drop them into a bowl of cold water for 5 seconds before placing on a tray. (You can make these pasta shapes a day in advance and store them in the refrigerator.)

4 Put the onion, garlic and fennel seeds into a pan with 150ml/¼ pint/⅔ cup of the stock. Bring to the boil, cover and simmer for 5 minutes until tender. Peel and finely dice the beetroot, reserving 60ml/4 tbsp for the garnish. Add the rest of it to the soup with the remaining stock, and bring to the boil.

5 Add the orange juice and cooked ravioli and simmer for 2 minutes. Serve in shallow soup bowls, garnished with the reserved diced beetroot and fresh fennel or dill leaves. Serve hot, with crusty bread.

VARIATIONS
Use cumin or caraway seeds in place of fennel seeds, for a slightly different flavour profile. Use mixed fresh wild mushrooms in place of standard mushrooms. Use brown or wholemeal breadcrumbs in place of white breadcrumbs.

Red Onion & Beetroot Soup

This beautiful ruby-red soup, with its contrasting swirl of white yogurt highlighted with green chives, will look stunning at any dinner party.

SERVES 4–6

INGREDIENTS
15ml/1 tbsp olive oil
350g/12oz red onions, sliced
2 garlic cloves, crushed
275g/10oz cooked beetroot (beet), cut into sticks
1.2 litres/2 pints/5 cups vegetable stock or water
50g/2oz/1 cup cooked soup pasta
30ml/2 tbsp raspberry vinegar
salt and freshly ground black pepper
natural (plain) yogurt or fromage blanc and chopped fresh chives, to garnish

1 Heat the olive oil in a large pan or flameproof casserole and add the onions and garlic.

2 Cook gently for about 20 minutes or until soft and tender, stirring the pan occasionally.

3 Add the beetroot, stock or water, cooked pasta and vinegar and heat through. Season and garnish with swirls of yogurt or fromage blanc and chives.

COOK'S TIP
Try substituting cooked barley for the pasta to give extra nuttiness to the flavour.

STAR-GAZER VEGETABLE SOUP

If you have the time, it is worth making your own stock for this recipe – either vegetable or, if preferred, chicken or fish.

SERVES 4

INGREDIENTS
1 yellow (bell) pepper
2 large courgettes (zucchini)
2 large carrots
1 kohlrabi
900ml/1½ pints/3¾ cups well-flavoured vegetable stock
50g/2oz rice vermicelli
salt and freshly ground black pepper

1 Cut the pepper into quarters, removing the seeds and core. Cut the courgettes and carrots lengthways into 5 mm/¼ in slices and slice the kohlrabi into 5 mm/¼ in rounds.

2 Using tiny pastry cutters, stamp out shapes from the vegetables or use a very sharp knife to cut the sliced vegetables into stars and other decorative shapes.

3 Place the vegetables and stock in a pan and simmer for 10 minutes, until the vegetables are tender. Season to taste with salt and pepper.

4 Meanwhile, place the vermicelli in a bowl, cover with boiling water and set aside for 4 minutes. Drain, then divide among four warmed soup bowls. Ladle over the soup and serve.

COOK'S TIP
Sauté the leftover vegetable pieces in a little oil and mix with cooked brown rice to make a tasty risotto.

WILD MUSHROOM SOUP

Dried porcini have an intense flavour, so only a small quantity is needed. The beef stock helps to strengthen the earthy flavour of the mushrooms.

SERVES 4

INGREDIENTS
25g/1oz/2 cups dried porcini mushrooms
250ml/8fl oz/1 cup warm water
30ml/2 tbsp olive oil
15g/½oz/1 tbsp butter
2 leeks, finely sliced
2 shallots, roughly chopped
1 garlic clove, roughly chopped
225g/8oz fresh wild mushrooms
1.2 litres/2 pints/5 cups beef stock
2.5ml/½ tsp dried thyme
150ml/¼ pint/⅔ cup double (heavy) cream
salt and freshly ground black pepper
sprigs of fresh thyme, to garnish

1 Put the dried porcini in a bowl, add the warm water and leave to soak for 20–30 minutes. Lift out of the liquid and squeeze to remove as much of the soaking liquid as possible. Strain all the liquid and reserve to use later. Finely chop the porcini.

2 Heat the oil and butter in a large pan until foaming. Add the leeks, shallots and garlic and cook gently for about 5 minutes, stirring frequently, until softened but not coloured. Chop or slice the fresh mushrooms and add to the pan. Stir over a medium heat for a few minutes until they begin to soften. Pour in the beef stock and bring to the boil. Add the porcini, soaking liquid, dried thyme and salt and pepper. Lower the heat, half-cover the pan and simmer gently for 30 minutes, stirring occasionally.

3 Pour about three-quarters of the soup into a food processor or blender and process until smooth. Return to the soup remaining in the pan, stir in the double (heavy) cream and heat through. Check the consistency, adding more stock or water if the soup is too thick. Adjust the seasoning. Serve hot, garnished with sprigs of fresh thyme.

BROCCOLI, ANCHOVY & PASTA SOUP

This tasty pasta soup originates from Apulia in the south of Italy, where anchovies and broccoli are often used together.

SERVES 4

INGREDIENTS
30ml/2 tbsp olive oil
1 small onion, finely chopped
1 garlic clove, finely chopped
¼–⅓ fresh red chilli, seeded and finely chopped
2 canned anchovy fillets, drained
200ml/7fl oz/scant 1 cup passata (bottled strained tomatoes)
45ml/3 tbsp dry white wine
1.2 litres/2 pints/5 cups vegetable stock
300g/11oz/2 cups broccoli florets
200g/7oz/1¾ cups orecchiette
salt and freshly ground black pepper
grated Pecorino cheese, to serve

1 Heat the oil in a large pan. Add the onion, garlic, chilli and anchovies and cook over a low heat, stirring all the time, for 5–6 minutes.

2 Add the passata and wine, with salt and pepper to taste. Bring to the boil, cover the pan, then cook over a low heat, stirring occasionally, for 12–15 minutes.

3 Pour in the stock. Bring to the boil, then add the broccoli and simmer for about 5 minutes. Add the pasta and bring back to the boil, stirring. Simmer for 7–8 minutes or according to the instructions on the packet, stirring frequently, until the pasta is *al dente.*

4 Taste and adjust the seasoning. Serve hot, in individual warmed bowls. Pass around the grated Pecorino cheese separately.

Hot-&-sour Soup

A classic Chinese soup, this is a warming and flavoursome start to a meal. Cloud ears (wood ears) are mushrooms that have been used in Chinese cooking since the 6th century. They are favoured because they soak in the flavours they are cooked with.

SERVES 4

INGREDIENTS
10g/¼oz dried cloud ears (wood ears)
8 fresh shiitake mushrooms
75g/3oz tofu
50g/2oz/½ cup sliced, drained, canned bamboo shoots
900ml/1½ pints/3¾ cups vegetable stock
15ml/1 tbsp caster (superfine) sugar
45ml/3 tbsp rice vinegar
15ml/1 tbsp light soy sauce
1.5ml/¼ tsp chilli oil
2.5ml/½ tsp salt
a large pinch of freshly ground white pepper
15ml/1 tbsp cornflour (cornstarch)
15ml/l tbsp cold water
1 egg white
5ml/1 tsp sesame oil
2 spring onions (scallions), cut into fine rings, to garnish

COOK'S TIP
To transform this tasty soup into a nutritious light meal, simply add extra mushrooms, tofu and bamboo shoots.

1 Soak the cloud ears (wood ears) in hot water for 30 minutes or until soft. Drain, trim off and discard the hard base from each one, and chop the cloud ears roughly.

2 Remove and discard the stalks from the shiitake mushrooms. Cut the caps into thin strips. Cut the tofu into 1cm/½in cubes and shred the bamboo shoots finely.

3 Place the stock, mushrooms, tofu, bamboo shoots and cloud ears in a large pan. Bring the stock to the boil, lower the heat and simmer for about 5 minutes.

4 Stir in the sugar, vinegar, soy sauce, chilli oil, salt and pepper. Mix the cornflour to a paste with the water. Add the mixture to the soup, stirring until it thickens slightly.

5 Lightly beat the egg white, then pour it slowly into the soup in a steady stream, stirring constantly. Cook, stirring, until the egg white changes colour.

6 Add the sesame oil just before serving. Ladle into heated bowls and garnish each portion with spring onion rings.

CONSOMMÉ WITH AGNOLOTTI

Prawns, crab and chicken jostle for the upper hand in this rich and satisfying consommé. The agnolotti – half-moon shaped ravioli – look elegant when stamped with a fluted pastry cutter, giving them delicate, notched edges.

SERVES 4–6

INGREDIENTS
75g/3oz cooked peeled prawns (shrimp)
75g/3oz canned crab meat, drained
5ml/1 tsp finely grated fresh root ginger
15ml/l tbsp fresh white breadcrumbs
5ml/l tsp light soy sauce
1 spring onion (scallion), finely chopped
1 garlic clove, crushed
1 egg white, beaten
400g/14oz can chicken or fish consommé
30ml/2 tbsp sherry or vermouth
salt and freshly ground black pepper

FOR THE PASTA
200g/7oz/1¾ cups plain (all-purpose) flour
pinch of salt
2 eggs
10ml/2 tsp cold water

FOR THE GARNISH
50g/2oz cooked peeled prawns (shrimp)
fresh coriander (cilantro) leaves

1 To make the pasta, sift the flour and salt on to a clean work surface and make a well in the centre with your hand.

2 Put the eggs and water into the well. Using a fork, beat the eggs gently together, then gradually draw in the flour from the sides, to make a thick paste.

3 When the mixture becomes too stiff to use a fork, use your hands to mix to a firm dough. Knead the dough for about 5 minutes until smooth. Wrap in clear film (plastic wrap) to prevent it drying out, and leave to rest for 20–30 minutes.

4 Meanwhile, put the prawns, crab meat, ginger, breadcrumbs, soy sauce, spring onion, garlic and seasoning into a food processor or blender and process until smooth.

5 Once the pasta has rested, roll it into thin sheets. Stamp out 32 rounds 5cm/2in in diameter, using a fluted pastry cutter.

6 Place 5ml/1 tsp of the filling in the centre of half the pasta rounds. Brush the edges of each round with egg white and sandwich with a second round on top. Pinch the edges together to stop the filling seeping out.

7 Cook the pasta in a large pan of boiling, salted water for 5 minutes (cook in batches to prevent them from sticking together). Remove and drop into a bowl of cold water for 5 seconds before placing on a tray. (You can make these pasta shapes a day in advance. Cover with clear film and store in the refrigerator.)

8 Heat the consommé in a pan with the sherry or vermouth. Add the cooked pasta shapes and simmer for 1–2 minutes.

9 Serve the pasta in soup bowls covered with hot consommé. Garnish with peeled prawns and coriander leaves.

OYSTER SOUP

Oysters make a delicious soup that is really special. This recipe calls for oysters that have been shucked – removed from their shells. They should never be heated too quickly or cooked for too long, because their meat is very tender.

SERVES 6

INGREDIENTS
475ml/16fl oz/2 cups milk
475ml/16fl oz/2 cups single (light) cream
1.2 litres/2 pints/5 cups shucked oysters, drained, with their liquor reserved
a pinch of paprika
25g/1oz/2 tbsp butter
salt and freshly ground black pepper
15ml/1 tbsp chopped fresh parsley, to garnish

1 Combine the milk, single cream, and oyster liquor in a heavy pan. Heat the mixture over medium heat until small bubbles appear around the edge of the pan, being careful not to allow it to boil. Reduce the heat to low and add the oysters.

2 Cook, stirring occasionally, until the oysters plump up and their edges begin to curl. Add the paprika and season to taste.

3 Meanwhile, warm six soup plates or bowls. Cut the butter into 6 pieces and put one piece in each bowl. Ladle in the oyster soup and sprinkle with chopped parsley. Serve immediately.

CLAM & CORN CHOWDER

When using fresh clams, discard any shells that remain closed during cooking as this means they were already dead. Canned or bottled clams in brine, once drained, can be used as an alternative to fresh ones in their shells.

SERVES 4

INGREDIENTS
300ml/½ pint/1¼ cups double (heavy) cream
75g/3oz/6 tbsp unsalted butter
1 small onion, finely chopped
1 apple, cored and sliced
1 garlic clove, crushed
45ml/3 tbsp mild curry powder
350g/12oz/3 cups baby corn
225g/8oz cooked new potatoes
24 boiled baby onions
600ml/1 pint/2½ cups fish stock
40 small clams
salt and freshly ground black pepper
8 lime wedges, to garnish (optional)

1 Pour the cream into a small pan and cook over a high heat until it is reduced by half.

2 In a larger pan, melt half the butter. Add the onion, apple, garlic and curry powder. Sauté until the onion is translucent. Add the reduced cream and stir the mixture well.

3 In another pan, melt the remaining butter and add the baby corn, potatoes and baby onions. Cook for 5 minutes. Increase the heat and add the cream mixture and stock. Bring to the boil.

4 Add the clams. Cover and cook until the clams have opened. Discard any that do not open. Season well to taste with salt and freshly ground black pepper and serve, garnished with lime wedges, if you like.

SAFFRON MUSSEL SOUP

This is one of France's most delicious seafood soups. For everyday eating, the French would normally serve all the mussels in their shells. Serve with plenty of French bread.

SERVES 4–6

INGREDIENTS
40g/1½oz/3 tbsp unsalted butter
8 shallots, finely chopped
1 bouquet garni
5ml/1 tsp black peppercorns
350ml/12fl oz/1½ cups dry white wine
1 kg/2¼lb mussels, scrubbed and debearded
2 medium leeks, trimmed and finely chopped
1 fennel bulb, finely chopped
1 carrot, finely chopped
several saffron strands
1 litre/1¾ pints/4 cups fish or chicken stock
30–45ml/2–3 tbsp cornflour (cornstarch), blended with 45ml/3 tbsp cold water
120ml/4fl oz/½ cup whipping cream
1 medium tomato, peeled, seeded and finely chopped
30ml/2 tbsp Pernod (optional)
salt and freshly ground black pepper

> COOK'S TIP
> To prevent cut fennel from turning brown at the edges, put the prepared fennel in cold water acidulated with a little lemon juice, until it is ready for use. Drain well and use as directed.

1 In a large, heavy pan, melt half the butter over a medium-high heat. Add half the shallots and cook for 1–2 minutes until softened but not coloured. Add the bouquet garni, peppercorns and white wine and bring to the boil. Add the mussels, cover tightly and cook over a high heat for 3–5 minutes, shaking the pan from time to time, until the mussels have opened.

2 With a slotted spoon, transfer the mussels to a bowl. Strain the cooking liquid through a muslin-lined sieve (cheesecloth-lined strainer) and reserve.

3 Pull open the shells and remove most of the mussels. Discard any of the closed mussels.

4 Melt the remaining butter over a medium heat. Add the remaining shallots and cook for 1–2 minutes. Add the leeks, fennel, carrot and saffron and cook for 3–5 minutes.

5 Stir in the reserved cooking liquid, bring to the boil and cook for 5 minutes until the vegetables are tender and the liquid is slightly reduced. Add the stock and bring to the boil, skimming any foam that rises to the surface. Season with salt, if needed, and black pepper and cook for a further 5 minutes.

6 Stir the blended cornflour into the soup. Simmer for 2–3 minutes until the soup is slightly thickened, then add the cream, mussels and chopped tomato. Stir in the Pernod, if using, cook for 1–2 minutes until hot, then serve the soup immediately.

VARIATIONS
Use 2 onions in place of the leeks. Use 1 courgette (zucchini) in place of the carrot.

CLAM & BASIL SOUP

Subtly sweet and spicy, this special-occasion soup would make an ideal appetizer for serving at the beginning of a celebration dinner.

SERVES 4–6

INGREDIENTS
30ml/2 tbsp olive oil
1 medium onion, finely chopped
leaves from 1 fresh or dried sprig of thyme, chopped or crumbled
2 garlic cloves, crushed
5–6 fresh basil leaves, plus extra to garnish
1.5–2.5ml/¼–½ tsp crushed red chillies, to taste
1 litre/1¾ pints/4 cups fish stock
350ml/12fl oz/1½ cups passata (bottled strained tomatoes)
5ml/1 tsp granulated sugar
90g/3½oz/scant 1 cup frozen peas
65g/2½oz/⅔ cup small pasta shapes, such as chifferini
225g/8oz frozen shelled clams
salt and freshly ground black pepper

1 Heat the oil in a large pan, add the onion and cook gently for about 5 minutes until softened but not coloured. Add the thyme, then stir in the garlic, basil leaves and chillies.

2 Add the stock, passata and sugar to the pan, with salt and pepper to taste. Bring to the boil, then lower the heat and simmer gently for 15 minutes, stirring from time to time. Add the frozen peas and cook for a further 5 minutes.

3 Add the pasta to the stock mixture and bring to the boil, stirring. Lower the heat and simmer for about 5 minutes or according to the packet instructions, stirring frequently, until the pasta is *al dente*.

4 Turn the heat down to low, add the frozen clams and heat through for 2–3 minutes. Taste and adjust the seasoning. Serve hot in warmed bowls, garnished with basil leaves.

SEAFARER'S STEW

Any variety of firm fish may be used in this recipe, but be sure to use smoked haddock as well; it is essential for its distinctive flavour.

SERVES 4

INGREDIENTS

225g/8oz undyed smoked haddock fillet
225g/8oz fresh monkfish fillet
20 mussels, scrubbed
2 streaky bacon rashers (strips) (optional)
15ml/1 tbsp olive oil
1 shallot, finely chopped
225g/8oz carrots, coarsely grated
150ml/¼ pint/⅔ cup single (light) or double (heavy) cream
115g/4oz cooked peeled prawns (shrimp)
salt and freshly ground black pepper
30ml/2 tbsp chopped fresh parsley, to garnish

1 In a large, heavy-based pan, simmer the haddock and monkfish in 1.2 litres/ 2 pints/5 cups water for 5 minutes, then add the mussels and cover the pan with a lid.

2 Cook for a further 5 minutes or until all the mussels have opened. Discard any that have not. Drain, reserving the liquid. Return the liquid to the rinsed pan and set aside.

3 Flake the haddock coarsely, removing any skin and bones, then cut the monkfish into large chunks. Cut the bacon, if using, into fine strips.

4 Heat the oil in a heavy-based frying pan and fry the shallot and bacon for 3–4 minutes or until the shallot is soft and the bacon lightly browned. Add to the strained fish broth, bring to the boil, then add the grated carrots and cook for 10 minutes.

5 Stir in the cream together with the haddock, monkfish, mussels and prawns and heat gently, without boiling. Season and serve in large bowls, garnished with parsley.

LOBSTER BISQUE

The blue and black clawed lobster is known as the king of the shellfish. When cooked, it turns a brilliant red colour. This is an extravagant soup – complete with the luxurious addition of brandy – worthy of any celebration dinner party.

SERVES 4

INGREDIENTS
1 cooked lobster (about 675g/1½lb)
30ml/2 tbsp vegetable oil
115g/4oz/½ cup butter
2 shallots, finely chopped
juice of ½ lemon
45ml/3 tbsp brandy
1 bay leaf
1 sprig of fresh parsley, plus extra to garnish
1 blade of mace
1.2 litres/2 pints/5 cups fish stock
40g/1½oz/3 tbsp plain (all-purpose) flour
45ml/3 tbsp double (heavy) cream
salt and freshly ground black pepper
a pinch of cayenne pepper, to garnish

VARIATIONS
Use 4 spring onions (scallions) in place of shallots. Use sherry in place of brandy. Use crème fraiche in place of cream. Use a well-flavoured vegetable stock in place of fish stock, if preferred.

1 Preheat the oven to 180°C/350°F/Gas 4. Lay the lobster out flat and split in half lengthways. Remove and discard the little stomach sac from the head, the thread-like intestine and the coral (if any).

2 In a large, heavy-based roasting tin, heat the oil with 25g/1oz/2 tbsp of the butter. Sauté the lobster, flesh-side down, for 5 minutes. Add the shallots, lemon juice and brandy, then cook in the oven for 15 minutes.

3 Remove the lobster meat from the shell. Place the shell and the juices in a large pan and simmer with the bay leaf, parsley, mace and stock for 30 minutes. Strain. Finely chop 15ml/1 tbsp of the lobster meat. Process the rest in a food processor or blender with 40g/1½oz/3 tbsp of the butter.

4 Melt the remaining butter, add the flour and cook gently for 30 seconds. Add the stock gradually and bring to the boil, stirring constantly. Stir in the processed meat, the cream and seasoning.

5 Ladle into individual serving dishes and garnish with chopped lobster, parsley sprigs and a sprinkling of cayenne.

Prawn & Egg-knot Soup

This is a delicious Japanese soup, just right for a festive occasion. The main ingredients – prawn (shrimp) balls, knotted omelette and spring onions (scallions) – look really special suspended in the translucent soup. Egg knots are very easy to make.

SERVES 4

INGREDIENTS
900ml/1½ pints/3¾ cups kombu and bonito stock or instant dashi
5ml/1 tsp soy sauce
a dash of sake or dry white wine
salt
1 spring onion (scallion), finely sliced, to garnish

FOR THE PRAWN SHINJO BALLS
200g/7oz raw large prawns (shrimp) shelled, thawed if frozen
65g/2½oz cod fillet, skinned
5ml/1 tsp egg white
5ml/1 tsp sake or dry white wine
22.5ml/4½ tsp cornflour (cornstarch) or potato starch
2–3 drops of soy sauce

FOR THE OMELETTE
1 egg, beaten
a dash of mirin
oil, for frying

COOK'S TIP
Japanese ingredients such as kombu, dashi and sake are available in some large supermarkets and in specialist food stores and delicatessens.

1 Devein the prawns. Process the prawns, cod, egg white, 5ml/1 tsp sake or wine, cornflour or potato starch, soy sauce and a pinch of salt in a food processor or blender to make a sticky paste. Alternatively, finely chop the prawns and cod, crush them with the knife's blade and then pound them well in a mortar with a pestle, before adding the remaining ingredients.

2 Shape the mixture into four balls and steam them for 10 minutes over a high heat. Meanwhile, soak the spring onion for the garnish in cold water for 5 minutes, then drain.

3 To make the omelette, mix the egg with a pinch of salt and the mirin. Heat a little oil in a frying pan and pour in the egg, tilting the pan to coat it evenly. When the egg has set, turn the omelette over and cook for 30 seconds. Leave to cool.

4 Cut the omelette into long strips about 2cm/¾in wide. Knot each strip once, place in a sieve (strainer) and rinse with hot water to remove excess oil.

5 Bring the stock or dashi to the boil and add the soy sauce, a pinch of salt and a dash of sake or wine. Divide the prawn balls and the egg knots among four bowls. Pour in the soup, sprinkle with the spring onion and serve.

VARIATION
Use haddock or monkfish fillet in place of cod.

SEAFOOD WONTON SOUP

While most wonton soups are traditionally prepared using pork as their main ingredient, this variation uses seafood instead, for a really special flavour.

SERVES 4

INGREDIENTS
50g/2oz raw tiger prawns (shrimp)
50g/2oz queen scallops
75g/3oz skinless cod fillet, roughly chopped
15ml/1 tbsp finely snipped fresh chives
5ml/1 tsp dry sherry
1 small egg white, lightly beaten
2.5ml/½ tsp sesame oil
1.5ml/¼ tsp salt
large pinch of freshly ground white pepper
20 wonton wrappers
2 cos lettuce leaves, shredded
900ml/1½ pints/3¾ cups fish stock
fresh coriander (cilantro) leaves and garlic chives, to garnish

COOK'S TIP
The filled wonton wrappers can be made ahead of time, then frozen for several weeks and cooked straight from the freezer.

1 Peel and devein the prawns. Rinse them, dry them on kitchen paper and cut them into small pieces.

2 Rinse and dry the scallops. Chop them into small pieces the same size as the prawns.

3 Place the cod in a food processor or blender and process until a paste is formed. Scrape into a bowl and stir in the prawns, scallops, chives, sherry, egg white, sesame oil, salt and pepper. Mix well, cover and leave in a cool place to marinate for 20 minutes.

4 Make the wontons. Place 5ml/1 tsp of the seafood filling in the centre of a wonton wrapper, then bring the corners together to meet at the top. Twist them together to enclose the filling. Fill the remaining wonton wrappers in the same way. Tie with a fresh chive if desired.

5 Bring a large pan of water to the boil. Drop in the wontons. When the water returns to the boil, lower the heat and simmer gently for 5 minutes or until the wontons float to the surface. Drain the wontons and divide them among four heated soup bowls.

6 Add a portion of lettuce to each bowl. Bring the fish stock to the boil. Ladle it on top of the lettuce and garnish each portion with coriander leaves and garlic chives. Serve immediately.

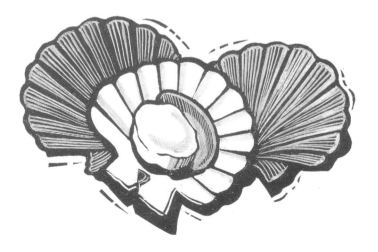

SEAFOOD SOUP WITH ROUILLE

This is a really chunky, aromatic mixed fish soup from France, flavoured with plenty of saffron and herbs. Rouille, a fiery hot paste, is served separately for everyone to swirl into their soup to add flavour.

SERVES 6

INGREDIENTS

3 gurnard or red mullet, scaled and gutted

12 large prawns (shrimp)

675g/1½lb white fish, such as cod, haddock, halibut or monkfish

225g/8oz mussels

1 onion, quartered

1.2 litres/2 pints/5 cups water

5ml/1 tsp saffron strands

75ml/5 tbsp olive oil

1 fennel bulb, roughly chopped

4 garlic cloves, crushed

3 strips pared orange rind

4 sprigs of thyme

675g/1½lb tomatoes or 400g/14oz can chopped tomatoes

30ml/2 tbsp sun-dried tomato purée (paste)

3 bay leaves

salt and freshly ground black pepper

FOR THE ROUILLE

1 red (bell) pepper, seeded and roughly chopped

1 fresh red chilli, seeded and sliced

2 garlic cloves, chopped

75ml/5 tbsp olive oil

15g/½oz/¼ cup fresh breadcrumbs

COOK'S TIP
To save time, order the fish and ask your fishmonger
to fillet the gurnard or mullet for you.

1 To make the *rouille*, process the pepper, chilli, garlic, oil and breadcrumbs in a food processor or blender until smooth. Transfer to a serving dish and chill.

2 Fillet the gurnard or mullet by cutting away the flesh from the backbone. Reserve the heads and bones. Cut the fillets into small chunks. Shell half the prawns and reserve the trimmings to make the stock. Skin the white fish, discarding any bones, and cut into large chunks. Scrub the mussels well, discarding any open ones.

3 Put the fish trimmings and prawn trimmings in a pan with the onion and water. Bring to the boil, then simmer gently for 30 minutes. Cool slightly and strain.

4 Soak the saffron in 15ml/1 tbsp boiling water. Heat 30ml/2 tbsp of the oil in a large sauté pan. Add the gurnard or mullet and white fish and fry over a high heat for 1 minute. Drain.

5 Heat the remaining oil and fry the fennel, garlic, orange rind and thyme until beginning to colour. Make up the strained stock to about 1.2 litres/2 pints/ 5 cups with water.

6 If using fresh tomatoes, plunge them into boiling water for 30 seconds, then refresh in cold water. Peel and chop. Add the stock to the pan with the saffron, tomatoes, tomato purée and bay leaves. Season, bring almost to the boil, then simmer gently, covered, for 20 minutes.

7 Stir in the gurnard or mullet, white fish, shelled and non-shelled prawns and add the mussels. Cover the pan and cook for 3–4 minutes. Discard any mussels that do not open. Serve the soup hot with the *rouille*.

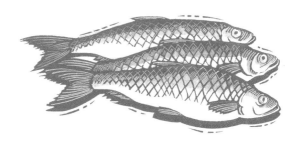

THAI FISH SOUP

Thai fish sauce, or nam pla, *is rich in B vitamins and is used extensively in Thai cooking. It is available in Thai or Indonesian stores and good supermarkets.*

SERVES 4

INGREDIENTS
350g/12oz raw large prawns (shrimp)
15ml/1 tbsp groundnut (peanut) oil
1.2 litres/2 pints/5 cups well-flavoured chicken or fish stock
1 lemon grass stalk, bruised and cut into 2.5cm/1in lengths
2 kaffir lime leaves, torn into pieces
juice and finely grated rind of 1 lime
½ fresh green chilli, seeded and finely sliced
4 scallops
24 mussels, scrubbed
115g/4oz monkfish fillet, cut into 2cm/¾in chunks
10ml/2 tsp Thai fish sauce

FOR THE GARNISH
1 kaffir lime leaf, shredded
½ fresh red chilli, finely sliced

1 Peel the prawns, reserving the shells, and remove the black vein running along their backs.

2 Heat the oil in a pan and fry the prawn shells until pink. Add the stock, lemon grass, lime leaves, lime rind and green chilli. Bring to the boil, simmer for 20 minutes, then press through a sieve (strainer), reserving the liquid.

3 Prepare the scallops by cutting them in half, leaving the corals attached to one half.

4 Return the stock to a clean pan, add the prawns, mussels, monkfish and scallops and cook for 3 minutes. Remove from the heat and add the lime juice and Thai fish sauce. Serve garnished with the shredded lime leaf and finely sliced red chilli.

PASTA SOUP WITH CHICKEN LIVERS

This is a soup that can be served as a special-occasion first course or main course. The fried chicken livers are absolutely delicious.

SERVES 4–6

INGREDIENTS

115g/4oz/½ cup chicken livers, thawed if frozen
15ml/1 tbsp olive oil
a knob of butter
4 garlic cloves, crushed
3 sprigs each of fresh parsley, marjoram and sage, chopped
1 sprig of fresh thyme, chopped
5–6 fresh basil leaves, chopped
15–30ml/1–2 tbsp dry white wine
2 × 300g/11oz cans condensed chicken consommé
225g/8oz/2 cups frozen peas
50g/2oz/½ cup small pasta shapes, such as farfalle
2–3 spring onions (scallions), sliced diagonally
salt and freshly ground black pepper

1 Use scissors to cut the chicken livers into small pieces. Heat the oil and butter in a frying pan, add the garlic and herbs, with salt and ground black pepper to taste, and fry gently for a few minutes. Add the livers, increase the heat to high and stir-fry for a few minutes until they change colour and become dry. Add the wine, cook until it evaporates, then remove from the heat.

2 Tip both cans of chicken consommé into a large pan and add water to the condensed soup as directed on the labels. Add an extra can of water, then stir in a little salt and pepper to taste and bring to the boil.

3 Add the frozen peas to the pan and simmer for about 5 minutes, then add the small pasta shapes and bring the soup back to the boil, stirring. Allow to simmer, stirring frequently, for about 5 minutes or according to the instructions on the packet, until the pasta is *al dente*.

4 Add the fried chicken livers and spring onions and heat through for 2–3 minutes. Taste and adjust the seasoning. Serve hot, in warmed bowls.

Duck Broth with Orange Spiced Dumplings

Using a very delicate touch when bringing together the mixture for the dumplings will create a light texture to match their delicious flavour.

Serves 4

Ingredients

1 duckling, about 1.75kg/4–4½lb, with liver
1 large onion, halved
2 carrots, thickly sliced
½ garlic bulb
1 bouquet garni
3 cloves
30ml/2 tbsp chopped chives, to garnish

For the spiced dumplings

2 thick slices white bread
60ml/4 tbsp milk
2 rashers rindless streaky (fatty) bacon
1 shallot, finely chopped
1 garlic clove, crushed
1 egg yolk, beaten
grated rind of 1 orange
2.5ml/½ tsp paprika
50g/2oz/½ cup plain (all-purpose) flour
salt and freshly ground black pepper

1 Set the duck liver aside. Using a sharp knife, cut off the breasts from the duckling and set them aside. Put the duck carcass into a large, heavy-based pan and pour in enough water to cover the carcass completely. Bring to the boil and skim the scum off the surface.

2 Add the onion, carrots, garlic, bouquet garni and cloves. Reduce the heat and cover the pan, then simmer for 2 hours, skimming occasionally to remove any surface scum.

3 Lift the carcass from the broth and leave to cool. Strain the broth, and skim it to remove any fat. Return the broth to the pan and then simmer gently, uncovered, until reduced to 1.2 litres/2 pints/5 cups.

4 Remove all meat from the duck carcass and shred it finely with a sharp knife, then set the shredded duck meat aside.

5 To make the dumplings, soak the bread in the milk for 5 minutes. Remove the skin and fat from the duck breasts. Mince the meat with the duck liver and bacon. Squeeze the milk from the bread, then add the bread to the minced meat with the shallot, garlic, egg yolk, orange rind, paprika, flour and seasoning, and mix together well.

6 Form a spoonful of the mixture into a ball, a little smaller than a walnut. Repeat with the remaining mixture to make 20 small dumplings. Bring a large pan of lightly salted water to the boil and poach the dumplings for 4–5 minutes, until just tender.

7 Bring the duck broth back to the boil and add the dumplings. Divide the shredded duck meat among four bowls and ladle in the broth and dumplings. Garnish with chives.

Chicken & Leek Soup with Prunes & Barley

This recipe is based on the traditional Scottish soup, cock-a-leekie. The unusual combination of leeks and prunes is surprisingly delicious.

Serves 6

Ingredients
1 chicken, weighing about 2kg/4¼lb
900g/2lb leeks
1 fresh bay leaf
a few each fresh parsley stalks and thyme sprigs
1 large carrot, thickly sliced
2.4 litres/4 pints/10 cups chicken or beef stock
115g/4oz/generous ½ cup pearl barley
400g/14oz ready-to-eat prunes
salt and freshly ground black pepper
chopped fresh parsley, to garnish

Cook's Tip
Pearl barley is whole grain barley with the outer husk removed. It is an excellent addition to many vegetable-based soups because it helps to thicken and flavour soups as well as adding an interesting texture.

1 Cut the breasts off the chicken and set aside. Place the remaining chicken carcass in a large pan.

2 Cut half the leeks into 5cm/2in lengths and add them to the pan. Tie the bay leaf, parsley and thyme into a bouquet garni and add to the pan with the carrot and the stock. Bring to the boil, then reduce the heat and cover. Simmer gently for 1 hour. Skim off any scum when the water first boils and occasionally during simmering.

3 Add the chicken breasts and cook for another 30 minutes, until they are just cooked. Leave until cool enough to handle, then strain the stock. Reserve the chicken breasts and meat from the chicken carcass. Discard all the skin, bones, cooked vegetables and herbs. Skim as much fat as you can from the stock, then return it to the pan.

4 Meanwhile, rinse the pearl barley thoroughly in a sieve (strainer) under cold running water, then cook it in a large pan of boiling water for about 10 minutes. Drain, rinse well again and drain thoroughly.

5 Add the pearl barley to the stock. Bring to the boil over a medium heat, then lower the heat and cook very gently for 15–20 minutes, until the barley is just cooked and tender. Season the soup with 5ml/1 tsp salt and black pepper.

6 Add the prunes. Slice the remaining leeks and add them to the pan. Bring to the boil, then simmer for 10 minutes or until the leeks are just cooked.

7 Slice the chicken breasts and add them to the soup with the remaining chicken meat, sliced or cut into neat pieces. Reheat if necessary, then ladle the soup into deep plates and sprinkle with chopped parsley.

VARIATIONS
Use red or standard onions in place of leeks. Use ready-to-eat dried apricots or dates in place of prunes. Use a dried or fresh bouquet garni in place of the bay leaf and fresh herb sprigs.

GINGER, CHICKEN & COCONUT SOUP

This aromatic soup is richly textured with coconut milk and intensely flavoured with galangal, lemon grass and kaffir lime leaves.

SERVES 4–6

INGREDIENTS
750ml/1¼ pints/3 cups coconut milk
475ml/16fl oz/2 cups chicken stock
4 lemon grass stalks, bruised and chopped
2.5cm/1in piece galangal, finely sliced
10 black peppercorns, crushed
10 kaffir lime leaves, torn
300g/11oz skinless boneless chicken, cut into thin strips
115g/4oz button (white) mushrooms
50g/2oz/½ cup baby corn
60ml/4 tbsp lime juice
45ml/3 tbsp fish sauce

FOR THE GARNISH
2 red chillies, chopped
3–4 spring onions (scallions), chopped
chopped fresh coriander (cilantro)

1 Bring the coconut milk and chicken stock to the boil in a pan. Add the lemon grass, galangal, peppercorns and half the kaffir lime leaves, reduce the heat and simmer gently for 10 minutes.

2 Strain the stock into a clean pan. Return to the heat, then add the chicken, mushrooms and baby corn. Cook for about 5–7 minutes until the chicken is cooked through.

3 Stir in the lime juice, fish sauce to taste and the rest of the lime leaves. Serve the soup hot, garnished with red chillies, spring onions and coriander.

Indian Beef & Summer Berry Soup

You can use any kind of fresh berries you like in this exotic Indian soup. They give the flavour a pleasant kick, as well as adding a vivid colour to the dish.

SERVES 4

INGREDIENTS
30ml/2 tbsp vegetable oil
450g/1lb tender beef steak
2 medium onions, finely sliced
25g/1oz/2 tbsp butter
1 litre/1¾ pints/4 cups good beef stock or bouillon
2.5ml/½ tsp salt
115g/4oz/1 cup fresh huckleberries, blueberries or blackberries, lightly mashed
15ml/1 tbsp honey

1 Heat the oil in a heavy-based pan until almost smoking. Add the steak and brown on both sides over a medium-high heat. Remove the steak from the pan and set aside.

2 Reduce the heat to low and add the sliced onions and butter to the pan. Stir well, scraping up the meat juices. Cook over a low heat for 8–10 minutes until the onions are softened.

3 Add the beef stock or bouillon and salt and bring to the boil, stirring well. Mix in the mashed berries and the honey. Simmer for 20 minutes.

4 Meanwhile, cut the steak into thin, bite-size slivers. Taste the soup and add more salt or honey if necessary. Add the steak to the pan. Cook gently for 30 seconds, stirring all the time, then serve.

VARIATIONS
Use lean lamb or pork in place of beef. Use 8 shallots in place of onions. Use maple syrup in place of honey.

Moroccan Spiced Mutton Soup

Three classic north African spices – ginger, turmeric and cinnamon – are combined with chickpeas and mutton to make this special main-course soup.

SERVES 6

INGREDIENTS
75g/3oz/½ cup chickpeas, soaked overnight
15g/½oz/1 tbsp butter or 15ml/1 tbsp olive oil
225g/8oz mutton, cut into cubes
1 onion, chopped
450g/1lb tomatoes, peeled and chopped
a few celery leaves, chopped
30ml/2 tbsp chopped fresh parsley
15ml/1 tbsp chopped fresh coriander (cilantro)
2.5ml/½ tsp ground ginger
2.5ml/½ tsp ground turmeric
5ml/1 tsp ground cinnamon
1.75 litres/3 pints/7½ cups water
75g/3oz/scant ½ cup green lentils
75g/3oz/¾ cup vermicelli or soup pasta
2 egg yolks
juice of ½–1 lemon, to taste
sea salt and freshly ground black pepper
fresh coriander (cilantro), to garnish
lemon wedges, to serve

COOK'S TIP
If you have forgotten to soak the chickpeas overnight, place them in a pan with about four times their volume of cold water. Bring very slowly to the boil, then cover the pan, remove it from the heat and leave to stand for 45 minutes before using as described in the recipe.

1 Drain the chickpeas and set aside. Heat the butter or oil in a large pan and fry the mutton and onion for 2–3 minutes, stirring, until the mutton is just browned.

2 Add the chopped tomatoes, celery leaves, herbs and spices and season well with ground black pepper. Cook for about 1 minute, then stir in the water and add the green lentils and the soaked, drained and rinsed chickpeas.

3 Slowly bring to the boil and skim the surface to remove the froth. Boil rapidly for 10 minutes, then reduce the heat and simmer very gently for 2 hours, or until the chickpeas are very tender.

4 Season with salt and pepper, then add the vermicelli or soup pasta to the pan and cook for 5–6 minutes until it is just tender. If the soup is very thick at this stage, add a little more water.

5 Beat the egg yolks with the lemon juice and stir into the simmering soup. Immediately remove the soup from the heat and stir until thickened. Pour into warmed serving bowls and garnish with plenty of fresh coriander. Serve the soup with lemon wedges.

INDEX